JOURNEY TO
SAFE HARBOR

JOURNEY TO SAFE HARBOR

MEMOIR OF THREE GENERATIONS
SELF LOVE, FORGIVENESS, RECONNECTION

Elizabeth Jacks Scott

Library of Congress Control Number: 2021909077
ISBN: Hardcover   978-1-6641-7282-1
                Softcover   978-1-6641-7281-4
                eBook   978-1-6641-7283-8

Family History and Memoir

Tenants Harbor, Maine
photo by Elizabeth Jacks Scott

Print information available on the last page.

Rev. date: 06/11/2021

To order additional copies of this book, contact:
Xlibris
844-714-8691
www.Xlibris.com
Orders@Xlibris.com
823566

CONTENTS

PART 1

PART 2

For Al

This has God given to all creatures,
To foster and seek their own nature.
—Mechthild of Magdeburg, in *Medieval Women Mystics*

GENEALOGY

Canada	America
Maritime provinces	Tenants Harbor, Maine
Rev. H. Y. Corey	Deacon Robert Long
Each generation picked one	Built sail loft, 1848
person to be a minister.	Shipbuilding business bankrupted in 1870

Rev. Hebron Corey---married 1894, missionaries in India---**Clara Long**
(1862–1928)   (1868–1947)

Five children of Hebron and Clara, all born in India
Cedric   **Albert**   **Charlie**   **Harry**   **Betty**
(1895–1947) (1898–1963) (1900–1928) (1902–1902) (1908–1973)

Betty Corey------------married 1936 in Chicago------------**Bob Hunter**
(1908–1973)   (1898–1997)

Four children of Bob and Betty Hunter
Johnny   **Bobby**   **Betsy**   **Margie**
(1936–)   (1939–)   (1940–)   (1944–)

Betsy Hunter--married 1968--**Bob Jacks**--Betsy married 1991--**Al Scott**
(1940–)   (1925–1983)   (1931–)

Two children of Betsy and Bob Jacks
Betsy-Bond Jacks   **Bob-Roy Jacks Jr.**
(1969–)   (1972–)

PREFACE

Journey to Safe Harbor is a work of nonfiction, a true story, but some names have been changed, some scenes have been imagined, and the sequences of some events have been altered for the sake of the narrative flow.

With my long experience as a grief therapist and a family and individual therapist, I can attest that it is possible for grieving and hurting families and individuals to heal and to find meaning and joy once more in their lives. Although this book is a particular family's history and my personal journey, I am publishing it with the hope the book will create possibilities for others to delve deeply into their own histories, emotions, and faith and find their own journey home to healing.

My extended family might not all agree with my interpretations and conclusions, but I have felt compelled to write my truth to the best of my ability. I hope others will write their own stories, for I claim this only as my own.

Elizabeth Jacks Scott

PROLOGUE

Tenants Harbor, Maine, 1975

The gentle southwesterly breeze blowing off the harbor filled my lungs with its fresh, pure sea air. In that moment, I had no idea I would spend decades struggling with what I would find onshore. My hair billowed in the soft breeze. The mellow light of the late-afternoon sun created reflections of the boat hulls in the water, bathing the water in multiple tones of lavender and blue, with the sailing boats, lobster boats, and cruising boats glowing a golden yellow. The beautiful harbor was named Tenants Harbor and located halfway up the coast of Maine.

As I looked away from the sea toward the land, the barren scene surprised me: no trees, a narrow gravel roadway, a couple of acres of land with scruffy grass, and no marked boundaries. A large, rectangular white building, an old sail loft, loomed in front of me. It was left over from the days of wooden shipbuilding in the nineteenth century, when sailmakers made sails for schooners plying the coastal trade and a ship's chandlery outfitted schooners for long trading journeys.

The building, my new inheritance, had been built by Deacon Robert Long in 1848 and used to be bustling, but on that late-summer day in 1975, the large plain white clapboard sail loft building looked abandoned, with peeling paint. No one lived there, and the building had been vandalized by local kids with pulled-down drain pipes. Two locked wooden store doors with square glass windows led into the former ship's chandlery, which later had been a grocery store. Peering in the window, I saw odd furnishings piled high, left over from when a later grocery store had closed in the 1930s with numerous debts unpaid. Outside, rickety stairs on the far left led to the second floor, where ancestors had built two small apartments now vacant. Yellowing lace curtains hung in the second-floor Victorian windows.

Other than the large old building and scruffy land, I saw only a town wharf; a fish wharf on the right, with wafting smells of red herring bait for the lobstermen; and a sprinkling of cottages and old sea captains' homes up on the hill, filled with folks, including a few who were angry at the losses of opportunity in the village after the demise of the shipping and quarrying industries. Some were angry at my family for coming back after being gone for so long and insisting on taking possession of their inheritance when local members of the family were already in place. People from away were not known, and our family felt unwelcome, but I felt I belonged, as seven generations of my mother's family had lived in the village.

Looking up to the Victorian windows, I spotted an old woman in widow's black and a younger woman in linen blue peering out the window. On second look, I realized the figures were just shadows, ghostlike shadows, maybe even imagined shadows suggested by the tricks of the setting sun, but for an instant, I had thought I saw Clara and her daughter, Betty. Clara, my grandmother, had been born in Tenants Harbor and spent nearly thirty years in India as the wife of a missionary. She had lived out the end of her tragic, faith-filled life in the barren building. Betty, my mother, though born in India, had considered the old sail loft building her heritage and her heart's home. She'd fought valiantly to keep her heart's home and to create a new life for herself, her children, and her community, but lurking underneath had been hidden pain and shame. Both Clara and Betty were dead.

But I was alive. I was a young matron from New York with a husband and two small children and the new owner of the old sail loft building. My widowed father, a chief judge in Chicago, had signed over the sail loft to me with the epigram "Why would you want that old place?"

The truth was, my father the judge didn't want that old place. He was already remarried.

I wanted it. Although it looked barren, it did not feel barren. It was filled with memories and history, six generations of them, a jumble of contradictory, conflictual, tragic, and happy memories. It held the promise of a summer home for my young children and my husband, as we lived in New York City and needed a place to spend the summer. Maybe more, it held the key to Mother, whose property it had been. Could struggling with the gift and the burden unlock the mysteries between my mother and me and within each of us? Would it help me with my own children? I came to realize the barren house reflected both how my mother had felt and how I felt deep inside, despite our sunny smiles like the harbor. I could not let the struggle go. The sparkling lavender blue and golden lights on the harbor beckoned me forward in hope, even in the midst of all the rancor onshore.

As I stood on the shore, contemplating the gift, I watched my young children, three and six years old, play on the rocky shore. How I loved them, and how scared I felt. The tension in my marriage was terrible for my children. I knew something was not quite right inside me. I had to figure out a way to solve the problems and to work them out. I was aware there had been a lot of problems in my parents' marriage, and there was a long history through the generations of tension and hurtful parenting. I desperately wanted to change the plague of children being hurt down through the generations. How could I be sure I would be different in order not to hurt my son and daughter? I had been given a great heritage in terms of education and community service but with a lot that was wrong and needed fixing with regard to parenting. I decided to go on a journey to find healing for myself and my family. I believed if I looked hard enough, I would find answers.

I had been curious about my family for many decades for it never made sense to me, and I started collecting family memorabilia even when I was a child. I kept letters and photographs. In college, I wrote a research paper based on my great, great grandfather's ship building records, Robert Long and Son, of Tenants Harbor. Those archives are currently located at the Bath Marine Museum in Bath, Maine. As a graduate student in history, I took an oral history of my father, Judge Robert L Hunter. While in seminary, I made a trip to Canada to visit the headquarters of the Canadian Baptist Foreign Mission of the Maritime Provinces and read the records of Rev. Hebron Young Corey, my grandfather who spent nearly thirty years in India. Before she died, my mom, Betty, handed me a pack of letters dating from 1894 to 1919 written by her mother Clara while in India as a missionary's wife to Clara's own mother, Elizabeth Bickmore Long, a refined woman of the small village of Tenants Harbor, who had been born and died not far from where I stood contemplating the sail loft I had just inherited. I kept all these records and read and transcribed the letters from Clara to her mother.

Out of all these collected records and my experiences, I have written a narrative of my journey. Part One narrates the saga of the origins of my family's trauma in Tenants Harbor, how it played out in India and on the south side of Chicago. I go back and forth between Tenants Harbor, India and Chicago to show the interweaving of three eras and three generations, and how they resulted in the family's fragmentation and great tragedy. Part Two, narrates the journey of healing through all the ups and downs of life resulting in myself, the family and our community being reconnected. Grace came to me by surprise in the midst of my searching.

PART 1

Part I

CHAPTER 1

India Visited, 1995

The car and driver bumped, swerved, and screeched lickety-split over the narrow dirt road in Andhra Pradesh in southern India, taking me to find the birthplace of my mother. It was a dusty search, as February was a dry time of year in southern India. It was 1995, eighty-eight years after Mom's birth in 1908 and twenty-two years after her death in 1973. It was thrilling to contemplate seeing a place I had heard about as a child. According to her passport, she had been born in Vizianagaram, Andhra Pradesh, India, as the daughter of Canadian Baptist foreign missionaries, the Reverend Hebron Young Corey from New Brunswick, Canada, and Clara Long Corey from Tenants Harbor, Maine. She had been their fifth child and only daughter.

Since it had been seventy-three years since Mom and her family left India, no one would have a fresh memory of them. Nevertheless, I was going to see what I could find out. I was the first one from my family to travel to Vizianagaram since they'd left in 1923. It seemed mysterious to me.

I was scared stiff to make the trip. Something about it was frightening— perhaps what I would discover about my mother. My mother, a foreigner even in her own birthplace, had looked for home for much of her life. I also looked for a place where I belonged.

I had traveled on several planes from New York City to reach the port city of Visakhapatnam on the eastern coast of India, and now I proceeded in a shiny black English car with a Hindu driver deeper into the hinterland of Andhra Pradesh. I entered agricultural South India and its primitive, isolated villages.

I had traveled to southern India on a tour with the American Museum of Natural History and had left the tour to visit sites specific to my family. Luckily, I was not alone on my journey to Vizianagaram, because I had run into an Australian woman who had married an Indian farmer. Her mother, the wife of a former missionary, had jumped at the chance to accompany me. When I'd met the mother, I had thought of my late great-aunt Harriet, whom I had seen teach the Bible Sunday mornings at Tenants Harbor Baptist Church when I was a child. The Australian woman's mother was white-haired, thin, and stooped over, with a bun and wire-framed glasses, wearing a flowered shirtwaist dress. She kept handing out Bible tracts, an embarrassment to me—an anachronism from the past, I thought.

The stooped-over lady had introduced me to a slightly plump middle-aged Indian couple who were part of the Christian network of the area. They had stood together in a shaded doorway and proudly told me, "We are economic Christians," explaining that becoming Christians had helped them find employment because they had been taught English. They had joined my entourage. Thus, there were four of us, plus the driver, going to Vizianagaram.

A hard part for me was listening to my traveling companions, who all still believed in the mission of my grandparents, whereas I no longer did. I thought one shouldn't try to change another person's religion. I felt speechless and just listened and observed. When one thinks what one believes is the whole truth, one can become dictatorial and controlling, exhibiting behaviors so different from listening and sharing.

We passed rice paddies with workers stooping over flooded fields, planting, and herds of cows blocking the road. The Hindu driver swerved around them without ever touching a single animal. Indian men in their whites drove oxen with fancily painted horns. Children working in the fields quickly swamped our car out of curiosity or seeking handouts—pencils. They peered in at me. I was told these children had never seen a white woman before. They stared without embarrassment. I was a foreigner in my mother's birthplace.

We entered Vizianagaram after two hours on the dusty road and were stopped by a train of oxen pulling carts with huge wooden wheels. The carts were filled with piles of newly cut sugarcane. We saw women in rickshaws driven by bicyclists. A group of schoolchildren in English-looking uniforms—blue pleated skirts and white blouses with Peter Pan collars—walked on the side of the road. They were among adults in Indian dress, except for the male guardians, who were in Western dress. Other women walking on the road wore brightly colored saris, and some men were in Indian turbans with dhotis and loose white shirts. There were no cars. A few open trucks and an open bus were all I could see. Eighty-eight years after my mother, Betty, had been born, the modern world still had not reached the town.

I wore Indian dress, trying to fit in. I felt ridiculous. I had bought an Indian outfit in a local bazaar on my way to Vizianagaram. It consisted of a purple, gold, and maroon patterned top with elaborate gold embroidery down the front. It fell to my knees over baggy pants tied at the waist, and a scarf was neatly slung over my shoulder, also extending to my knees.

I had planned to wear my khakis, but the stares of the children at a tourist site where we had stopped had made me decide that women in India didn't wear pants without skirts covering their seats. It just was not done. I had turned around and seen fifty little girls in saris trying not to stare at me, with their hands over their mouths to keep down the giggles. I might have done the same thing on the topless beaches of France as a child. Mom always had been concerned about wearing the proper thing—but what was proper changed. She had been so English.

I tried to remember what I knew about my grandparents Clara and Hebron's family. Their fourth son, my uncle Harry, had died as an infant from cholera. Their first son, Cedric, had been injured at birth and never learned to talk. When, many years later, my son almost had been injured at birth, Mom had talked about Cedric's injury as an unbearable heartache for her parents and said she was grateful I had been spared so much suffering. Their first and third sons had grown to adulthood, but one of their lives had ended in tragedy. Their last child, born when Clara was in her forties, their only girl, Betty, had been raised by the ayahs, who'd taught her Telugu before she learned to speak English. Neither of her parents had been able to spend much time with their baby daughter, because her mother had been worn out and sickly, and her father had been overworked by his mission.

Goodness, so much sadness in one family trying to do good in the world, I thought.

My entourage had arranged for us to go first to a Western-style white stucco Baptist church with a steeple to meet the Indian Baptist minister. There were no longer any Western missionaries in India: the Indian government had thrown them all out in 1970, deciding they did more harm than good. A whitewashed brick-walled enclosure surrounded the Baptist church. Outside the walls were straw-and-mud huts of the Indian villagers. Clay pots sat outside open doorways in the sunshine with cots of woven rope nearby. I watched villagers sweeping, sitting, washing, and carrying water jugs or huge piles of greens on their heads. My only reference was the diorama of village life in the Bronze Age at the Natural History Museum.

I thought about my grandparents back in 1895, when they'd arrived in Vizianagaram: Clara had been pregnant, and Hebron, her husband, had struggled to care for his wife. They had arrived by oxcart, traveling two miles an hour, a much longer and bumpier ride than I had just experienced. What had taken me two hours would have taken them four or five days, and there would have been no roadside comfort stops. The driver must have stopped and boiled water over a charcoal fire, cooking a little rice and maybe a few vegetables for sustenance. Clara must have worried about the safety of her soon-to-be-born baby and her own health. They had come to serve God, but I could imagine they'd had no idea of the consequences. They had been young, newly married, and committed to the mission of spreading Christianity to the Hindus of the Telugu-speaking part of southern India, whom they called heathens. My thinking had progressed a hundred years beyond their thinking. I wanted to keep studying the ancient Hindu scriptures for all their wisdom, knowing they had a great deal to teach. But I lived in a different time. The missionaries sacrificed their lives and their children for their faith, but India, a predominantly Hindu country, had its own faith thousands of years old.

It is hard for me to reconcile my grandparents in India evangelizing the Hindus while their own children suffered. Their faith and their calling were that powerful.

The minister and his wife greeted us warmly with hot tea and biscuits. He wore Western-style pants and a shirt in sparkling white, and his wife wore a traditional sari. We sat in their comfortable Western-style living room. It all looked out of place to me. He told me he was an Indian Christian whose father had been baptized by the missionaries, but since the 1970s, the churches had been staffed entirely by Christian Indian nationals. He had had to carry on without the support of the West. For all the missionaries' diligent work for more than 150 years, only 3 percent of India was Christian at the time. India had heard the faiths of many conquerors over its long history and had assimilated parts into their Hindu religion. About 30 percent of India was Muslim, but Islam did not have a big presence in the Telugu area of Andhra Pradesh, where the Canadian Baptist missionaries had their mission field.

I asked the Indian minister about the Reverend Hebron Young Corey, my grandfather, since that was why I had come all this way. He told me he knew nothing about my grandfather but looked him up in a book called *History of the Canadian Baptist Foreign Mission to the Telugu of South India*. He read me the story of my grandfather baptizing the lepers at the riverbank which went something like the following: The Rev. Hebron Young Corey was riding his bicycle one day along a riverbank and heard a great commotion. He stopped and got off his bicycle to see what was going on. He found out that a group of lepers wanted to be baptized but that everyone was afraid to touch them. The Rev. H.Y. Corey then jumped down into the river and himself baptized all the lepers that wanted to be baptized. Thus began the mission of the CBFM to the lepers of South India.

My grandfather, out of compassion for the lepers, jumped into the river and baptized them all. Tears welled up in my eyes. My grandfather had risked his health and maybe even his life for his faith and his compassion for these most forsaken and untouchable of souls of India, of the Bible, and of history. My grandfather had shed the fear of thousands of years and touched, loved, and saved. He'd chosen to risk his own health to help the lepers, the lowest rung of Indian society. What a wonderful thing he'd accomplished. It was amazing for me to listen to this story I had never heard before, but I couldn't help but think how his choice had had consequences for his children. The Reverend H. Y. Corey and his wife, Clara, had ended up losing three sons because of their mission work in India.

The Indian minister asked me if I would like to walk to see the old missionary compound. We discussed dates, history, and where my mother might have been born. He said there were two possibilities among the houses where the missionaries had lived at the time my mother was born, but after further debate, he settled on one of them.

We walked through a walled compound of large houses with thick walls to keep out the heat. In the middle of a square was a rectangular house in ruins. The structure had no roof and had crumbling sides of brick covered with stucco. I walked from room to room, perhaps six rooms in all, wondering which had been the living room and which had been the library. I was told a large veranda had wrapped around outside, where the missionaries could sit in their rocking chairs to cool themselves. I remembered Mom telling me about the cook who'd crouched in the corner of the veranda over a grill to cook dinner and the punkahs—large fans—waved back and forth all day to keep air circulating in the heat.

I picked up some bricks and stucco pieces to take back with me to New York and thought again about my mother's life. She had been born to a forty-year-old mother in the middle of nowhere, in a compound surrounded by mud huts. Much tragedy had already happened to her family by the time she arrived, and her mother had been sickly and worn out. She must have seemed like an added burden, just as I must have seemed to my parents as the third child born a year before Pearl Harbor.

Seeing my mother's birthplace for the first time, the first time for anyone in my generation, made me try to imagine what her life must have been like. She had gone far in her life after starting out in this isolated, strange place.

My reverie was interrupted by the Indian Christian minister, who asked me if I would also like to see the Christian cemetery. I agreed with trepidation, having my mother's brother Cedric's sad story on my mind and wondering if I would find his grave. No one ever had told me where he was buried, so I had no idea if the grave was in Vizianagaram.

After a short walk, I found myself wandering among the Christians' headstones in the poorly maintained cemetery. I had to push away tall grass in order to read the stones lying on the ground: the Reverend Smith had died of malaria in 1910, Mrs. McHenry and child had died in 1900 of typhoid, and the Reverend Giles had died in 1885. I wondered what had killed the Reverend Giles. I looked for Mom's brothers' graves, for Cedric's or baby Harry's, but I did not find them. Mom had always been vague about what had happened to Cedric. It must have been too painful to try to explain. The walk in the cemetery felt like walking among the carnage of the missionary life in tropical southern India. I kept thinking about the promise they had clung to of a reward in heaven. I had come to believe we were meant to have an abundant life here on earth. *But we all live in different times. It is not up to me to judge my ancestors; rather, I seek to understand them so I might better understand myself and my family.* But seeing the cemetery made me begin to understand my mother's anger. There had been much tragedy in her young life, yet her parents had explained to her they were in India to serve God. It was too confusing to even mourn.

My minister guide interrupted my thoughts again and suggested we move on. After all, there was more to the story than a cemetery. He wanted to show me the schools, the orphanages, and the other churches and to have me meet more of the people whose families were helped by the missionaries.

We continued the trip to a village called Bobbili, where the girls' high school had been told we were coming. It was the school where my grandfather had been principal in the second decade of the twentieth century. The teachers, in their saris, were lined up to greet us, as though we were celebrities, and the students gave us garlands of flowers, putting them around our necks as a sign of welcome. They threw handfuls of rose petals onto the path where we walked to honor us and sang, "We welcome you. We welcome you. We welcome you to our school," in their stilted English. We walked into a courtyard with open classrooms all around and dirt floors. A group of smiling students in white blouses and red skirts, with red ribbons in their hair, came out to recite the Twenty-Third Psalm in English, in a military-like cadence. A group in white gym costumes, holding large metal circles covered with white flowers, performed impressive dance formations in the outdoor square of the school. They were charming and glowing. I was solicited for funds and gave them a donation.

The school demonstrated the pioneering work of the missionaries, providing a high school education for girls at a time when many girls did not attend a school at all, a lasting monument to the work of the missionaries. The happiness on the faces of the teachers and students of this pioneering girls' high school warmed my heart. I was glad to see the glowing school but couldn't help but think about the children of the missionaries, who all had been sent far away to school, not ever to a local day school like this one.

After leaving the girls' high school, we were driven to the home of Mr. Sharma, a Brahman whose grandfather had been converted by the missionaries and thereafter devoted the rest of his life to running orphanages. The Indian minister told me the missionaries had gone to the villages, picked the unwanted baby girls out of the gutters, and brought them to the orphanage, where Mr. Sharma and his family had taken care of them, fed and clothed them, and taught them Bible stories and English. After his death, the work had been carried on by his son and, subsequently, his grandson.

As hard as I tried, I could not picture a place where a baby girl could be lying in a gutter. What these missionaries had confronted I was here to try to understand: the desperation of the people and the great compassion of the missionaries.

My reverie was once again interrupted by the present Mr. Sharma coming out to greet me. A tall, elegant man clad in sparkling white bowed in a welcoming namaste gesture with his hands together in front of him. I bowed to him in return with my hands together in a namaste gesture. By the light and kindness beaming from his face, I felt I was in the presence of a truly holy man. He invited me into his comfortable home, where his daughter-in-law served tea and homemade crumpets to me, his wife and son, and the rest of my entourage. We talked about the orphanages he ran, and he told me how hard it had been since the Canadians all were asked to leave India, for they had lost their base of support. I asked what I could do to help, and he told me it would be a big help if I could build a church in one of the isolated villages.

I happily offered to give him the donation, knowing that a little money went far in India. He said he would build a redbrick church to the memory of the Reverend Hebron Young Corey's years of service in India, 1894 to 1924, and said it would help the villagers have a place to meet. I liked thinking about the memorial to my grandfather's life's work, despite all the tragedy to his own family and to the many Hindu converts who had been thrown out of their own families. Yes, it was true: if a Hindu villager converted to Christianity, the rest of the villagers banished the convert from the village because he or she had become defiled by eating with a noncaste person, since all foreigners had no caste. Thus, when Hindus converted to Christianity and took communion, they were defiled. The villagers banished husbands, fathers, grandfathers, and grandmothers when they converted to Christianity. *How hard it is to understand this history, except when one remembers the missionaries believed they had the only true religion and were sacrificing their lives and those of their children to save the Indians.* But there I was, their granddaughter, thinking it wasn't right, until I met Mr. Sharma's holy family. For generations, they had given loving service to the orphans.

This Indian family were at home with all their family together, caring for each other and the orphans, a different model from my grandparents, who had been halfway around the world from their families in a foreign land and had sent their children away.

After saying goodbye to lovely Mr. Sharma and my traveling companions, I flew to Tamil Nadu in the south of India, where I was driven in a car with a driver up the Nilgiri Hills to Coonoor and the original home of the girls' Hebron School, the boarding school Mom attended from age eight to fourteen.

The former Hebron School For Girls in Coonoor, which currently is an orphanage but still has the monkeys Mom used to talk about.

The old Hebron School of Coonoor had become an orphanage with a campus of small yellow buildings. Monkeys greeted me as I walked up the roadway. I remembered Mom telling me, "Although monkeys look cute, they are nasty. Never try to play with them." I steered clear. A teacher greeted me at one of the classrooms and offered to show me around. She took me into a dormitory. I stood still in shock. There were rows of narrow brown double-decker wooden bunk beds looking spare and barren. I shivered, wondering if this was where Mom had slept as a small eight-year-old crying herself to sleep with homesickness.

Brown bunk beds at the orphanage in Coonoor, India.

I could only imagine how scared and lonely Mom must have felt. I saw a swimming pool filled with rancid water and classrooms with small desks lined up in rows. Wondering what I could do to help, I asked my guide what they would like. She said a merry-go-round. I gave her my second $1,000 check I carried with me—half from my sister, Margie—for things to be built in Mom's memory.

Afterward, I went to Ootacamund, called Ooty, the current location of the Hebron School for boys and girls, still a boarding school. It looked like an English boarding school, with the children in English uniforms, located in what looked to me like a traditional Indian town. How strange it seemed to me to see traditional English boarding schools in the midst of Hindu India. This was the last stop on my visit to India.

It was time to pack up my Indian clothes, put on my khakis, and head back to New York, where I would no longer be the foreign one. I left behind the mud huts, orphans, money to build a new little redbrick church in memory of the Reverend Hebron Young Corey, money for a merry-go-round, and the economic Christians. Seeing the missionary compound where mother had been born and the Hebron School where, at age eight, she had been sent away for ten months a year allowed me to glimpse her isolated and lonely childhood in a foreign land. I had walked the ground my mother had walked and had seen the rickshaws, rice paddies, monkeys, and elephants. I had not needed to be so afraid.

Mother, dear, I have grown closer to you in my journey to your birthplace. It has revealed to me our common humanity, things I never saw when I was a child. I only saw things in terms of myself and how lonely I felt, not understanding the adorable little girl you were or realizing that you yourself had such a confusing, lonely, and painful entry into this world. I did not understand why it was hard for me to get close to you.

CHAPTER 2

Betty and Bob in Chicago, 1935

In the library of our home on South Kenwood Avenue in Chicago, a large embossed sterling-silver picture frame held my parents' wedding picture. Mom, born in India in 1908, and Dad, born in western Iowa in 1898, had married in 1936. I loved staring at the photo, although I could never imagine my parents looking that way. Mom, dressed in a creamy white lace wedding dress to the floor with a perky hat and a long veil, stood with Dad in his tails and and their wedding party at the Northwestern University Chapel. They looked elegant and tense, not smiling.

Betty and Bob's wedding photo, Evanston, Illinois 1936.

I would say, "Mom, could you tell me about how you met Dad and about your wedding?"

Mom, surprisingly, would answer me in detail and didn't seem to tire of telling me about how she had met my father and about her marriage to him, although it was a puzzling story. She used to say, "Men usually have cold feet when they marry, which is why they have a best man." Mom's story went something like this.

"In the fall of 1935, Jo"—Mom's best friend—"and I were living in Gary, Indiana, working as speech therapists. We'd spent the previous summer in England, being entertained in many country houses—friends of Jo's family—but one evening at six o'clock, we were getting ready for our dates with two thirty-six-year-old bachelor Chicago lawyers. We were in high spirits, still in the afterglow of our big trip to England, which even the Depression hadn't dampened. We were twenty-six years old, and I was having a blind date arranged by Jo. I put on the braided hairpiece I had worn in England that had made such a sensation and just enough makeup to still look natural." Looking natural was always of paramount importance to Mom.

"When Bob and Frank entered the living room, we greeted them in our flowered knee-length silk dresses. Bob seemed taken with me right away, but my face fell when I saw your father for the first time. He was too old."

I could imagine that was not a great way to start a relationship.

"On the way to the restaurant, I sat in the front seat. At dinner, Bob told his favorite stories about growing up in Iowa and how he had had to work since he was twelve, picking cockleburs in the fields for fifty cents a day and taking care of the horses on a nearby farm.

"I found Bob's stories entertaining, but the life he described of a small-town Iowa farming community was worlds away from anything I had ever known in India or Canada.

"In his small town of Mapleton, young people liked to arm-wrestle. Their hero was a man who could lift an anvil with one hand. Bob told me he had coached the winning football team in Cherokee, Iowa, and, during law school in Chicago, had joined the pro football team that became the Chicago Bears, playing guard for fifty dollars per game, which was enough for him to live on. I did admire his ingenuity but still thought him too old.

"At the end of the evening, the two men asked Jo and me if we would come into Chicago the following week to have dinner and attend the theater. We accepted.

———

12

"The next week, Bob was late for that second dinner, as he had to first attend a political fundraiser. Jo was annoyed at waiting for him, but I didn't mind.

"When Bob took me to dinner by himself the following week, I made clear my concerns about his being too old for me. 'Yes, I agree,' Bob replied, 'and you are a bit old for me. I'm used to dating women who are twenty-two, and you're twenty-six.'

"The next time we met, Bob asked me about this age thing, and I replied, 'I don't think it makes any difference.'"

That was always one of Dad's favorite stories.

"Twelve months after we met, your dad presented me with a handsome diamond ring and asked me to marry him. I accepted. I still had a Canadian passport but started proceedings to become a naturalized American citizen. It was hard for me to give up my Canadian citizenship, but I felt confident Bob and I could build a life together.

"We planned a formal evening wedding set for February 1936. I invited friends from Chicago and Northwestern and all of Jo's family to the wedding, which I wanted in the handsome chapel at Northwestern, where I had done graduate work. Out of my own savings from working as a speech therapist, I purchased an all-lace bridal gown with a veil to the floor, ornamented with an orange blossom bouquet. Of course, I had to do it myself the way I had to do everything myself. My mother was sickly and helpless, living in the old sail loft in Tenants Harbor, Maine, too far to help or even come to the wedding, and my father was deceased.

"Suddenly, out of the blue, the night before our wedding, your father got cold feet and decided he didn't want to get married after all. He said, 'I have been a bachelor for a long time and want to keep it that way. Let's call off the wedding.'

"I was furious and mortified and told him, 'You are not going to embarrass me in front of all my friends. You are going to marry me tomorrow. You can divorce me the next day if you wish.'

"We were married in a candlelight ceremony the next evening."

That was Mom's story, and she didn't seem to mind repeating it, a part of family lore, but it troubled me.

CHAPTER 3

Beginnings in Chicago, 1940

What lies behind us and what lies before us are tiny matters compared to what lies within us.

Ralph Waldo Emerson

After the peculiar wedding, Mom and Dad proceeded to have four children together. Their third child, I was born nearly five years into their marriage. My name, Elizabeth Bond, came from a previous Elizabeth Bond on my mother's side of the family, who had been the daughter of Revolutionary War hero Colonel William Bond, an officer among George Washington's troops who fought at Bunker Hill. The name had been passed down through the generations in Mom's family in Massachusetts and then Tenants Harbor. In naming me, Mom claimed her American roots. She wanted a new life through me, even though she had been born in India and had just become a naturalized American citizen. I was brought home as a newborn to a house my parents had just purchased on South Kenwood Avenue in Chicago.

Having three babies—a newborn, nearly two-year-old Bobby, and four-year-old Johnny—Mom was worn out. Dad needed his sleep, so every time I, the new baby, cried in the middle of the night, Mom had to get up, no matter how tired she was. "Sometimes you were left just too darn long in that crib," an analyst said to me years later.

Pearl Harbor came less than a year after my birth. Dad was already a veteran, and at age forty-three, he was not called back. He and Betty found a couple who would live on the third floor and assist with chores in return for rent. The war brought rationing and shortages, but Mom and Dad soldiered on. Dad continued to spend long hours away at work. Mom usually dragged her three children with her on errands. She didn't like it when strangers made a fuss over me. "You were so pretty as a baby," Mom told me many years later, "with your blonde curls all over your head, big blue eyes, and a peaches-and-cream complexion. Complete strangers would walk up and give you gifts. I decided that was a terrible way for my baby girl Betsy to grow up—to think she would be just given things—so I asked everyone to stop giving you presents."

In 1944, five days after D-Day, a fourth child arrived: my younger sister, Margie. If three children were difficult, four were impossible. In India, her mother had an ayah (a nursemaid) for each child, but Mom could not do that. Though she was given money to run the household, she would not ask Dad for more. She never asked for anything. After Mom and Dad's tense wedding, Mom told me, she decided she would not ask for things. Having given up her career as a speech therapist, she did not have money of her own. "You four children did not ask to be brought into this world," she told me when I was older. "I brought you all in, so I had to take care of you." She was a highly educated woman, particularly for her time, having done all the work for her PhD from the School of Speech at Northwestern, yet she spent much of her life doing housework.

Dad inherited his mother's farm in Iowa upon her untimely death. As he became more successful, he decided to sell the Iowa farm and buy a bigger one nearer Chicago. Dad had grown up doing hard work from the time he was a young boy. His first job had been picking cockleburs—prickly, round seed balls that cling to clothing—when he was eight years old. Now he dreamed of owning his own farm, not just managing one, as his father had. Some weekends, he went alone to his farm, leaving Mom and all four of us children alone for the day on Saturday. He climbed into his new tan Oldsmobile and drove an hour and a half to get there. Sometimes he took the two boys so they could learn to work, but many times, we all were left waving from the front door as he drove off.

I had a pit in my stomach upon seeing him drive off, wishing he would spend the day with me and teach me all about the farm. Mom excused his absences by saying, "It is good Dad is going. He is building up something, and all four of you kids should have an inheritance one day." But the truth was that Dad loved his livestock and his land. His prize Holstein bulls sired cows that won records for milk production. He never seemed happier than when he was scratching the head on one of his beloved cows or talking with his manager about the right mix of silage.

Meanwhile, Mom busied herself with chores back on Chicago's South Side. I watched her go upstairs in her light blue housedress, gather all the dirty clothes and linens from the bedrooms, and come downstairs like Santa, only Mom's sack was dirty laundry wrapped up in a sheet. I felt awful in seeing her struggle with the heavy load, and I pleaded with her, "Mom, let me help."

"No, no, Betsy, you go play," she replied repeatedly.

I tried again. "But, Mom, I really want to."

"No, I don't want you burdened the way I was as a child. I had to do all the work around the house because I had a helpless, sickly mother. I never want to do the same to my children."

Frustrated, resigned, and sad, I tried to think up something to do.

I always thought it was my fault my parents didn't want me around, because that is what all children think. I had no way of understanding Mom's depression and inability to cope with the needs of all her children. Mom must have been enormously angry at being left with all the drudgery, but her sense of duty made her keep going. But more than that, her parents had shooed her away in India; her sickly mother had been in bed, and her father had been away working as a missionary.

My oldest brother, Johnny, didn't even try to help. He mostly stayed in his room with his door closed. He read a lot of science fiction. I was scared to knock on his door, because he got so angry. "Go away. Leave me alone" was all he ever said. When he did play a game with us and the neighborhood kids who sometimes came over, he was so rough it wasn't any fun. Also, Johnny would say things that sounded outlandish to us kids: "Man will land on the moon one day." Everyone made fun of him. Johnny stamped angrily upstairs to his room and slammed the door. Of course, he was right and knew more than the rest of us because of his wide reading. Mom, busy in the house, was unaware of what was taking place in her own backyard.

Bobby, on the other hand, was kind and full of dumb jokes at which we all laughed. I was secretly jealous of him because he was the only one Mom would let help her. She would say, for example, "Bobby, here's a quarter. Please go to the store, and get us some bread." She even let Bobby help carry some of the heavy laundry. When he wasn't helping Mom, Bobby loved to make up experiments. He attached a string that ran all around the room to an alarm clock, which would set off several contraptions, including a mousetrap, to help him wake up in the morning. I loved Bobby, but he was often too busy to play with me.

My sister, Margie, was three and a half years younger. She always wanted to do whatever I was doing, and that wasn't much fun either. Besides, Mom kept a close watch on her and usually kept her in a playpen in the kitchen. One time, we were playing doctor up in my room, and Mom came and snatched Margie away. "Don't play with my baby," she said sternly.

We four kids did not learn to play with one another; we were isolated despite living under the same roof. The tension between my parents kept us apart as well.

On Sunday mornings, we four kids were sent to Sunday school at Hyde Park Baptist Church. The Sunday school teacher hugged me when I arrived and read Bible stories to the class. She showed us a picture of Jesus with lots of hair and piercing blue eyes. "Jesus loves you and forgives your sins. Believe in Jesus, and obey," the teacher told us. I sat quietly and listened. At the end of class, Mom came to pick me up. "Your daughter is an angel," said the teacher.

Mom always told me I was an easy child to raise. She kept saying to Margie, "Why can't you be more like Betsy?" Of course, that made Margie furious.

I liked the praise, but it confused me. It was not the way I felt inside. I was confused, not knowing what to do, not wanting to upset Mom, wanting Dad's approval. I sensed Mom's burden and hurt. I was always looking to Mom to try to understand, but of course, I had no idea what made her so angry. I did not want to add to her hurt and did not want her to get angry at me. I wanted to make things better for her and wanted to make her happy, so I smiled and obeyed, even when I didn't feel that way. Secretly inside, I wanted to have an exciting life like Dad's and wanted him to teach me, but he only wanted me to be quiet, obedient, and pretty and leave him alone.

I succeeded in getting praise and not anger but felt hollow inside. I became what is classically known in family systems theories as the lost child: the compliant, quiet one who is lonely and alone. I did not feel connected to myself or to others, but with a smile on my face, I tried to please. It was a role reversal for Mom and me, with my trying to care for

Mom and developing into what has been called the parentified child. When a child concentrates on protecting the mother, the child's own development suffers.

* * *

Whenever Dad returned from the farm, he was in his farming clothes, and his shoes smelled like manure. With a big smile on his face, he brought bushels of whatever produce was in season: tomatoes, apples, or brussels sprouts. When he sent a pig or a heifer to the meat packer, he would return home with meat wrapped in white paper. The freezer in the basement was then filled with the bounty of the country. Mom put the tomatoes in jars for the winter and made the apples into applesauce. Dad understood how to feed his family. Farming had taught him about nutrition for his cattle. "Don't eat that Wonder Bread; it's just white paste," he warned. "Whole wheat bread is better for you."

Dad exuded energy and life and had an imposing presence. He had been a fullback on the Iowa University football team and for the Chicago Bears in their early years. He had put himself through the University of Iowa and the University of Chicago Law School, earning money by wrestling, boxing, and playing football. He was my hero. His unwavering belief that women belonged in the home as wives and mothers sometimes turned to anger or derision when I got in his way or when I exerted myself. He would lash out unexpectedly and be critical, as his mother had done to him. I continued to learn to be quiet and invisible and stay out of the way.

One day, however, I decided to make Easter baskets for everyone and was proud of the cute bunnies I cut out of Dad's old shirt cardboard. I had found a stack of last year's Easter baskets and purple cellophane in our dark and dusty basement. I was sitting on the steps to the second floor, staying out of the way, assembling the baskets, when Dad happened to walk up. He had a hard time passing me on the stairs and became annoyed since he was in a hurry. Looking at the baskets, he surprised me. I thought he would say how nice they were, but instead, he wrinkled up his nose in disapproval, shook his head, and said, "They're not much good."

Stunned, I didn't speak up. I made no answer. As Dad walked on up the steps, I laid my head on the red-carpeted steps, and a black fog crept into my soul. I loved my big, important dad. How could I win his approval? What was wrong with me?

On Easter morning, I put out my baskets for everyone anyway. They did look puny compared to the big baskets Mom had put together and the huge chocolate bunnies and handsomely decorated eggs that Dad's clients had sent. No one said much to me about my baskets. My father found me crying in the kitchen and was annoyed because he wanted everyone to be happy at Easter. Once again, he wrinkled up his nose and shook his head, saying, "Betsy, wipe that silly expression off your face, or go to your room until you can come downstairs with a smile."

I went up to my room and lay on my bed. Eventually, I came back downstairs with that smile. "That's better," Dad said, but I did not feel better.

I never could understand my father's criticism and cruelty. I thought I was unacceptable. I had no way to understand as a little girl that my father was projecting onto me and many others the way he felt deep inside himself. It was intolerable to him the way he felt about himself, coming from his own childhood with a cruel, critical, and neglectful mother. He got rid of those feelings by being critical and cruel to others. Then he felt better. This cycle of abuse, which passes on from one generation to the next, is hard to break, for it is unconscious, but I took it on as my task in life to try to break the cycle.

My brother Bobby had his own way to describe Dad. Bobby loved to quote things he heard. One was something he must have heard on the radio: "Before one is married, a woman is courted with roses. Afterward, she is barefoot and courted with cabbages." Bobby thought he was hilarious.

"That's not funny," Mom fumed. "Don't ever say that again."

Some weekends, Dad did take us all to the farm. Once, in the fall, we were there all day. Dad talked to the hired hand who took care of his cows. He let John and Bobby ride the tractor to help with the fieldwork, but I was told to stay out of the way. Boys needed to be toughened up by hard work, but girls needed to stay in the home and be protected. I wished he would spend time with me. I wanted to know about the cows like Daddy did, but he wanted me to be out of the way.

I suddenly decided I would mow the big lawns in front of the manager's and farm hands' houses. (We never had a house for ourselves at the farm.) I found the old motorized mower and managed to get it started. I went up and down the big lawn, enjoying working. "Look at Betsy!" Dad exclaimed. "I didn't know she could do it."

On the way back to Chicago that Sunday afternoon, I was stuck between my two older brothers in the back. I never liked the long, boring rides. Margie was in front, on Mom's lap, making noise, and Dad was driving, singing his favorite songs: "Old Man River" and "Home on the Range." Mom didn't say much. Dad tried to keep us quiet by telling us to look for red cars. When that got tiring, Dad just told us to quiet down. At one point, I asked, "Daddy, will you please stop at the gas station?"

"No, wait till we get home," he replied.

"Dad, please, please stop," I pleaded.

"No. Quit whining. No one will want you when you grow up if you are a whiner," Dad said.

Finally, we turned into our driveway. I jumped out of the car and ran up the steps to the second floor two at a time. I was as desperate as I could ever remember being.

"Look at Betsy run." Dad chuckled. "I never knew she could move that fast. That's a pretty funny sight."

When I came back downstairs, Mom was in the kitchen, unpacking groceries. Dad was reading his newspaper. I snuggled in one corner of the oversized sofa. It had been brought down from the farm and recovered in rose canvas. I couldn't think of anything to do and curled up to make myself small.

The smells from Mom cooking supper—fried apples, fried tomatoes, and fried pork chops—awakened me. "Mom, can I help?" I asked.

"No, Betsy, I'm busy. Go play till I call you," replied Mom.

I gave in. "Okay, Mother."

I went back to the rose sofa in frustration. I tried to get myself to obey and wait for supper, to figure out a way for me to be better, but my mind went blank.

I went into the backyard and climbed to the top of the six-foot wooden fence, using the mulberry tree's branches as a ladder. The fence separated us from our back neighbors. I walked carefully along its small ledge a foot below the top of the fence in order to reach the tree of heaven that grew near the fence. A branch of the tree hung just a few feet from where I was standing. I figured I could make it and flung myself off the fence toward the branch, grabbing it. Since the tree of heaven was a bendy tree, once I had hold of the branch, my weight pulled it down toward the ground, and I jumped off. It was fun. I repeated the maneuver over and over.

I went back inside, and Mom told me to wash my hands because dinner would be ready in ten minutes. I dutifully washed up and came back to sit and wait for the others to arrive so dinner could be served.

There was free time after supper before bedtime. I went out again to the backyard and climbed the wooden fence and the same old tree that would lower me gently to the ground. It felt good to be in the air between the fence and the tree. I kept doing the same thing repeatedly. Time finally passed.

At bedtime, I went in to say good night to my parents in their salmon-painted bedroom with frilly white curtains. I wanted to sit on Daddy's bed and talk. My parents slept in twin beds. I did not want to be sent away again. But Dad said, "Good night, Betsy. Good night. Go to bed."

I went over and gave Mom a kiss in her bed. Reluctantly, I left my parents' bedroom and walked down the narrow, dark hallway to my bedroom and crawled into my bed, which had little rails on each side so I couldn't fall out. Margie was sleeping in her crib.

I was curled up, trying to be invisible, when I happened to look outside my window and see the most amazing sight: a vision of a huge figure lighting up the darkness, looking through my small window, bringing light into my room and onto me. It was standing on the tree of heaven outside the window. The figure glowed, giving off a beautiful, soft light in the tone of coppery blue green. I cried out to my mother to come, but she didn't. She must not have heard me, I thought, so I tried again. "Mom! Look what's in my window! Please come!"

It was so real. The figure outside my window seemed warm and kind. It glowed from within. It looked like the Statue of Liberty with her arm outstretched, blessing me, reassuring me. As I kept staring at this great figure glowing with reassuring light, I noticed men, small in comparison to the great figure, dressed like my father in white business shirts, brown pants, and brown suspenders, climbing up the outside of the figure's huge robe. I couldn't tell why they were there, but I wanted my mother to come see.

The vision comforted me. Mom did not come, and eventually, I fell asleep. I wasn't more than five years old at the time. The figure never reappeared, nor did I have other visions afterward, but I became curious about my family's history and the meaning of the vision. From the time I was a little girl, I started collecting any information I could find, and eventually, I wrote out the history as I had come to understand it.

When, many years later, I studied theology and psychology, I could understand one interpretation of the vision as my father seeking comfort from a loving presence, as he himself was extremely needy. The vision showed my wish to be the strong and caring one.

CHAPTER 4

Clara and Hebron 1868 - 1895

Tenants Harbor, the tiny village where Clara, my grandmother, was born in 1868, had been both her mother's and her father's ancestral home. Halfway up the coast of Maine, on the St. George Peninsula, it was one of innumerable similar villages that were infinitely important to those who called them home. The village had one main street with small white clapboard houses and a few stores. Halfway up the hill stood a white schoolhouse with a bell tower, and at the top of the hill, gracefully surveying the village, stood the Baptist church, with its tall white steeple and elegant stained-glass windows dedicated to Clara's relatives, the pride of Clara's extended family.

Dependent on the sea and its safe, well-situated harbor, the villagers created a prosperous life out of their relationship to the sea but had to survive its inevitable tragedies. Clara's grandfathers on both sides were shipbuilders, and she heard of the sturdy wooden coastal sailing vessels they built. Sent on voyages laden with lumber, granite, and ice from Tenants Harbor, they traded for goods the villagers needed.

Clara's grandfather Deacon Robert Long, a second-generation Irishman, went to sea at age ten to learn the trade of sailing, made captain at age twenty, and retired at forty to build a commercial building for his growing businesses on the shores of Tenants Harbor. He built the Sail Loft in 1848, the very building I inherited in 1974. It is a large white wooden rectangular building with a commanding view of the harbor. Robert Long had a ship's chandlery on the first floor and a loft on the second floor that he rented out to a sail maker. Out in front was a wharf for all the ships coming in and out of the harbor to do business with him.

Clara's grandfather's success went beyond his businesses, for he successfully wooed and married Margaret Smalley, the daughter of the oldest family in town, a *Mayflower* descendant. Clara was proud of that ancestry and might have inherited a bit of their attitude. "The Smalleys thought they were better than anyone else," the town manager said to me many years later.

The new groom became a deacon of the Baptist church, a designation he proudly kept for the rest of his life. Thus, Clara was brought up with a mix of the social snobbery of her *Mayflower* ancestors, a dedication to the church, and the rough-and-tough of the Irish shipbuilders. The mix stuck to the family for three generations.

Clara's own father and mother were like her grandparents. Deacon Robert and Margaret's son, Whitney, went into the shipbuilding business with his father and married Elizabeth Bickmore, a refined and college-educated woman from a distinguished family in town with important relatives in Boston and New York, such as Albert Bickmore, the father of the American Museum of Natural History in New York City.

Clara's parents, like the previous generation, had made their life in Tenants Harbor and built a modest white clapboard Cape with green shutters. The house had an attached woodshed and a barn overlooking the harbor on High Street. They could see the sailing vessels coming in and out of the harbor, carrying goods to ports near and distant. Many of the ships docked at the family's wharf. The provisioning officers walked up the hill to the Long and Son chandlery to outfit their ships for voyages, buying everything from blocks and pulleys to coffee, sugar, and boots.

The white Baptist church, with its tall steeple, on the highest hill, served as a beacon for the sailors and villagers. The Long family attended the Baptist church for Sunday service, a Bible study hour, and Wednesday night prayer service, as I did three generations later. The minister preached the Bible as the Word of God and a strict code of morality: keep the Sabbath holy; no dancing, no cards, and no alcohol allowed; live by the Golden Rule and the Ten Commandments; believe, and your life will be saved; and God will provide for his flock. Life prospered in the tiny village, until it didn't anymore.

This tiny village and these ancestors were the people both Clara and Betty clung to all their lives, their Camelot, a prosperous, highly educated, accomplished, churchgoing, socially elite family, but it wasn't perfect even back then.

Grandmother Clara Watts Long was christened Clarissa after her aunt who had died at nineteen just six years earlier. As Clara grew older, she was told the story: Clarissa loved to help at her father's ship chandlery in the sail loft. Her parents were too busy to spend time with her. At the chandlery, she came to know Albert Elwell, the sailmaker who rented the upstairs loft. Albert had a wonderful smile, and Clarissa felt he understood all she said. Once, while Clarissa and Albert were alone up in the loft, Albert held Clarissa's hand. She had never felt such happiness before.

But her parents disapproved of their spending time together and tried to stop Clarissa from coming to the sail loft. Clarissa and the sailmaker fell in love despite her parents' objections. Deacon Robert Long and his wife, Margaret, forgetting for the moment that Deacon Robert himself was a self-made man, were horrified that their cultured Clarissa, just eighteen, would want to marry a lowly sailmaker. They forbade the marriage.

Clarissa, however, was determined and eloped with Albert. They might have escaped to the next town and rented a small house. They were happy together, even though the new groom couldn't provide the style of life Clarissa was accustomed to. Clarissa didn't seem to care, but the house was drafty, and Clarissa caught pneumonia. Despite everyone's best efforts, she died within a year of her elopement.

Heartbroken, her husband used his meager savings to build a magnificent monument in the Tenants Harbor cemetery: a Gothic white marble arch with a broken urn inside, carved with the following inscription:

> The silver cord is loosed, the golden bowl is broken
> Clara W.
> Wife of William A. Elwell,
> Died Feb. 12, 1862: Aged 19 years.

At the base of the monument was written, "God's Will Be Done." The pure-white monument, the only one ever built in Tenants Harbor, gleamed in the moonlight and reminded all the people of the village of the tragic story of the lovely young Clarissa and her beloved William.

Deacon Robert and Margaret spent the rest of their lives greatly humbled and sad, wondering whether Clarissa might still have been alive if they had not forbidden the marriage. Clarissa's mother, Margaret

Smalley Long, the *Mayflower* descendant, had thought she was better than everyone else, but the death of her lovely young daughter put everything in perspective. Social standing felt irrelevant in the face of the stark reality of their daughter's death. They warned everyone around them not to interfere with the marriages his or her children wanted to make. Clara heard the message clearly and passed it along to her daughter, Betty, my mother, who in turn told me she did not intend to interfere with my decision to marry, because of the story of tragic Great-Aunt Clarissa.

Clara's own life was another powerful lesson for Betty in the effect that one's choice of a husband has on one's own life—and on the lives of their children. Her mother's choice led her far away from the village where she was born, into an extraordinary life of sacrifice and willing deprivation that we can barely conceive of today, as well as many unintended and tragic consequences.

Clara, having been born into a charmed family in Tenants Harbor, witnessed it all change when she was just a tiny girl. A crisis changed everything in her life, the life of her family, and, eventually, the whole village of Tenants Harbor. Long and Son's shipbuilding business went bankrupt. Clara's father, Whitney, had arranged to build three ships all at once. The capital to build the ships came from Long and Son's, but once the ships were built, shares to finance each voyage were sold to families in the village, who in turn would share in the profits when ships successfully returned to Tenants Harbor. Of course, a number never returned.

That year, however, in the middle of the construction of the three new ships, the workers went on strike, demanding higher pay. The carpenters, joiners, blacksmiths, and painters walked off the job, with the wooden ships left partly finished on the shore. The labor strike bankrupted the Longs' business, but it was also part of the bigger story of the demise of the wooden ships along the coast of Maine and, indeed, the whole eastern seaboard—a catastrophe.

The strike never settled. The number of customers coming to the chandlery declined quickly since the economy of the entire village had been affected. Tradesmen left the village to find jobs elsewhere. The old chandlery closed and became a grocery store for the villagers. Few sailing vessels came in and out of the harbor, and the ships' captains had no more work. The family no longer had a business to support them. They and the entire village became poorer. The unfinished ships were left to rot on the shore. Steam-driven ships replaced the wooden sailing vessels, and the train bypassed Tenants Harbor. The whole way of life the people of Tenants Harbor had known for generations collapsed.

Ships' graveyard—five-masted schooners left to rot as the sailing ships of the coastal trade were made obsolete by the introduction of the steam engine.

Thus came the true start of my long saga. The economic collapse of Tenants Harbor led to a struggle for the villagers to maintain their identity and values in the face of growing poverty. The generations who followed kept looking back at the so-called golden age, trying to rebuild their lives based on this story. At the same time, their struggle led to economic and social distortions.

I thought it my duty to turn the old abandoned sail loft, the last vestige of the glory days of the wooden ships, back into something beautiful, a reincarnation. This would be a fulfillment of my mother's dream of a return of something solid in her life, but she was long dead. What would it mean to me in my life and for my children? Perhaps a link to the past.

Clara's family stayed on in the village and struggled. Her father, handsome and sensitive Whitney Long, felt like a failure. He had not been able to keep the business going and felt he couldn't live up to his father's expectations. He couldn't adjust to the reality that not only had his shipbuilding business gone bust, but the whole wooden ship industry had become obsolete down the whole eastern seaboard of the United States and, indeed, around the world.

Except for lobstering, fishing, and granite quarrying, the villagers of Maine who lived on building ships and shipping never found another industry to bring them a second golden age like the great era of the wooden ships, except perhaps today in the era of retirees and second homes. There were a few individuals who thrived in Clara's family's story, such as Clara's cousin Lillius Gilchrest, also of Tenants Harbor. Lillius, while on one of her father's ships in South America, walked off the gangplank into the arms of William R. Grace and married him in 1859. William R. Grace founded Grace and Company in Peru in 1854, became extremely successful, and became mayor of New York City—but this was not my family.

Clara's father, Whitney, took the failure of his business personally and began to drink. When he couldn't see a way out, he kept up his drinking. Clara's mother, the fine Elizabeth Bickmore, struggled to hold the family together and do her best for her girls under the difficult circumstances. Luckily for the family, their cousin Lillius helped them out. The proud family accepted her gifts.

Elizabeth, their fine mother, was determined to see her girls educated the way she had been educated. Her firstborn, Clara, considered homely, went to the ladies' collegiate course of Coburn Classical Institute in Waterville, Maine, and graduated in 1888. The tallest of the sisters, with a plain face and hair tied back in a bun, Clara was called Deacon because she looked like her grandfather, the blustery Deacon Long. She was determined to do something with her life. She taught school for a few years but had always been interested in missionary work, as she wrote much later:

> The winter following my 14th birthday, I was converted and soon united with the Baptist Church at home, being one of many who were converted during the great revival. From a child I was interested in Missions as my mother from an early age told me about missionaries … Indeed, so early did she begin this instruction that the second thing I remember her telling me about was Judson's work in Burma. My grandmother also was interested in mission work and for years was president of the Women's Missionary society of our church, and yet when I wanted

to be a missionary, they almost wondered how I became interested in the work.

However, from the time I was converted I felt the call to the foreign field and although I taught school for several years yet I kept this in view always and finally applied to the UBFM [United Baptist Foreign Mission] Society of the United States to be sent to the foreign field and was accepted as a candidate and went to Mrs. George's home at Newton Centre with several others who are now in Burma to prepare for the work there.

She physically left the village of Tenants Harbor and her alcoholic father, though emotionally, it remained forever her heart's home. When she was just twenty-four years old, in late August 1892, her mother helped her pack her domed trunk to set off from her small white clapboard home on High Street down the hill in a horse cart to the family's wharf on the harbor's edge in front of her grandfather's sail loft to start a new chapter of her life. I can imagine that she wore a newly made floor-length gray cotton dress with a matching gray woolen shawl to throw around her shoulders while at sea. Everyone came to see her off, and they waved white handkerchiefs as the ferryboat moved out of sight of land and became just a spot on the horizon.

Filled with apprehension and excitement, she traveled by steamer to Boston and then to Mrs. George's home, part of Newton Theological Seminary. While settling at the seminary, she met another student, Hebron Young Corey, a tall, handsome Canadian with penetrating blue eyes and a kind face. It seemed to be love at first sight. The ugly duckling Clara from Tenants Harbor was transformed.

Hebron, who'd been born on March 31, 1862, in Butternut Ridge, Kings County, New Brunswick, Canada, was one of thirteen children in a family of farmers. His ancestors had been Tories during the American Revolution and escaped to Canada, where they'd had to start over. Hebron distinguished himself by becoming a star student and athlete, winning the governor's medal in his province.

Hebron's family attended church in Petitcodiac, which, like Tenants Harbor, had a prominent white-steepled Baptist church that was the center of family life. For generations, Hebron's family had sent one of its offspring to Acadia University and to Newton Theological Seminary to be trained for the Baptist ministry, not unlike Irish Catholic families sending one of their sons to be a priest.

Hebron's uncle Charles Henry Corey, his hero, had graduated from Acadia in 1858 and Newton Theological Seminary in 1861 and become a Baptist pastor. He'd fought in the Civil War and, afterward, become a missionary among the freedmen of South Carolina. In 1868, he had been named president of the Richmond Theological Institute for the training of African American preachers and teachers. He served as the president of the Negro Seminary, as it was often called, until just before his death in 1898.

Reverend Charles Henry Corey believed the best way to lift society was to start with those who suffered most, spending his career teaching and preaching to the poor former slaves in the South, many of whom had not been allowed an education and had limited vocabularies. He enabled them to found Southern Baptist churches in the South, where some of the parishioners were so poor when they married they could only pay the preacher in eggs—three was the going rate. Hebron, deeply impressed with such stories, wanted to model his life on that of his uncle: to teach and preach to the poor and outcast.

Following in his uncle's footsteps, Hebron graduated from Acadia in 1891 and from Newton Theological Seminary in 1894. He accepted the call from the Canadian Baptist Foreign Mission Board to serve as a missionary among the Telugu people of poor, isolated southern India. In his own words, he said, "I dedicated my life to doing good in India."

The year 1894 was the time of the Second Great Awakening, the call to go out to all corners of the earth to evangelize the heathens, save their souls, and bring light to the darkness. Clara and Hebron became caught up in the movement.

When Hebron asked Clara to marry him and accompany him to India, Clara accepted. Both Baptists, they shared the missionary's zeal deep in their bones. She decided that instead of being a missionary herself in Burma, she would be the wife of a missionary in India. It meant giving up her own career and going far from Tenants Harbor and her beloved mother, but at the same time, she would escape her father's drinking and the bankruptcy of her family.

In preparation for marriage, Clara left seminary, leaving her studies unfinished, and returned to Tenants Harbor for a year to teach and get ready for her new life as a spouse in a foreign land. Like her namesake, Clarissa, Clara was going with her love. The young couple's wedding took place on August 23, 1894, in Tenants Harbor Baptist Church, the same church that today has a coatrack and umbrella stand in her memory, given by her daughter.

They sailed off to India shortly after their honeymoon. Clara had just turned twenty-six, and Hebron was thirty-two. Clara wrote her mother letters nearly every day on board the ship and regularly during all the years she and Hebron served in India, from 1894 to 1923. Ten years of letters are missing, 1900 to 1910. Her daughter, Betty, might have removed them to write a play called *The Choice* about their first son, Cedric, and his tragic life. Unfortunately, the play has been lost. In all her letters, Clara called Hebron Mr. Corey, but in all the official correspondence, he is called Reverend H. Y. Corey, and she is Mrs. Corey.

The new missionaries were equipped with Bibles, hymnals, and New Testament tracts. They had not studied Hinduism or learned the Telugu language. Their domed trunks were filled with handmade long summer dresses with petticoats, woolen shawls, linens with lace trim lovingly made or given by their family and fellow members of Tenants Harbor Baptist Church, linen handkerchiefs, her mother's favorite recipes for apple chutney and fish stew, and cotton suits for Hebron. On the steamship, they saw great sights, met cultured people, and had their first experience with Hindu Indians, who were for the most part the ship's porters. She wrote, "Am getting quite used to the native servants on board. All the men except for the officers are Hindus." Clara was continually seasick, and Hebron cared for her.

They changed steamers in London to sail through the Mediterranean. They arose one morning early to see Vesuvius in action but did not go ashore with the others in Capri because it was a Sunday, and one had to keep the Sabbath holy. They were amused by the traders bartering on board the ship. Clara was amazed that flowers that would have cost five dollars in Rockland, Maine, could be had for twenty-five cents. There were some pleasant families on board, especially a tea planter with his well-behaved children.

They arrived in Madras (now Chennai), four hundred miles from their destination, in early December 1894, the cool season. They were heading for Vizianagaram in the state of Andhra Pradesh, located on the eastern coast of India. There the Canadian Baptist Foreign Mission Board (CBFMB) had their mission field, the area designated for the Canadian Baptists by the American Baptist Convention for outreach to the Telugu people and a few tribes. Their mission field hugged the Bay of Bengal and included around seven thousand square miles, thousands of villages, and several cities, four of which already had compounds where Canadian missionaries lived. In their thirty years in India, Clara and Hebron were moved around to different towns within the mission field, including Parlakimidi, Bimlipatam, Bobbili, and Waltair, but they returned often to Vizianagaram, their main station.

The plains of South India were tropical and hot, vastly different from Tenants Harbor. The heat was punishing during the dry season in the spring months until the rainy season in August. Farther south, up high in the Nilgiri Hills of Tamil Nadu, there were cooler areas where the missionaries escaped in the worst of the heat. In these English hill towns, as they were known, the missionaries held their annual conference.

The Maritime Canadian (i.e., from the eastern Canadian provinces) Baptist Mission was established in 1874 and ended in 1970, when the Indian government demanded all foreign missionaries leave the country. In the one hundred years the Canadians worked in their mission field in Andhra Pradesh, they established hundreds of small village chapel schools, city boarding schools for caste girls, day schools for no-caste children (held on the missionaries' verandas with boys and girls separated), girls' high schools, an industrial school, orphanages, hospitals, leper asylums, a theological seminary, and both English and Telugu churches. In 1894, when Clara and Hebron arrived, the work had been in progress for twenty-some years.

To get to Vizianagaram from Madras, Clara and Hebron took a steamship to the port city of Vizagapatnam and, from there, an oxcart ride on a dusty one-lane dirt road that swerved around herds of goats, wandering cows and bulls considered holy, women in colorful saris, and rice paddies. Pulled by a pair of oxen with a driver, an oxcart traveled two miles an hour, carrying people and belongings on a wooden platform with wooden sides and large wooden wheels.

"THE LONG TREK"
Three hundred miles: two miles an hour

Oxcart in a river in India

Clara and Hebron would have had to bring their food with them and sleep on the oxcart. The driver probably doubled as a cook and gathered wood along the way to build a fire to boil water for tea and for curried rice. There were no sanitation facilities along the way, and one can only imagine the proper young New England matron embarrassed but making do along the dirt roads of India. In 1894, the trip took four or five days. Today it takes two hours by car.

Clara and Hebron were part of the second wave of Canadian Baptists to arrive in India from the Maritimes. The first wave of seven had arrived in 1874, and another seven came in 1894. Their new home in Vizianagaram was a missionary bungalow of brick covered in lime whitewash, with large rooms with tall ceilings. A spacious covered veranda where the cook would crouch over a charcoal stove ran around the outside of the house. It had a courtyard surrounded by a tall whitewashed brick wall.

The bungalow had been built by the London Missionary Society, a group who had left India in 1870 and sold their properties to the Canadians. The land had been given to the missionaries by the maharaja, the local ruler. The maharaja appreciated the Christian charity and social consciousness of the missionaries and occasionally loaned his carriage to make their transportation faster and easier. Funds for salaries, Bible tracts, and buildings were sent by the Baptist churches of Maritime Canada. The schools the missionaries started in Telugu were for Indian Christians, some for high castes and some for Dalits, the lowest caste, previously known as untouchables, while the maharaja established schools for Hindus.

Clara and Hebron might as well have been going to the moon. Their missionary bungalow was in an isolated, hot, dusty, poor preindustrial town in the Telugu-speaking state. Their part of Vizianagaram was a village of mud huts with grass roofs, rickshaws, and oxcarts, which contrasted sharply with the maharaja's palace on the far side of their compound. Villagers wore traditional Indian garb: dhotis (long white loincloths) and loose-fitting shirts for the men and saris for the women. The men often carried piles of agricultural products on their heads, and the women carried a water jug or sometimes two. Children swarmed the newly arriving missionaries. They seldom saw white people, except for other missionaries or British colonial officials. The loneliness and isolation must have been unfathomable.

The Canadian Baptist Mission, dedicated to religious and humanitarian purposes, was securely part of the British raj, a world utterly separate from Indian life. Hindus were born into a caste they could leave only upon death. The accompanying belief in karma dictated that one's past deeds determined his or her current caste, and his or her current actions would determine his or her caste in the next life. Caste dictated one's work; whom one could marry; and whom one could associate with, eat with, and go to school with. The castes did not mix. The missionaries, however, believed that all people were created equal in the sight of God and that humans should love one another, help one other, and be together in community. It was a clash.

Although the missionaries were poor in comparison to the British officials, the lowest-caste Indians, the Dalits, saw them as rich, which created a conflict in status hard to reconcile in India. When the white Western missionaries preached to the lowest-caste Hindus, some of their audience couldn't help but think that following the faith of the rich white men might make them rich and free. At the same time, however, many others, both Dalits and a few high-caste Indians, converted to Christianity out of true belief.

The most difficult aspect of becoming a Christian was that the rules of caste forbade it. Converts had to leave their villages and everything they knew. Wives would not tolerate having husbands who converted, because they felt defiled. Their mothers would come take their daughters back home. Hindus who took part in the Eucharist with a missionary were defiled, because they had eaten with a no-caste person. Caste Hindus could not go to school with Dalit Indians for the same reason: they would be defiled.

Hindu villagers would not tolerate having a Christian convert in their midst. When Hindus converted to Christianity, the Hindu villagers broke the converts' cooking pots, tore down their houses, and ran them out of the village, sometimes stoning them. Nor would the Baptist missionaries tolerate the newly converted continuing to live in their traditional ways. Evangelizing the Indians had the unintended consequence of breaking up the Hindu families. The missionaries' beliefs took precedence over the maintenance of family relationships, and that too, unintentionally, contributed to the breakup of village society.

Hebron and Clara had followed their calling, going into a Hindu culture they had not studied. With my eyes today, it seems a tragedy all the way around, even though they left some things for which India is still grateful, such as schools, hospitals, and the English language. But how was their daughter, Betty, ever to make sense of her parents' life in India? She never could. She ended up unconsciously duplicating much of it on the South Side of Chicago.

Chapter 5

Tenants Harbor, Maine 1947 -1948

By the time I was six, it was clear that Mom's mother, Clara, the wife of the missionary, could no longer stay in her home in the sail loft house in Tenants Harbor, and Mom brought her to live in Chicago. Grandmother Clara took over the back room on our second floor. There were three other bedrooms on the second floor: I shared a room with my sister, my brothers shared a room, and my parents had the front bedroom.

I had little interaction with my grandmother, but one afternoon in the early fall, I was lonely and wanted to find out about Grandma. I knocked gently on the door of her room. "Come in," said a faint voice, and I cautiously entered the back bedroom.

According to Mom, Grandma and I had met before on trips to Tenants Harbor, but I did not remember her. She seemed like a stranger when I saw her sitting by the window in a black leather chair with wooden arms and legs. She was dressed head to toe in black. Her small silver wire glasses and ashen white hair pulled back in a bun made her pale face look round and puffy. We stared at each other with blank expressions, neither seeming to know the other. I wanted to go closer, but my curiosity was overshadowed by fear. Would she be my friend?

I sorely wanted a friend, yet I froze before getting any closer than five feet from the big chair. Her gaze never left mine, but she felt cold, like a heap of black ice. We just stared at each other. After what felt like a long time, I backed away slowly and quietly, until I closed the door behind me.

I had received no hugs or kisses from my only living grandmother. I went back to my room and snuggled up on my bed.

A few weeks after our encounter, Grandma Clara was moved to a nursing home in southern Illinois. She'd broken her hip by falling down the stairs, and looking after her was more than Mom could do. Besides, Clara was showing signs of senility. Keeping a home, shopping, cooking for Dad and four children, and sewing clothes for herself and her children kept Mom busy. Then there were all her other activities: directing the church pageant, in which I was cast as one of the angels; participating in a garden club flower-arranging contest, for which Mom decorated an old wooden wheelbarrow with pots of red geraniums and a yellow watering can; and organizing the mothers of the PTA safety committee to see that children were safe when crossing streets on their way to and from the local school.

But she saw her mother as often as she could. "I went to visit Grandma yesterday," said Mom one day while doing the dishes at our huge white farm-style sink. "She asked me why I hadn't been to visit in so long, when I had just gone two days before. Can you imagine, Betsy? She'd completely forgotten. Poor thing."

We were silent for a minute. I wanted to help, to be with Mom, but she said I should go play, and she would dry the dishes. I stayed around because I wanted to be with Mom.

"It was just so hard when she was living here," Mom said, looking out the dark window, as if speaking to no one in particular. "She'd seen a fly on the window and tried to swat it with a frying pan. Of course, the window broke, and so did my patience. She just didn't know what she was doing anymore."

On a cold, blustery winter day, I came home from school and found Mom crying in the kitchen with her head down and her hands on the side of the sink. It was unexpected and looked out of place in our crowded kitchen. I'd never seen her cry before. I was beside myself, with an indescribable tightness in my stomach. She was wearing a pale blue housedress and standing with her back to me by the mangle near the wall. I wanted to hug her, but I couldn't bridge the gap and make it happen. "Mom, what happened? What's the matter? What's going on?"

"Grandma has died," she answered, and after a moment, she added, "Someday you'll understand how sad it is."

* * *

Dad was too busy with work to accompany Mom as she escorted Grandma's body back to Tenants Harbor. She'd be buried at Seaside Cemetery, next to nearly all the relatives who'd died before her. I wondered how Mom fared on the all-night train ride to Boston. She'd have to transfer to an older, ricketier train for a three-hour ride to Rockland, Maine, where she'd be met by a hearse for the half-hour drive to Grandma's final resting place.

I felt lighthearted and happy when Mom arrived back home. She quickly changed into her turquoise housedress and white apron and busied herself with dinner preparations: fried chicken, fried apples, and fried potatoes and always a green salad. The aroma was dizzying, and I wanted to help her.

"No, Betsy, you go out and play," she said in her typical response.

But I got a wave of courage, along with concern, and I persisted. "Mom, what was it like burying Grandma?"

She continued minding the pans over the six-burner gas stove for a few moments and then started to choke up again. "It was very sad, Betsy," she said gingerly. "She was only seventy-eight and had a very hard life. Her body seemed so old." She paused to wipe her eyes with a tissue. "And yet she had a beautiful, radiant smile on her face while lying in her open coffin at her funeral at the front of the Baptist church in Tenants Harbor. It was amazing that her old, wrinkled face could be so transformed. I thought she must have seen something that made her very happy when she died. Even the undertaker said no makeup artist could have created such an expression of joy."

I remained still with no expression as I thought about what she was saying. I tried to imagine the old, wrinkly face I had seen in the back room transformed into something beautiful.

Mom continued, saying she was pleased that her mother was buried with the family and that they all had matching gravestones. "There are two additional stones for her other sisters when they pass," she added.

I found this news alarming. "They make stones before people die?"

"Yes, it's better that way. It makes it easier when someone dies."

To my surprise, my mother continued, adding details about the funeral and how she wanted her mom to be remembered. She told me the service had been held in Tenants Harbor Baptist Church, where stained-glass windows in memory of Clara's ancestors looked beautiful. She'd felt as if she were surrounded by her family from generations back. She told how she wanted Grandma to be remembered and said she had given money for the purchase of a coatrack and umbrella stand with her name to be put on a small plaque. Mom's talking to me so openly wasn't her usual way, and I treasured every moment.

* * *

After Grandmother Clara's death, Mom would leave Dad at home and take my siblings and me to stay for summers in Clara's old apartment in the sail loft in Tenants Harbor, Maine. Everyone seemed happy with the arrangement, although I always had a pang in my heart when leaving Dad for the summer. We took the train from Chicago to Boston and from Boston to Rockland. Sometimes we had sleeper cars, but other times, Mom walked us four children past all the sleepers to the coaches bound for Boston, where we settled into our seats and waved out the window to Daddy.

"Dad will try to get up there the last two weeks of August," said Mom, "perhaps bringing Miss Railton, his old bookkeeper, whom he thinks could benefit from the sea air."

It was a long night when trying to sleep on the seats. The seats pushed down partway, and Mom rented us pillows and blankets from the porter. Since it was hard for me to fall asleep, I peeked out the windows at Cleveland, Buffalo, Syracuse, Albany, and, finally, Boston, where we piled into a taxi to change stations and catch the rickety train with wicker seats to Rockland, Maine. We arrived in the late afternoon, and a taxi drove us the ten miles down the St. George Peninsula to Tenants Harbor. We were without a car till Dad arrived at the end of the summer.

Staying in the small apartment where Clara had lived as a widow, I saw her black coat still hanging in the closet in her sitting room and bedroom. It gave me the shivers. It looked to me handmade of a beautiful silk material fitted at the waist but with all the buttons cut off. I imagined she had had the special coat made out in India and kept it as her best coat for special occasions. Her glass-fronted desk overflowed with letters she had kept, scraps of paper, and several long cream tubes that Margie later speculated had held some sort of birth control. Mom hadn't the heart to clean out any of it ever.

It was all a tribute to the life that had been: the front parlor with Clara's Bibles and books, the summer kitchen with its wooden icebox and barrel of kerosene, the winter kitchen with the cream-and-apple-green kerosene stove, the bedroom with the flowered wallpaper, and the small yellow bedroom. Even the cabinets in the summer kitchen were stuffed with Clara's careful thriftiness: brown paper bags neatly folded; spools of yarn she had carefully recovered from no-longer-usable sweaters; spools of thread and materials saved from a worn-through dress to make into quilting squares; and piles of worn-out soles of shoes neatly tied with white string. I don't know that any of these were treasures to Mom, but she never touched them. Mom left her mother's apartment untouched because she didn't want to deal with all her feelings toward her mother. Better not to touch it. Thus, the black coat of Clara's from India continued to hang in Clara's closet until many years later, when Betty herself was long gone.

Three of us slept in the yellow room in the corner. It once had been the cloakroom for the village school held at the sail loft, but when I was little, it had an antique iron crib for the baby, a cot with a feather mattress for me, and a daybed with a thin mattress for Bobby. It was cozy, warm, and fun. We loved being together. Johnny had to sleep in a different room because the tiny yellow room was too small for a fourth bed. He had a daybed in Clara's parlor, and Mom had the flowered bedroom. We three in the yellow room told ghost stories to one another. Johnny joined in only when Mom came in and read stories; otherwise, he was alone in the front parlor.

The iceman came once a week with a huge block of ice he carried with big tongs and placed in the top of the icebox. There was a cistern in the basement that frequently ran dry. When it did, Mom walked across the field to fill two buckets of water and carry them back. She told us she loved the exercise in the fresh morning sea air. She cooked on a hot plate, not wanting to light the kerosene stove in the summer.

Mom had had indoor plumbing put in for Clara so she would not have to go out in the cold, but she had not had a water heater installed. To warm up the cold water for our weekly bath, Mom put a teakettle on the hot plate to boil water and poured the hot water into the tub along with cold water until just the right temperature was reached. Three of us would get in and play "Rub-a-Dub-Dub, Three Men in a Tub."

Mornings were dedicated to the daily chores: sweeping the steps, making beds, and assembling a picnic lunch. Our favorite lunch was cucumber sandwiches with mayonnaise, but bologna, peanut butter and jelly, or marshmallow and peanut butter were also in the mix. Kool-Aid and water went into an empty milk jug.

We didn't care that we were without a car. Walking in the village was fun, and occasionally, a friendly neighbor would take us to Rockland for something big, such as the Lobster Festival or the sardine-packing contest. Women with big aprons and scarves wrapped around their heads who worked in the sardine factory would compete to see who could pack the most cans in, say, five minutes.

Most days, we were confined to Tenants Harbor. We put bathing suits on under shorts and T-shirts; took a towel each; and walked down the small gravel roadway known as Front Street (which would cause great angst in the future), past Skinny Morris's fish wharf stinking with redfish lobster bait, past the closed-up and abandoned hotel, and up the hill along High Street, where great-aunts Fannie and Harriet lived in the same small Cape house where Clara had been born. Our great-aunts, maiden old ladies, usually waved out their front parlor window.

We continued up the steep hill to a path through the woods covered with pine needles, which we collected to make sachets. At the end of the path lay Barter's Point, a sandy beach with large, flat rocks, where we spread out our towels for sunning and reading. At low tide, we walked across the sand and rocks to tiny Mouse Island and its single house. Summer people owned the house but were seldom in residence. We were careful not to scrape our knees on the barnacles or slip on the seaweed. We wore old sneakers for protection and found snails, crabs, starfish, and sea urchins, which we put in tidal pools for observation until they were swept back to sea at high tide. We swam in the freezing-cold water and had our picnic lunch. Mom always had a book with her.

As the afternoon wore on, Mom shepherded us back through the woods, down the hill past the great-aunts' house, by the abandoned hotel, past Skinny Morris's wharf, and back to the sail loft, where we had a quiet hour on our beds, a time to read. After the quiet time, we made our daily trip to the grocery store and the post office, and twice a week, we went to the library, which Clara and her sisters had helped found.

Other times, I didn't know what to do with myself and started bouncing a small pink rubber ball against the side of our clapboard house or, whenever possible, snuck off across the field behind the sail loft to Mrs. Baker's white Victorian house with white-and-green gingerbread trim. It had a sweet covered front porch with two green rocking chairs and was a sanctuary for me. Mrs. Baker was grandmotherly, with a gently curving, roly-poly figure; salt-and-pepper hair curled and pulled back; and wire glasses. She was always glad to see me, and I considered her my special friend. She sat in her rocker in the afternoons and crocheted multicolored squares for an afghan. She taught me to crochet, and I started making blue variegated squares, which I dreamed of sewing together one day into my own afghan when I went to college. I collected the squares I completed and felt a sense of accomplishment and pride in what I had made. Before I went off to college a decade later, I made those afghan squares into an afghan with a frilly embroidered edge, helped along by Mom—which made me mad because I wanted to do it myself.

Mom fixed dinner on the two-burner hot plate, often baked beans, hot dogs, and brown bread or Maine fish chowder with potatoes, onions, fresh haddock, butter, and milk. After dinner, we gathered to play hide-and-seek in the tall grass in the field out back with the neighbor kids.

Tenants Harbor was different from Chicago: we four children played together. On rainy days, we went into the summer kitchen, took a pole that had a hook on the end made from a coat hanger, and pushed open the trapdoor into the attic. We used the hook to pull down a ladder balanced by iron weights—heavy old ship's iron hooks and hardware. Upon scampering up the ladder, we found a treasure trove of leftovers from the ship's chandlery, which had closed in the nineteenth century, and from the grocery store, which had closed in the 1930s, along with domed trunks from India and furniture that everyone had left.

The most fun was to play train, pushing together old wooden store platforms covered with pieces of woven carpet. We designated an engine, coaches, a dining car, and sleepers. Someone would imitate the noise of the engine coming to crossings, and others would be the waiters in the dining room, the porters in the sleepers, or even the man who walked up and down the coaches to sell sandwiches and lemonade.

On Sundays, clean from our weekly Saturday night baths, we four children and Mom marched up the hill the opposite way from the swimming rocks to the white-steepled Baptist church at the top. We girls wore cotton blouses and skirts handmade by Mom, sometimes from old feed sacks from Dad's farm. The boys wore clean shirts and long pants, all freshly ironed. Mom seemed to love to iron, and I was actually allowed to help. I started with handkerchiefs and was proud that I learned to iron a man's shirt. I never figured out why I could help in Maine and not in Chicago, but I was much happier in Maine, helping. Mom seemed to want us around her in Maine, unlike in Chicago.

The Baptist church at the top of the hill had been built by ships' carpenters and had a simply carved maple-framed interior. In addition to the stained-glass windows on the sides in memory of our sea captain ancestors, there was a large and elaborate stained-glass window in the center, depicting a woman with a water jug standing before a seated figure of Jesus with his hand outstretched. Below was written,

> Jesus answered and said unto her
> Whosoever drinketh of this water
> Shall thirst again.
> But whosoever drinketh of the water that I shall give him
> Shall never thirst again
> But the water that I shall give him shall be in him
> A well of water springing up into everlasting life.

The window was in memory of my grandmother's great-grandfather Captain Watts, who had died in 1841. Clara must have seen the window as a little girl the same way I did. All my life, I have loved that verse, and it has guided me. I have always had faith that if I sought long and hard enough, I would find the love, connection, and happiness I sorely missed.

In the vestibule of the church were the brass coatrack and umbrella stand in memory of Grandmother Clara. The adults stayed in the main sanctuary to attend the service and Great-Aunt Harriet's Bible lessons. Harriet, Clara's sister, was thin in her flowered cotton shirtwaist dress and had short, curly white hair and wire glasses. She and all the church members were earnest. Mom felt connected there at church with that umbrella stand and coatrack dedicated to her mom and with the many people who knew her great-aunts or even remembered her mother.

In the Sunday school rooms, we children were taught Bible stories from both the Old and New Testaments, such as Joseph and his many-colored coat or the Good Samaritan who stopped to help the man in need. We ended with homemade cookies and lemonade made by volunteers. At the close of Sunday school, we went to the main sanctuary and shook the hands of the villagers, who told us stories of seeing Mom as a little girl when she came from India with her parents. I listened to these stories about Mom and her parents with delight, feeling special that these people knew my family. I tried hard to picture Mom as a little girl, but it seemed impossible that she was ever as little as I was. I was curious and wanted to know more about the people they talked about. Never did it occur to me that one day I would spend a great deal of time trying to find out about my mother's life and write about it. Many years later, my sister gave me a photo of Mom as a small girl. I was shocked to see how much she looked like me.

After church, Mom took us to the cemetery. She walked us up and down, holding our hands, telling us not to step on the graves, out of respect. We walked along the grass-mown roadways among the monuments and headstones. "You come from a very long line of distinguished people," she would say, and then she'd rattle off the familiar stories as we came to each headstone of a person related to us. They were familiar to me because Mom repeated them over and over: "Captain Bickmore, a ship's captain, lived in a big house at the top of the hill. His son played with matches in the barn one day, and it burned down. Deacon Robert Long, another ship's captain, built the sail loft upon his retirement from the sea. Charles Stearns was the first doctor of Tenants Harbor and your great-great-great-uncle."

In addition, Mom often repeated her list of important ancestors to me or to people she met. "I come from the leading family in Tenants Harbor," she would say. "The family had been there for seven generations. My uncle was a trustee of Vassar College, and my great-grandfathers built ships. I am descended from Stephen Hopkins, who came over on the *Mayflower*, and Colonel William Bond, who fought in the Revolutionary War." I felt I knew these people even better than some living people around me.

The stories sometimes made me feel special, but I wasn't sure. That Mom kept emphasizing our ancestors didn't make any sense to me, but it was important to her that we know about the people in the cemetery. She kept saying we should remember their names; otherwise, they would all be lost. I wondered if she'd thought of these people as her family when alone at the boarding school in India.

I wondered what I would do in the future to carry out Mom's wishes, since it remained a primary goal of mine to make my mother happy. I kept trying to be a good girl and listen, but I would have liked to leave the cemetery and go swimming. Mom was so earnest; she would have been hurt and angry had I run off to play.

After the required visit to the cemetery, we ran down the hill and along the street, passing a candy store, two gas stations, and a grocery store, until we reached High Street to pay a visit to Great-Aunt Fannie, who was in bed, being taken care of by her sister Harriet. "Children, remember, Aunt Fannie won't know you," Mom said. We walked into the small white clapboard Cape with a woodshed and barn attached on the back and sat obediently in the front parlor. Quietly and with ceremony, we were ushered into Aunt Fannie's room, where she was lying in bed with a yellowing lace-trimmed white nightcap, a nightgown, and a bed jacket of tan silk and lace. She reminded me of the drawings of the wolf in bed in *Little Red Riding Hood*. I felt the hush upon entering the room. We were paying respects to one of the living whom everyone feared was on her way to being among the dead.

With the duty of the second required visit finally over, we were released to run down the hill to our apartment in the sail loft. On those occasions, Mom would put on the red plaid skirt and halter top she had made for herself and sit out on the flat rocks in the sun by the side of the sail loft overlooking the harbor. She was tanned and relaxed in the warm sunshine. It was cozy to be near her. She read out loud *Ivanhoe*, *Robinson Crusoe*, *Little Women*, and the Greek myths. At those moments, she was surrounded by all she loved: Maine, the sea, her heritage, literature, and the place where her mother had been. I was content.

The weeks wore away happily in similar fashion until the third week of August, when Dad arrived from Chicago in his big tan Oldsmobile with frail Miss Railton, his bookkeeper from his law office in Chicago. Miss Railton dressed in black shoes and stockings, a long black shirt, a maroon jacket, and a black hat over her white hair pulled into a bun. She rocked and looked out to sea the same way Clara had before her. Dad felt sorry for Miss Railton and wanted her to have a vacation. That seemed more important to him than having time alone with his wife and four children he had not seen all summer.

After Dad arrived in Tenants Harbor, he started going off again alone to the Union Fair to watch the pulling, a contest to see which ox or workhorse could pull the heaviest weight, and to inspect the livestock. On the occasions when he took me along, I was happy to share something he loved with him and happy to spend some time with him. We watched together the greased-pig contest, in which kids would try to catch a greased pig in the shortest amount of time, and the 4-H exhibits and contests for the biggest squash or pumpkin. I particularly liked to see the handicrafts with the completed afghans. Later, we walked up and down the barns to see the livestock, inhaling the strong smells of straw, fresh hay, and manure. I never liked the odors but enjoyed seeing the calves and took notice of the cute farmer boys.

Ten days later, we piled into the tan Oldsmobile and drove back to Chicago's South Side, leaving cozy, warm Maine and returning to cold, lonely Chicago life. Tenants Harbor was the place where Mom felt happy, and it spilled over onto us kids.

CHAPTER 6

Cedric and Harry Perkins
in India 1895-1902

Clara, the young woman from Tenants Harbor, Maine, set about making a home in poverty-stricken, hot traditional Hindu India. Clara and Hebron settled down into their house in the missionary compound, though it was not their own house and not for them alone. They shared the house with other missionaries, single women, and, occasionally, another family. It sat among other large, thick-walled stuccoed brick houses with high ceilings in their walled-off area of the village. When I visited there, an Indian Christian minister explained to me that people from a cold country had to have thick walls, or they could not stand the heat. They needed high walls to keep out thieves and wandering animals.

The couple set up a bifurcated life. Their fellow Canadian missionaries were their friends and community. They would not socialize with the Hindus in their mud huts with thatched roofs or with the maharaja in his large, elaborate palaces ornamented with silk rugs and opulent hangings. Neither side wanted to mix. The two cultures were too different and too racist for them to make friends. The missionaries dedicated their lives to "saving" the Indians, not to getting to know them. It was the same attitude my mother had had on Chicago's South Side when I was a child, leading to isolation and a sense of dislocation. My quest had become how to bridge the gap and make friends.

Clara wanted India to be more like Tenants Harbor. In a letter to her mother, Clara wrote, "Why can't these people put a price on anything instead of bargaining for everything?" and "I finally received my white wicker front parlor furniture, but nothing happens on time in this country." Labor was cheap in India. Even though missionaries were paid little, there was money for a cook, a houseboy, errand boys to go to the market, and coolies to pull their cart when they wanted to go out. In 1946, for example, when missionaries were paid $1,500 per year, the Indians earned only fifteen dollars per year. The caste lines were so strict that each person could do just one specific job. Clara could not convince a high-caste person to move a chair for her. No one could be persuaded to do anything other than what his or her caste dictated. Clara found it infuriating.

Hebron spent his time the first year learning Telugu, but Clara didn't have time to learn the language. She had to cope with morning sickness and the birth of her first baby, a boy they named Cedric, who was born within a year of their arrival. Her letters were filled with homey details about spending her days making tomato chutney or not feeling well and going to bed. Clara spent much of her time in bed.

December 13, 1895
My dear Mama,

> Mr. Corey was very busy all the time I was sick, for with caring for me and trying to keep on with his studies he has hardly a minute to himself, and right here I will say if you should hunt the world over you would not find a better, kinder husband anywhere. He just waited on me by inches while I was sick and is very kind to me all the time, and until lately he has even taken all the care of baby at night. He is just kindness itself.

Clara told Mama that the Indians got mad when the missionaries mispronounced Telugu words, but the words were similar to each other. The word for *teacher* and the word for *cat* were the same except for a vowel that was pronounced short or long. Thus, one night, the missionaries prayed for the cats instead of the teachers.

Clara was amused at the caste system and tried to figure out where she fit in the social hierarchy, perhaps as her grandmother had before her back in Tenants Harbor.

> I hardly know myself how the natives consider white people. I think the Brahmins consider themselves the gods of the earth, so they think they are much better than white people, but as the English are the ruling class and in their religion the ruling class is superior people, they have to admit when much pressed that we are superior in that way.

"Any Brahmin would sooner starve to death than do any manual work," wrote Clara in another of her letters.

Clara sent her mother a photograph of some Indian children without clothes but told her mother to "keep the picture under wraps." The children who could afford it wore gold jewelry, and Clara wrote that it was not uncommon for children to be murdered for the gold.

Clara's main activity in India, besides trying to set up a home like the one she had known in Maine, was to have children—five in total. After Cedric was born in 1895, she had Albert in 1898, Charlie in 1900, and Harry in 1902. Clara wrote to Mama about her babies, describing Cedric as a nervous child "crying pitilessly at night until it is time for his milk." She said he was slow to walk or talk but supposed he would eventually learn. Finally, when she was forty and tired, her fifth child and only daughter was born. She was named Elizabeth after Clara's mama back in Tenants Harbor and called Betty. Betty, born in 1908 in a large brick house right next to the Indians' mud-and-straw huts in Vizianagaram, Andhra Pradesh, South India, eventually gave birth to me in Chicago.

After the year of language study, Hebron became a bicycle evangelist, riding to tiny villages, including some so remote that the only access was a dirt road that often washed out in the rainy season or a river crossing without a bridge. He had to ford the rivers the best he could. One letter described his tying a rope to a tree, throwing the other end across to another tree, and securing it I know not how. He then held on through the raging waters.

The remote native villages were nearly self-sustaining with a few animals and crops. They cooked over an open fire. Women gathered the wood for the fires and brought it home piled neatly on their heads. They fetched water daily from nearby wells and carried the water in silver-colored jugs on their heads. Their only pieces of furniture were rope beds they made themselves and a clothesline where the women hung their saris.

Hebron wore Western-style clothing to the remote villages, as did all the Canadian missionaries. The female missionaries wore long dresses to the floor, and the male missionaries wore suits, often dark blue cotton suits, and white shirts and ties. They all tried to keep cool in the tropical heat in their Western clothes.

Hebron arrived in the poor villages of mud huts with his newly acquired language skills on his bicycle, clad in a suit and tie, wanting to preach the gospel of salvation: "Believe, and your life will be changed, and your soul will be saved." When he rode up to a remote village, the women hid, afraid of the stranger, used to a life of seclusion. Over time, the children would grow curious and come out and eventually would persuade their parents to come. Hebron tried to make friends of the villagers despite their fear of being contaminated by the white man of no caste. He took an interest in them and said he would like to come back to teach them about how their lives could be made better.

When villagers' hearts were moved by the New Testament scriptures and they desired baptism, Hebron would baptize them in a local river. When people were baptized, water was not just sprinkled onto their heads; they were immersed, just as I had been immersed. Since the Baptists only baptized those old enough to choose, they didn't baptize babies.

Once the converts were baptized, Hebron had to help them find a place to live since they could no longer stay in their villages. Hebron would have to endure watching their suffering as they had to leave their homes. The new converts would be invited to a nearby center where a chapel schoolhouse had been built. They would be taught English and the scriptures with the hope that they would take over the chapel schoolhouse and preach and teach other converts. The Canadians had to raise the money to pay the new teacher and preacher.

Hebron came to see what bringing "light into the darkness" of village India really meant. Baptizing converts was painstakingly slow work. He was pleased if they had ten in a year. The hardships and problems they had known at home shrank in comparison to the human misery he encountered in India. For example, the lepers were shunned and cast out of their homes. No one would touch them, but Hebron took great pity on the lepers he saw who wanted to be baptized. He was the first to enter the river with the lepers and baptize all that wanted to be baptized.

One hundred years later, while walking down Park Avenue in New York City, I ran into the husband of a good friend, a highly successful New

York businessman. When I told him the above story, I watched in surprise as his eyes welled up with tears, and he said, "There is a man who did something with his life."

When Hebron visited remote villages, he often found abandoned baby girls on the ground. Impoverished families knew they would not be able to afford the dowries they would have to pay for their daughters to be married, and if the girl did not marry, she would be just one more mouth to feed. Thus, the girls were abandoned. The missionaries picked up the babies and brought them to an orphanage, where they were fed, clothed, and educated. Some Indian Christian converts of higher caste followed the missionaries' example and started orphanages of their own.

The orphanages held hundreds of little barefoot girls in a big open courtyard with a veranda around the sides. Each girl had a straw mat and a suitcase that contained all her earthly belongings. At night, they rolled out the mats to sleep on. In the morning, the mats were rolled up and stored behind their suitcases. The older children took care of the younger ones. An enormous cauldron filled with rice and vegetables sat on a raised open fire pit. The vegetables were raised right on the grounds.

The girls were taught to read, write, do simple math, study the scriptures, and perform a trade, such as sewing, so they would be able to find work to take care of themselves. They learned to recite the Twenty-Third Psalm in English and perform a simple dance, but not many of them were baptized.

When Hebron went to the missionary conference in the spring in Ooty, according to their history, *The Enterprise*, the missionaries recognized the need to build many institutions to uplift the Telugus out of "poverty, ignorance and superstition, caste and karma". They saw the need to start more schools, including boarding schools for high-caste girls, day schools for Dalits, and separate boys' schools, as well as hospitals and a seminary. Children were taught a regular school curriculum and religion. They did not have to convert, though the missionaries always hoped some would convert.

The Canadian missionaries in India found themselves spread thin in trying to oversee their growing number of mission fields and institutions. The conference wanted Canada to send more missionaries to India, but that was fraught with difficulty because so many of the missionaries they did send came down sick and had to be sent home.

Hebron was appointed to the building committee to help oversee the enormous number of building projects, but it was a challenge in Telugu-speaking India. Hebron had to become both the architect and the contractor overseeing the process. In 1924, the Canadians published a book called *The Enterprise,* in which they described the scene when building a new structure:

> The stone is drawn, the trenches for foundations are dug ... In a large shed are thirty or more men and women making tiles. They all, including children, must live on the compound during labours. They made nearly 300,000 bricks ... Then there were thousands of arch and pillar bricks to keep count of. Nearby in another shed was the sawmill, and the carpenter shop.

The CBFMB (Canadian Baptist Foreign Mission Board) increased their number of stations from four to twenty-two and built more than thirty-six missionary bungalows for one hundred missionaries, seven hospitals, boarding school dormitories, high schools, two leper asylums, nineteen caste girls' schools, an industrial school, and chapel schoolhouses for the Dalits.

Besides being on the building committee, Hebron continued visiting villages whenever he had time, but increasingly, he was asked to take on the administration of some of the institutions the Canadians were building, as *The Enterprise* records:

> Mr. Corey had oversight of the Bobbili from 1908 to 1910. From 1915 to 17, he had charge of Bimlipatam and in order to carry on the boys' school effectively, lived there ... Mr. Corey had oversight of Vizagapatam and in order to conduct that High School, moved there. Two cities of 50,000 each, a high school of 900 boys, an English church, two Telugu churches, did not leave much time to tour among more than 700 villages ... Stations undermanned, not only hindered the work, but imperiled the health of the missionaries burdened with a double task.

When Hebron had charge of the Bobbili field, one of his responsibilities was the oversight of the CBFMB's girls' high school for Dalit girls, which represented an incredible revolution in India for the prospects of women. Still, the missionaries always had to deal with caste. A lady missionary who worked with Hebron in Bobbili one day decided to invite two of the brightest Dalit girls to attend school at the high-caste girls' school she ran. She sat them by themselves on one side of the room, far away from the high-caste girls, but as soon as the mothers of the high-caste girls heard about the situation, they withdrew their daughters from the school.

The female missionary tried to explain to the mothers that she was keeping the Dalit girls separate, but the girls' mothers said the Dalits' presence was defiling, and it was too much trouble to have to bathe and purify their daughters before allowing them to enter again into their own homes. The mothers further explained that if the missionary slapped one of the Dalits—an accepted form of discipline at the time—and then slapped their girls with the same hand, their daughters would be defiled.

Hebron struggled on with all the challenges, believing that despite the long Hindu custom of keeping the Dalit women at the bottom of society, there was hope for them to have a better life. Most of the girls were there to get an education, and since India was a British colony, their chance of employment in the government was enhanced if they knew English. Ninety percent of the people with whom Hebron worked came from the Dalits, and he developed a more sympathetic understanding of the traditions and beliefs of the villagers than some of his fellow missionaries.

The CBFMB met regularly to discuss their work and to set policy. One of the arguments at a board meeting was whether an Indian man had to cut off his *juttu*, a tuft of hair on top of his head, when he converted to Christianity. Hebron's fellow missionaries said the juttu meant he was Hindu, but Hebron argued that it was cultural, not religious, and if the men were to cut off their juttus, they would be a laughingstock.

Hebron was overruled, and villagers who converted to Christianity not only couldn't go home again but also looked ridiculous to the traditional village Hindus. As a compromise, Hebron suggested the native Indian Christian church leaders decide for themselves about cutting off the juttu, but the Baptist mission board in Canada ruled that it alone had the right to decide. Hebron received a strict letter from his home missionary board reprimanding him for not making male converts cut off their juttus.

Hebron decided he had to obey his board. Later, he received a letter from the mission board asking him to inform another missionary, Mr. Hardy, that he agreed to the statement "I will refuse to baptize any native whose juttu has not been removed." A second letter confirmed that Mr. Hardy agreed, so the board decided Hebron could continue his missionary work in India.

It is hard to read such accounts of how lacking and uninterested the board of the mission were in understanding Hindu culture. The conviction that the board knew the whole Christian truth, which they had their missionaries preach as the only way to get to heaven, with all others damned, dominated the mission and spilled over into family life. They felt others were wrong. My mother, Betty, always told us she knew, and we did not. Such control took away one's sense of agency.

Hebron was often gone for a week at a time but came home faithfully to his growing family and sickly wife, Clara. Albert and Charlie were doing well, but Cedric had still not learned to talk or walk. They could not ignore this fact and tried to figure out what could have happened. Hebron contacted the district physician, who came to examine Cedric the next time he was in their village.

Cedric as a baby, 1898.

Eventually, one of their Indian housekeepers converted to Christianity and confessed: she had dropped Cedric on his head when he was a baby. Hebron and Clara were heartsick. It would never be clear if the fall was the cause of Cedric's problems, but Hebron and Clara dug deep into their hearts to find forgiveness for the servant. Cedric stayed at home, always needing someone to care for him, never able to talk. He was able to communicate through hand signals and some noises.

Clara and Hebron heard about a doctor in England who was known for an operation to relieve a subdural hematoma, a collection of blood between the surface of the brain and the dura that covers the brain. They thought this operation might help Cedric. They had saved a little money out of their small missionary's salary and planned to take their son to England, when a terrible famine broke out around them. The famine began with the failure of the summer monsoons and eventually killed around half a million people. Villagers were dying in droves. Not only did the missionaries pick up the baby girls left to die, but they watched babies die in their mothers' arms from malnutrition. Even though they lived behind brick walls, they could not shield themselves from the misery.

Clara and Hebron had a terrible decision to make. Could they turn their backs on these people they had come to serve and watch them starve, when they had the means to help, at least a little? Should they take their son to England for an operation, or should they give the little money they had to the relief effort for food to alleviate the misery they saw all around them? They dedicated the evening prayer service to pray for guidance. What was God's will for them now?

Their hearts had chosen Cedric, but their duty dictated giving their money to buy food. They were in India to serve God. They had left their own families back home. Christian charity meant offering unselfish, self-sacrificing love and being a suffering servant. One gave everything away so all might be saved. It was the example of their heavenly Father and his choice with his own Son. It had been the choice of Abraham with Isaac, though Isaac had been spared. Cedric was at least alive and fed.

Surely God would care for them all. Clara wrote in the back of her Bible, "I know not the way I am going, but well do I know my Guide, with a child-like trust I give my hand to the mighty friend at my side." Cedric struggled and suffered all his life, never getting better. He remained a source of heartache for all their lives. They arranged for his care, but their choice never ceased to wear upon them. Cedric's baby sister, Betty, wrote a play years later called *The Choice*, but it has been lost.

Children in a family for whom the needs of strangers in the community take precedence over their own needs often react by becoming deeply depressed. That was what happened to the children of Hebron and Clara and to the children of Betty and Bob. It is an example of the illegitimate split between doing God's will and loving one's family.

*   *   *

In 1902, Clara was pregnant with what would be her fourth son. The monsoon rains were over. The temperature was rising, and cholera season was approaching. The sky was bright blue and cloudless, and the sun was relentless. Clara stayed in her thick-walled house as much as possible, having a sulky servant pull the punkah—a large swinging fan attached to the ceiling with strings to pull it back and forth—for her all day. She would have gotten rid of him, but it was the job he was born into, so he stayed. So much for Clara thinking she was the boss. She was trying to gain control, but with a fourth baby on its way, she was worn out and in bed. Though she had been working on learning the language, her language skills were still poor, and the servants spoke only Telugu. She had to depend on them to look after her three boys, who all were under eight years old.

It was hot, and she was uncomfortable in the last weeks of her pregnancy. The houseboy came in with her lunch of rice, dal (cooked lentils with spices), and a cut-up mango the cook had been lucky enough to find in the market that morning. Cooks in India certainly knew how to make dal, but did they understand sanitation? It was impossible to explain that fruit had to be washed in sterilized water and that everything had to be cooked well to kill the inevitable germs.

Clara's labor pains suddenly started. She and Mr. Corey had given strict instructions to the cook to start boiling big kettles of water to sterilize anything that could meet her or the baby when the time came. Everyone was in a hustle. The two younger boys, having finished their lunch, came in to be with their mother but were shooed away.

"But, Mother, we would like to stay. I don't want to leave you," said Albert, who was four years old.

"Please, boys, you have to go out and play," replied Mr. Corey sternly.

Outside, oxen and camel carts trundled past, and the village women chattered away as they came back from collecting wood for their fires and water for their families. The boys ran around outside but within the walls of the compound. They didn't seem to mind the heat much. Indian children had climbed over the wall from their mud huts and joined in, shouting.

The midwife came to assist Mr. Corey, and the sterilized water was set in big bowls by the side of the bed. The labor lasted five hours. A five-pound-and-two-ounce son was born, whom they named Harry Perkins. The midwife washed the baby and wrapped him in a blanket for the mother to hold. Clara had planned not to nurse her baby but, rather, to begin by feeding him sugar water and then, in a few days, homemade formula made by the cook under the direction of the ayah.

A few weeks later, Clara felt well enough to get out of bed, got dressed, and took the new baby out onto the veranda, where she placed Harry in a rocker bassinette. As she gently rocked him, he started to vomit continuously. Clara panicked. She called the missionaries in the house next door for help. Although maiden ladies, they knew cholera when they saw it.

Harry got better and then worse. The skin on his little hands wrinkled, and his face sank. They couldn't keep him hydrated. The little fellow didn't survive. India's terrible diseases were too much for him. God took him back.

Mr. Corey made the simple pine coffin himself. The boys could hear him hammering away, pounding the nails into the wood to make the plain pine box. When it was finished, Clara lined the pine coffin carefully with pure-white cotton she was able to buy in the market. Together they picked up the stiff, small, precious body of their six-week-old deceased son and placed him in the box.

The boys were meant to be kept away by the ayah, but they managed to break free and run to see what their parents were doing. "Mother, what are you doing to our baby brother?" cried the older of the two young brothers, who were four and two. "You can't put our baby brother in that box." Too young to understand death, the small boys were beside themselves with fury and confusion. Clara and Mr. Corey wept, never having known life could be so hard. Clara once said that was the hardest moment of her life.

Clara's favorite hymn came into her mind:

> O Beulah Land, sweet Beulah Land,
> As on thy highest mount I stand,
> I look away across the sea,
> Where mansions are prepared for me,
> And view the shining glory shore,
> My heaven, my home forevermore.

Clara told her two sons, "On earth, there is tribulation, but in heaven, there is our home."

The theology that emphasizes life after death is often the theology of a stricken people. The excruciating tragedy of their current life was made bearable by the hope of happiness in the next life. Clara and Hebron felt duty-bound to continue their missionary work in India in allegiance to a harsh God.

CHAPTER 7

South Side of Chicago, 1947–1951

The four Hunter kids could have formed another Brady Bunch, but we didn't; we cocooned and fought instead. My sister, Margie, and I had not learned to share. When I was six years old and Margie was two and a half, she got into all my things and wanted to do everything I did. What a tragedy that we didn't keep each other company, but the strains in the house kept us four children apart.

Since Clara had died earlier in the year, a room was available. Mom moved Bobby into the back room that Clara had occupied, and she moved me to the third-floor garret room, which had been previously occupied by a couple who were supposed to help the family. The man, Bob, was to shovel the coal into the furnace, shovel the snow in the winter, and do other heavy work. The woman, Goldie, was to help iron, clean, and babysit. I attached myself to Goldie, until one evening, I came downstairs to find the police in our front hall. Mom had called them because her diamond ring and other jewelry were missing. The police found the jewelry on Bob and Goldie and handcuffed them both.

I didn't know what to think or do. I hated to see Goldie go, but Mom said she wasn't going to have any more live-in help. She would rather do the work herself and feel safe. As a result, Mom went back to doing the laundry herself. Mom moved me to the third floor so she could have peace and quiet, so the fighting would end.

I was alone on the third floor. The only access was a set of windy, narrow dark steps. It was scary and lonely to be separated from my family. Sometimes I curled up into a ball, and my mind went blank. Sometimes I tried to read, but something uncomfortable would happen. My eyes, after a while, wouldn't focus. The page of the book would look like a TV screen that was turned on but without a picture, just lines zigzagging.

My childhood was saved by Marilyn, at least for a while. Three years older, she lived two doors down in an elegant limestone town house with a nanny, a maid, parents, and an older sister. Marilyn attended the University of Chicago Laboratory School, and I was going to be sent to Kenwood Elementary School. For kindergarten, I attended Miss Faulkner's School for Girls down the street and around the corner from our house on Forty-Eighth Street and Dorchester Avenue.

After school, we found each other. Marilyn had dark hair and big dark brown eyes that sparkled whenever she saw me. She was pretty in her freshly starched and ironed dresses. I loved her, and she made me happy; I had a friend. I admired and imitated all she did. I didn't know and didn't care she was Jewish, and I was Christian; she was my best friend in all the world.

In her backyard, behind its high wrought-iron fence, Marilyn had a log cabin playhouse, where we played for endless hours—the kind of play I had wanted with my siblings. The log cabin playhouse had a miniature play kitchen with a stove, a refrigerator, a table and two chairs, small dishes, and pots and pans. It felt as if we were the Boxcar Children and had run away from home.

One time, on a Saturday, the nanny, Miss Yu, invited me to have lunch with Marilyn and served us egg salad sandwiches, cookies, and milk in their fancy glassed-in breakfast room overlooking the garden. Accidentally, some of the egg salad from my sandwich managed to land on the floor. Marilyn whispered to me the next day that the whole floor had to be washed as a result of my egg salad. I was filled with shame.

On rainy days at my house, we loved doing what Mom warned against. She'd say, "Don't play in the eaves, and don't get into my trunks," but as soon as she was safely in the basement, doing laundry, and out of earshot from my third-floor garret bedroom, we pulled open the door to the attic in the eaves, excited to be naughty.

There were no windows, so it was pitch black there, and the ceiling sloped down to the floor. We had to crawl on our hands and knees, feeling our way along the paper-covered insulation, past the dusty row of old trunks and hat boxes, careful not to lift our heads, or we might bump into a nail. We kept reaching up in the dark, hoping a hand would touch the string we could pull to turn on the bare lightbulb. By trial and error, we would finally find the string.

In the dim light, we could see the domed trunks with the steamship company stickers from India: "Mrs. H. Y. Corey of Wolfville, Nova Scotia." The flat trunks had stickers for "Elizabeth Corey, Acadia University," "Northwestern," or "Tenants Harbor, Maine." The trunks weren't locked, and Marilyn and I pushed them open. The domed one had scraps of silk and cotton materials, old dresses taken apart, photographs of missionary houses, laces taken off slips and blouses, letters, and more scraps of material. Browning photographs showed Mom as a schoolgirl in India, wearing a navy-blue pleated skirt and a navy sailor blouse with a white bow and brown shoes.

Marilyn and I pawed our way through all the stuff, thinking it was funny. After closing the trunk as best as we could, we went on to the flat, rectangular trunks. These were filled with Mom's flapper dresses, which were bright red with ruffles and so different from her navy-blue school uniforms. She must have worn them when she went to dances in the 1920s, though it was hard to imagine Mom ever having that much fun. We then stared in wonder at Mom's long gowns. Particularly beautiful were the long white-flowered silk organza trimmed with mink and the red crepe silk with fabric flowers sewn along the edges. I loved the sleek turquoise lounging robe and nightgown and the red velvet evening wrap trimmed with ermine. I couldn't resist trying on the red velvet with ermine trim. I felt elegant.

When had Mom, often in her turquoise housedress, ever worn the ermine-trimmed evening wrap? It must have been with her best girlfriend, Jo, whom she met at Northwestern and with whom she later shared an apartment. Together the two girls had taken a driving tour of England with Jo's parents. They'd had introductions to many members of the English upper classes, who'd entertained them in their grand country houses at private balls. One English lord had even wanted to arrange for Mom to meet the queen, but it never had happened—too expensive, and she'd had to get back to the USA.

Marilyn and I did not try on the dresses. They were way too big for us. We stuffed them all back into the trunks and closed the tops.

Finally, we opened the big hat boxes. The hats were amazing, and we wanted to try them on. We couldn't resist and carried one of the boxes out to my bedroom. I adored a large, wide-brimmed straw hat trimmed with white daisies, blue cornflowers, and red poppies, with its bright grass-green velvet ribbon to tie under the chin. The hat was the prettiest thing I had ever seen. It looked brand new. I never asked Mom if she ever wore it. Margie and I were always given straw hats with flowers for Easter, but they never came close to being that beautiful. We put the big hat away and tried on smaller hats, including one with pink flowers all over. We laughed at each other as we put on the various ones, pretending to be grand ladies.

"Betsy and Marilyn!" Mom's voice rose from the bottom of the stairs. "Are you into my trunks again after I told you not to go there?"

"Oh, Mom, we're just playing."

"Well, please don't go there."

We listened carefully, hoping she would not come up, and we were relieved when we heard her footsteps go away. On those days, it was an advantage to be on the third floor, since Mom didn't feel like walking up the extra set of steps. Quickly, we crawled in to return the hat box to the attic and turn off the light. We felt no remorse, only glee.

Another day, we went into the linen drawers in the second-floor bedroom hallway and found colorful glass bracelets from India. They were beautiful, in colors of red, blue, white, and green patterns. I tried them on, but they barely fit over my knuckles. Mom had many hidden treasures, which she had put away for fear we would break them. We found them anyway.

Thus, Marilyn and I rummaged through Mom's treasures and remnants from a happier life she had had for a short time while living with her friend Jo before she was married. Mom once told me, "Betsy, don't you give up everything the way I have given up everything."

* * *

In January 1947, I entered the first grade at Kenwood Public Elementary School, three blocks from home. My brothers were there, and finally, it was my turn. With my December birthday, I was told to start in midyear for first grade. I sat for the first time in a little desk with an inkwell in a row of seven, one of thirty-five desks, all bolted to the floor, and yes, the boy behind me tried to put my pigtail in the inkwell. Miss Breamer, my first-grade teacher, was tall, blonde, and nice. She sat us in alphabetical order and told us to fold our hands neatly in front of us on the desks. I wore a white blouse with a Peter Pan collar, a navy sweater, a skirt, and knee socks, like Mom's schoolgirl uniform in India. The boys wore long cotton pants and plaid shirts with belts at the waist. We all wore sturdy brown leather oxford shoes. I didn't know a soul.

A local park provided a gathering place for all the children of the neighborhood: we went skating in the winter and played baseball or tennis in the summer, and there was a costume party at Halloween. Mom made me a butterfly costume out of wire and black net with sparkly bright colors. It was beautiful! But my favorite thing to do at the park was to climb to the top of the large tree, where I could watch everyone below.

Mom decided it was time for me to learn to swim and walked me up to the Fifty-First Street YMCA, which had a separate program and even a separate entrance for women. Through twice-a-week swim lessons, I learned to swim, and by fifth grade, I joined the swim team at the Y. I specialized in the breaststroke, though I was never the star.

I also took arts and crafts and gymnastics. One spring day, Mom seemed upset while walking me home. "What's up, Mom?" I asked.

"Your crafts teacher took me aside and told me you acted helpless. Her talking about you that way made me mad. You don't act that way. How dare she!" Mom said with rage in her voice.

I just listened and thought Mom should have listened too, for in acting helpless, I was seeking the attention I did not receive at home. I had no self-confidence.

* * *

The sweet neighborhood gatherings, such as the Halloween block parties, came to an end soon after the night with the sparkling butterfly costume party when a momentous ruling was passed. In 1948, the restricted covenants were lifted from the Chicago neighborhoods. That meant real estate agents were required by law to show properties to anyone who could afford them, without excluding anyone because of race, color, or creed. I had no idea at the time, but this good ruling would drastically change the neighborhood and my life.

Soon after, Marilyn announced terrible news: her family was moving to Los Angeles. Her father, a successful older businessman, realized that Chicago's South Side was going to change. He decided to retire and enjoy sunny California. "How can that be?" I cried. "You can't go. I won't let you go." I couldn't imagine life without Marilyn. What was I going to do?

Within a few weeks, an enormous moving truck parked outside Marilyn's elegant town house, and men started carrying out boxes and furniture. I stood on the sidewalk and watched. It was true. It was happening. When the truck started driving away, I ran down the sidewalk, waving my hands, screaming goodbye, inconsolable. My best friend was gone.

I did not see Marilyn again until I was in college. She came to Chicago with her husband, John, one Christmas vacation to look me up twelve years later. In my college knee socks and loafers, I felt awkward with her, but she was her old lovely self, happy to see me.

* * *

After the sad day when Marilyn left, other white families fled to what my mother called "the lily-white suburbs." Kenwood changed almost overnight, fueled by unscrupulous real estate companies who participated in block-busting. Real estate agents contacted owners of property and told them that their property values were going down and that they should sell right away. Whole blocks of houses went on the market. African American families fleeing the southern United States and its discriminatory laws had come to Chicago to look for work. It was called the Great Migration. Former sharecropping families moved into the grand old houses of Kenwood and turned them into rooming houses. Property values fell further, but my family stayed put. Through all the revolutionary change in the neighborhood, my parents never even thought of moving away. The home on South Kenwood Avenue, where I had been brought home as a newborn, continued as our family home for all my years of growing up and beyond.

In addition to Kenwood, where I lived, nearby Hyde Park, the location of the University of Chicago, changed more slowly but eventually had to go through a major program of urban renewal to save the university, because the neighborhood, with its high crime rate, had become unsafe for students. They bulldozed blocks of run-down buildings and built new apartments and dormitories. When I went back to walk around after a few years, I could hardly find my way, as so much had changed.

Mom always had a clear line about socializing, something she had been taught as a child in India. "You only socialize with people of your own kind. Mixing is just not done," Mom would say. It was okay for Mom and Dad to help our African American neighbors but not okay for me to have them as friends. When Mom told me not to socialize with the African American people living around us, she taught me to be afraid, but I could not have articulated of what I was afraid. Even if I had ever met an African

American child, which I never did, I would have known better than to ever bring one home. It was just not done. I never came to know one.

As the neighborhood changed, trash began to be thrown onto the streets. "A sure sign of a deteriorating neighborhood," Mom said. My mother warned me that the neighborhood was unsafe. We were told not to walk outside alone after dark, to always be vigilant when walking around in daylight, and never to wear anything that could attract attention to oneself, but our family remained.

Living in our house became frightening. I felt as if we were living in a fortress surrounded by strangers. Several times, my sister and I saw a Peeping Tom in one of our living room windows. For example, one night, we were sitting in our living room, reading, and became aware of something or someone outside our window. We froze. Who could be looking in our window? What did they want? I reached up and turned off the reading lamp on the table. We both sat still. I crawled along the red-carpeted floor and pulled the cord on the white venetian blind so whoever was out there could no longer look in at us.

We called out to Mom, who called the police. We heard the sirens and the knock on the door and watched several big white policemen come in with their flashlights. It further disconcerted me to see the policemen in our house. The police reported they could see from the marks in the dust that someone had been sitting on the railing outside the living room window, but they didn't catch anyone. This kind of incident was repeated several times. No arrests were ever made.

One summer morning, it was Chicago-summer hot, and I was getting dressed in my third-floor bedroom, which had no air-conditioning. The night before, I had pulled the frilly white curtains apart and pushed open the casement windows to get some air. In the morning, I had gotten out of my bed with the pretty white bedspread, washed my face in the little anteroom, and walked back into my bedroom with its pink-and-gray wallpaper. I pulled off my white pajamas to put on a white blouse and light blue patterned skirt and happened to look up. Five big African American men were standing on the third-floor balcony of the house next door, staring in at me. They appeared amused. I was petrified and embarrassed. They were just twenty feet away. I dropped to the floor and crept to my little dressing room, pulling my clothes behind me.

I finished dressing, crawled along the floor so I couldn't be seen, and went down the narrow dark brown steps to where the rest of the family slept. It didn't occur to me to ask for help, but after that, I was careful to dress in my anteroom, and I did not see those scary men again.

Mom justified our continuing to live in the drastically changed neighborhood: "It's good for your father's political career. He needs the black vote to win." At the same time, Dad was home so little that the deteriorated neighborhood did not affect his quality of life. Dad was gone not only on weekends but also on weekday nights. He kept running for political office, such as county sheriff, congress and county judge; but as a Republican in a Democratic city, he kept losing. He remained comfortable as a South Sider with weekends at his farm. He wanted to spend his hard-earned money on his farm and perhaps to save for the coming college bills for his four children.

"The one thing I could never understand about Uncle Bob" (my Dad), said my first cousin Ellen after Dad died years later, "was how he could leave his family down on the South Side of Chicago in that deteriorated neighborhood. Other than that, I loved my uncle Bob and thought he was fabulous. We always got along so well together."

But Ellen didn't understand that Dad wasn't there. He came home to sleep. Mom noticed because she had to cope every day but kept going without complaint, as her missionary parents had done before her.

Our family's staying in a neighborhood where we no longer had a community that was known and loved, where we were the minority, and where we weren't safe was hard on me; but it was similar to the way Mom had lived in India as a child, and my father was preoccupied with his political ambitions. We all need to live in communities where we have friends and places that can nurture us, but my parents, like my grandparents in India, put the needs of the community and the father's career before the needs of the children. Economic necessity must have played a part.

Dad ran for judge of the county court of Cook County in 1946, around the same time Marilyn and many other families were moving. "It was an important position because that judge controlled the election machinery," Dad said to me years later in the oral history I took of him one summer in Maine. He told me the story of how he had won the race but lost the job.

"It became apparent during the campaign that the Republicans were going to do very well," Dad said. In the years after the war, he said, "There was meat rationing and wheat rationing and a lot of public indignation. It was quite evident when the ballots were counted that I had been elected county judge, but Edmund K. Jarecki, the incumbent since 1922, controlled the election machinery and could manipulate the count. He claimed he had won. We started a recount, but the rules were so outmoded and complex that it soon became apparent that the term would be over before the recount was finished."

Dad spent two years in the recount effort and managed to get a recount in only 1,000 precincts out of the 4,900, and in the process, he spent $26,000, a big sum then. According to the *Chicago Tribune*, the 1,000 precincts had added votes to Dad but not enough to overturn the election. There was not enough time remaining in the term to recount the remaining 3,900 precincts. Dad gave up the recount effort in 1948.

Mom became incensed that the recount law in Illinois was so poorly written and kept after her husband to write a new one. Dad didn't want to. He told me, "I was busy trying to make my living in the law practice, and I told her, 'Well, I don't have the time to draw up a recount bill; you draw it up.' She said, 'All right.' She proceeded to go through the information that we had assembled from other jurisdictions and do some reading and finally came up with a good recount bill. The bill was introduced at the state legislature in Springfield and voted out of committee but killed on the floor."

Mom had been right that in marrying Dad, she would be able to get involved in important matters in the government. The two of them worked to accomplish things for the broader community. I began to watch TV in the afternoons: *Howdy Doody*, *Hop-along Cassidy*, and *The Lone Ranger*. The Hunter family was an island unto itself, like the missionaries in India—perhaps even more than the missionaries, who at least had a community within their isolated compounds.

* * *

On a bright fall Saturday, Mom decided to take me shopping for winter clothes in downtown Chicago, an L train ride away. Dad was at the farm, as usual, and Bobby was practicing football. Johnny and Margie were left at home under the watchful eye of Florrie, the black part-time cleaning lady Mom had decided to hire. Ample and smiling, Florrie always wore a white apron and a white kerchief tied around her head.

Mom took me by the hand and walked to the South Fifty-First Street elevated station to ride up in the air to the Loop, where we got off near Carson Pirie Scott and Marshall Field's. We went right to the children's floor, where I saw a red, black, and white woolen plaid skirt with big squares in an A-cut pattern. I tried it on. It was the perfect thing for me. "I really love it. Mom, I want this one."

"That is not the one that is right for you," replied Mom.

"Why not? I really, really want it," I said.

"Because it's not right. I know," said Mom.

"But, Mom, this is the skirt I want," I said louder.

"We should buy for you a navy-blue pleated skirt, not that red, black, and white one," replied Mom firmly.

"But I want this one," I pleaded.

"We are going home," said Mom, getting irritated.

Mom took me by the hand and marched me out of the store, down the escalator, and up the stairs of the elevated train to head back to the South Side. When we got on the L, she had her arms crossed in front and her face in a frown. We were on opposite sides of the elevated car, and Mom faced away from me. I looked on with puzzlement, confusion, and anxiety. When the train arrived at the Fifty-First Street station, we walked home in stony silence.

Mom went to the kitchen to fix dinner. I went to my desk and tried to do homework but could not focus. I tried to read my favorite book, *The Boxcar Children*, in which the children run away from home and live in an abandoned railroad car, find old dishes in a dump, and pick wild blueberries for supper. Margie wanted to come up to play, but I told her to go away. Bobby arrived and went to help Mom. Johnny stayed in his room alone, reading science-fiction books. He continued to predict that man would go to the moon, but no one believed him.

When Mom called us all downstairs for dinner, I went down, but I didn't know what to say, so I said nothing. I felt sheepish that I had caused Mom a hard afternoon. Mom spoke up. "You know, I hear mothers sometimes ask their children what they would like to do, but children have no experience, no perspective. How do they know what to do? That is what they have parents for. You children are being brought up carefully, more like the princesses of England than the ragamuffins down the street."

We all listened to Mom, and Margie decided to question her. "But, Mom, how do you know?"

"If I didn't know, I wouldn't say so," replied Mom.

That marked the end of the conversation. I didn't cross Mom. I never wanted to make her life worse. I didn't understand it at the time, but Mom kept us all tightly under control to control her own anxiety.

* * *

In 1951, life changed for the Hunter family, for the Republicans asked Dad to run for mayor against Martin Kennelly, the incumbent Democrat.

"Margie and Betsy, hurry. Put on your green-and-red wool plaid dresses. The reporters are expected soon," said Mom.

I was ten years old. Dad had just announced his candidacy, and reporters from the major Chicago newspapers filled our living room. Our family sat in the living room, on a graceful Victorian couch covered in yellow silk damask, not the rose-colored one I always curled up on in the room with the TV. Bobby and Johnny were in their white shirts, ties, and suits, and Margie sat on Mom's lap. By our squeezing, there was room on either side of us four children for Mom in her beautifully tailored light turquoise suit and Dad in his tweed sports jacket, white shirt, and tie. The photographers carefully arranged our pose, showing us how to cross our legs and where to place our hands. The picture appeared in the newspapers and on campaign cards passed out all over Chicago: "Bob Hunter, Family Man, Candidate for Mayor." It was exciting.

MEET THE HUNTER FAMILY

Campaign card for Dad running for mayor of Chicago in 1951.

Our house became a sea of activity, with all the attention focused on Dad. It was fun for us four kids to watch but sort of scary at the same time, as we had to have a police car parked continually out in front of our house because of threatening letters Dad received. Several people wrote that they were out to get Dad because of the stands he was taking. Dad, however, made light of them, saying they were just some crackpots.

Sometimes I got to miss school, like the time I was taken to the circus and allowed to ride an elephant for a picture op. The kids at school told me they saw my picture in the newspaper. I felt a little like a celebrity.

The reporters came to our house for a picture of Mom showing off her collection of antique Worcester teapots she had brought down from Maine. Mom loved them, and so did I. My favorite was the strawberry-patterned teacup with a handle-less cup and saucer. I always wondered why people didn't burn their hands when they held them. The picture of Mom admiring her teapots made a big spread in the Sunday style section. The antique Worcester was kept carefully in a glass cabinet in our dining room.

The subject of tea became a familiar theme. Mom was invited to many ladies' organizations for tea. It seemed in keeping with what Mom preached to her two daughters: "Behind every successful man is a good woman," "One home cannot have two careers," and "A woman is happiest in being a helpmate to her husband."

On the other hand, I watched Mom every day in her housedress, cooking and doing the laundry, and she seemed sad to me or even angry. I kept wondering what I could do to make her happy. I was careful not to do anything that would make her sadder.

Dad, of course, didn't want Mom to depart from her traditional wifely role, but one time, things changed. Dad was invited to speak at an important meeting of a big ladies' organization at the LaSalle Hotel, but he wasn't free to attend. Reluctantly, Dad said that Mom could go.

Mom worked on a speech for days. "I studied public speaking at Northwestern, and just because I have not done it for a long time does not mean I cannot do it now," Mom said. "Your daddy is so used to seeing me do the dishes that he doesn't realize what else I can do."

The night came, and a ward committeeman escorted Mom to the big political gathering. At first, the people were disappointed to see Mom arrive instead of Dad. They changed their minds, however, because she gave an exceptional speech. The headline in the newspaper the next day said, "Hunter Has a Secret Weapon, His Wife." After that, Mom was asked to make speeches nearly every night. Dad quipped, "The *Tribune* ran a story that she was a more effective campaigner than I was, a better speaker. I said that was perfectly understandable—she could talk about me, and I had to talk about the issues." I loved all the things Dad said, but Mom said she felt Dad continued to resent her. Mom was hurt.

On Sundays during the campaign, we all marched up to Hyde Park Baptist Church in our Sunday best, but Dad didn't go with us. Mom said he was off campaigning in the black churches. She was proud of all the good works he accomplished for black people, which made him popular in the black wards. Dad told me how he had integrated the YMCAs of Chicago when he was chairman of the board of the Y. "I told them it was the young man's association, not the young white man's association. They changed the rules after I made my point." Dad also told me how he had gotten rid of the requirement for a photograph on job applications in Illinois when he was president of the Better Business Bureau and head of the State Civil Service Commission.

However, the results of his work for African Americans were mixed. "I did such a good job in the black wards that it hurt me in the white wards," he said. "I had to go out to the white wards and let them see me to straighten them out."

In order to try to defeat Dad, the opposition started rumors that Mom was black. Several people rang our doorbell, and when Mom answered, they exclaimed, "Well, you aren't black!" Even during the exciting campaign, living on the South Side bothered me because I had to be so careful. The neighborhood scared me, but Mom still always took Dad's side.

The campaign was building steam, and Dad had a big gathering in the International Amphitheatre to close out his campaign. We kids were picked up by police escort and, with the sirens blaring, were taken to the amphitheater, all of us but Margie. My parents considered her too young at six and a half, and she was hurt by that decision and remains so even to this day.

I thought the police escort and sirens were exciting, and I loved sitting in the front row with my blue-and-white dress and bows in my hair, along with my mother in her trim turquoise suit and my two brothers in their blazers, white shirts, and ties. Our next-door neighbor Mrs. Jackson, whom I called Jacknie, took charge of us three children to free my mother. We were escorted through the back door of the amphitheater and taken to our front-row seats so as not to go through the crowds. Cameras popped, balloons flew, and excitement rose. Sitting there looking back at the crowd, I was excited to see the enormous number of people holding signs: Hunter for Mayor.

The Purdue Glee Club sang. Margaret Chase Smith of Maine and Senator Everett McKinley Dirksen of Illinois gave speeches endorsing Dad. People kept coming and overflowed the auditorium. Dad gave a rousing campaign speech, promising to overhaul the water department and the police department, make the schools better, straighten out the traffic in Chicago by making one-way streets, and much more. He received a standing ovation.

Afterward, at home the next day, I heard Dad remark, "I wish my dad could see me now." Dad loved the gathering and all the attention, and I was living off his reflected glory.

After all that, Dad lost the election, but he was the first Republican to win the African American wards since Big Bill Thompson, who served as mayor from 1915 to 1923, and from 1927 to 1931. There had not been a Republican mayor of Chicago since Big Bill.

"The white wards mostly sat on their hands and did not get out the vote," Dad said. "We could have won that race if only we had had a better organization and another six weeks." I heard other people say that Dad had underestimated the power of the Democratic machine. I was sad for Dad, sensing his bitter disappointment, but the kids in school kept identifying me as the girl whose dad had run for mayor. Dad at least made Mom happy after the campaign, because he finally acknowledged what a help she had been.

Mom was invited to join a prestigious women's club on the North Side of Chicago. From time to time, she would get all dressed up and go to lectures and teas. We also joined the Fourth Presbyterian Church in the fashionable near North Side of Chicago, where Dad was soon made a trustee, but we continued living on the South Side of Chicago.

Our family never moved away from the South Side and never made friends with our African American neighbors. Mom kept telling my sister, Margie, and me that we were different, not like the kids who lived around us. She must have heard the same thing in India, where her family worked among the Indians but did not socialize with them.

The lack of connection among our family members was reflected in the isolation of our family in the community in which we lived. Both my mother and father were busy serving their communities. It was not unlike Hebron as a missionary in India, baptizing the lepers but not spending time with his own children, as he was away doing his work.

CHAPTER 8

Betty in India, 1908–1923

Clara, my grandmother, rested in the soft breeze of the punkah, waiting for Albert to return home for his school holiday. At forty, Clara was tired, especially with the surprise fifth child about to be born. The baby, her only girl, arrived on November 11, 1908, and Charlie, just eight years old, took to her immediately. He spent hours watching her and, when allowed by the ayah, held the baby carefully, sitting in a rocking chair.

Just a few months after Betty was born, Clara and Hebron decided it was time for Charlie to join his older brother Albert in the English school in Bangalore, hundreds of miles from Vizianagaram. Charlie didn't want to leave home. After he left, his new baby sister cried a lot, and Charlie was homesick while away at school at just eight years of age.

But this was the course that many missionaries followed in India. Albert too had begun boarding school at age eight, taking an oxcart across the mountains to Bangalore. Like many English back in England, the boys were gone for ten months a year. Clara and Hebron wanted them to be in a Christian school, preferably a Baptist one, with fellow missionary children, with English schoolteachers. Having Albert and Charles in the right school was more important than keeping them close at home. Travel was so difficult and slow that for two-week breaks, they couldn't come to see their parents.

Cedric needed constant care and remained at home. Clara tried to keep her household running smoothly but was heartbroken at seeing Cedric and thinking about having lost Harry, often taking to bed. She did the best

73

she could for her little daughter but was so tired that mostly, the ayah took care of the baby. Betty learned Telugu from her ayah before she learned English from her mother.

When Clara was feeling well enough and the tomatoes were ripe, she made chili and tomato preserves. Sewing clothes for all her family was a big part of her life. She wrote home to ask her mother for dress patterns and black buttons, which weren't sold at the market; she only could buy white ones. She asked her mother to tell her the latest fashions at home, so she could keep up with the trends.

When Hebron was at home, he conducted worship services on Wednesday evenings and Sunday mornings and taught Bible classes. Clara wrote home about the mistrust Hebron encountered when he worked with the Brahmans:

> Yesterday, three Hindu students from the rajah's college (in the native town three miles away) came to see Mr. Corey, and he and Mr. Churchill had a long visit with them. They listened well while they read passages from the New Testament and seemed interested in hearing about our Savior and answered questions and asked questions.
>
> The students from the college often come to see Mr. Corey Sunday afternoons. There are two young Brahmins who seem very bright and interested too. They can speak English quite well so Mr. Corey once when they came, gave them a copy of the gospels. One of them wanted to know if it was just the same reading in Mr. C's Bible, so he showed them in his bible the same gospel, so they were both satisfied, as they saw it for themselves.

In the hot months, the plains became unbearable, even though they used a punkah all day. Clara, Hebron, Cedric, and the baby Betty moved up to the English hill station, a city named Ootacamund, known to the English as Ooty, a five-day trip. Ooty was in the Nilgiri Hills of South India, where it was cool compared to the hot plains. The English had established the hill towns, called stations, to have a place to go to escape the heat. The vacation was a lot of work for Clara, as she wrote in a letter to her mother:

We are always obliged to move everything wherever we go, we get accustomed to it so it does not seem as much work as one would think it was at home. Even coming here—you would have laughed to see the number of articles we had to bring. One large box in which we placed the large bottles full of milk, two bowls, two cups, saucer, spoons, quart dipper, half-pint dipper, large bottle of salt, large bottle of brown sugar, medium-sized bottle of white sugar, bottle filled with water, the basket [of] clothes which were to be in use on the way, a box of tea, one dozen linen, one bottle lime water, small package of ginger, bottle of castor oil, common bar soap, good soap, tin soap dish and sponger, also little sponge, nurse bottle, clot milk strainer, tea, pot bread, boiled eggs, towel for ourselves, besides our pillows, sheets, and travelling rugs. Also, Ayah's belongings. There are no sleeping cars in this country. The seats, three in number, run along the length of cars. At night we sleep on the long seats. Fortunately, we had a car to ourselves although we had to change five times and wait at one place nearly a day.

In Ooty, they enjoyed fresh vegetables and the company of missionaries who were together for the missionary conference. Ooty had a shop that sold English boots and the English Hotel, with its wood-paneled dining room, a bit of England on top of a hill in Tamil Nadu, amid its villages of white stucco huts and red-tiled roofs. At the foot of the hill stood one of the great game preserves of South India, filled with monkeys and featuring an elephant hospital.

Despite the presence of the English and their shops, Clara did not write about socializing with them. The colonial rulers, who enjoyed their big-game hunts, gaming, and drinking at the English Club, undoubtedly considered the Baptists to be no fun. But Clara longed to be part of the upper-crust English society. She considered herself to be one of them since she came from the upper crust of Tenants Harbor. But she would never have agreed to the drinking, the gaming, and all the rest.

At the missionary conference, Hebron was assigned to oversee the Bobbili field since the missionary leading that field had died. Clara, Hebron, Betty, and Cedric were packed up with all their belongings and returned on the tiring five-day train ride back to Vizianagaram, just to have to pack up again and move to Bobbili, traveling farther away from independent Albert and sweet, homesick Charlie in Bangalore. Clara and Hebron kept reassuring each other that the boys were better off at the boarding school.

Hebron emphasized that it would build his children's characters and that they would receive a fine English Christian education, but Clara couldn't help missing her children. It would be many months before they saw Charlie and Albert again. Clara wrote the following in a series of letters:

> Charlie stood second in his class this term and Albert third, so they both have done well.
>
> Three weeks from today the children's school closes, and they will probably leave the next day, and reach here December 2nd. We will be so glad to have them with us again.
>
> Albert and Charlie arrived Friday afternoon the second. They are both looking well. Both have grown considerably since I last saw them in May. Albert is old for his age while Charlie is young.

They stayed for two years in Bobbili, until 1910. Clara sewed or rested, and Hebron ran the schools, preached, and oversaw the construction. Baby Betty and Cedric spent their time mainly with their Indian caretakers. A story came down to me that one time, Betty managed to escape the compound by herself and attend a Hindu Indian wedding taking place outside the wall. She saw the priest crouching before the ceremonial fire and watched as the bride, clad in a beautiful red sari, and her groom walked around the fire seven times. The priest put incense in the fire, and the bride and groom gave each other leis made of flowers. Betty always remembered this amazing spectacle, even though she was such a small child. But Clara and Hebron were upset she had attended a Hindu ceremony.

When Hebron had time, he went off on tour, starting churches and schools in remote Indian villages. The areas often were so remote that there were no roads or bridges. Once, Hebron was stuck for several days after a monsoon rain because of a raging river. He had to throw a rope across and improvise a way to get home.

At the end of their two years in Bobbili, the family packed up again and returned to Vizianagaram. In 1912, Hebron began to plan for a sabbatical year in Canada. Every seventh year, missionaries could return home to see their families, raise funds, and reconnect with their mission board. Hebron and Clara planned to go to Wolfville, Nova Scotia, where the headquarters of the Canadian Baptist Foreign Mission of the Maritime Provinces of Canada was located, and, of course, to Tenants Harbor for a visit to Clara's family.

Hebron secured steamship tickets leaving on April 19, 1913, from Calcutta and then continuing from Liverpool on June 5 on the *Devonshire* of the Leyland Line. Clara and Hebron decided to take Betty with them but leave Cedric in the care of kindly Mrs. Gullison for the year, a middle aged missionary. They also took Albert and Charlie out of school in Bangalore. They planned to leave the boys in Canada when they returned to India after the sabbatical year, reasoning that a Canadian education was best and that the boys ought to grow up with their own kind. They knew retired missionaries and farm families who could take the boys during school vacations in Canada. Thus, Charlie, age eleven, and Albert, fourteen, were enrolled in school in Wolfville, Nova Scotia.

Once in Wolfville, they put Betty in kindergarten. According to a letter from Clara to her mother, "Betty enjoyed going to school, also to church and Sunday school. The last was held at 3 PM and as Albert and Charlie went to Bible-class at the college, it left no one to go with Betty so she went alone." The five-year-old opened the door and walked herself down the street to Sunday school, and when it was over, she walked herself home. The tiny girl of five was determined not to miss Sunday school, even though no one had the time to take her. She felt capable, independent, and proud but, at the same time, hurt and resentful. Mom's character as a mother was formed as a tiny girl going courageously on alone.

Clara wrote to tell her mother she would only be able to come to Tenants Harbor for a month. She used the excuses of travel being too expensive and of the boys needing to work, but perhaps the real reasons were her nerves and her desire not to leave her sons again. On the other hand, Clara was always trying to be economical. When she visited, she wanted to sew and to get her old dresses out of the boxes in the barn. "I want them done over," she wrote. In the same letter, she shared with her mother a new recipe for apple pie, made with applesauce instead of real apples. It was much quicker, she remarked.

Two other things happened during their sabbatical year. Firstly, Clara confided in a letter to her mother that she was checking herself into a sanatorium outside Boston for two weeks to help calm her nerves. She said none of the other missionaries knew about this, but she needed to be well before returning to India.

Secondly, when Clara visited her family in Tenants Harbor, she saw how much her mother, sisters, and cousins struggled to keep their heads above water. With her mother having been a widow for so many years, money was tight. After the visit, roles switched. Instead of asking Mama for all the things they could not get in India, Clara and Hebron sent Clara's mama a money order for Christmas and for her birthday. One Christmas, the money order was for twenty-five dollars. Clara wrote to her mother to ask if she would like a purple dress with embroidery that Clara could buy in India to send home. Clara and Hebron became helpers not only for the poor of India but also for their own struggling family in Maine.

Clara wrote that she could hardly believe she was returning to India, but Hebron was directed by the board to return, and she would go with him. This time, they had no illusions about what India would be like. They were no longer young and had already lived through great tragedies of their own and great suffering among the Telugus. They knew it would wear on their health; nevertheless, they went. Duty called them. When they sailed back to India, they left two of their sons in Canada to go to school.

Hebron and Clara had come to Canada with Albert, Charlie, and Betty but were returning just with Betty, who was not quite six years old. They had come during peacetime and were leaving amid World War I, which had broken out in August, one of the deadliest wars in history. It was as if the whole world were going mad, with the terrible trench warfare and millions killed and injured. *I find it surprising they would return to India during a world war.*

They had planned to go by the Atlantic route and had made reservations to leave Quebec on October 18, 1914, and London on October 31. However, the Atlantic route was closed to travel, and they changed their plans and went by the Pacific, which was open for travel. They felt the western route would be safe, as it was "the mail route and well patrolled by cruisers."

As Clara wrote to her mother on November 23,

We are to leave on the quarter to ten train in the morning and cross the Bay to St. John, then go direct to

Toronto arriving there Thursday morning. Be there a few hours then go on to Chicago, taking another 24 hours and from there to San Francisco. Will be there or ought to be the morning of the fourth day from Chicago, so it will be the morning of the 7th day from here.

Five days later, while on the train, Clara wrote to her mother,

Betty is the only child on either of the two Pullman cars. There are two tourist cars on, but we did not know about them until after we had paid for our sleepers, otherwise we would have gone on them as they are cheaper and have a little stove at one end where we could eat food and drink water. We are going to get one meal a day and provide the rest ourselves, as we have plenty of goods and fruit with us.

It took about two months to travel back to India, with stops along the way in Hong Kong, Singapore, Penang, and other ports. Clara wrote that the most dangerous part of the journey was from Penang, Malaysia, to Calcutta, where "the Captain had to keep a sharp lookout for the enemy." Clara enjoyed the sights but hated travel by sea, as she frequently succumbed to seasickness.

Once they were back in India, Hebron went to get Cedric, the child they had not seen in more than a year and a half. He was now twenty. "He looks much the same, only is thinner than when we went home. He is a good boy and makes no trouble. He and Betty get on nicely together," wrote Clara. Cedric still could never be educated, nor was he able even to talk, but he resumed his quiet place in their home, a constant heartache for his parents.

Clara and Hebron found India peaceful when they arrived, and where they were in India, there was little talk of the war. India remained loyal to England, as Clara explained to her mother before they left for India:

The Nizam of Hyderabad has issued a proclamation saying that England is the friend of Mohammedans and Germany only got Turkey to join for her own benefit and it will mean Turkey's ruin, so he orders all his subjects to remain loyal, and he is the biggest Mohammedan ruler in India. So far India has been very loyal and has sent troops who are fighting for the Allies.

During the war, communication became difficult among Andhra Pradesh, Wolfville, and Tenants Harbor because many ships carrying mail were torpedoed. Clara and Hebron received sporadic letters. Clara wondered how her boys were doing in faraway Wolfville. They did not see Charlie or Albert again for almost eight years. Clara tried to oversee their care from faraway India:

> Mrs. Manning of Wolfville wrote me that both Albert and Charlie are growing stout and look well and happy. While I think of it, I will write about Albert. Won't you please look over his clothes and see what he will need for the next year. As Mrs. Peck cannot keep the boys any longer. I do not know who will look after their clothes. I think he needs some new summer drawers (little short ones) and some new cotton stockings. He must get quite thick cotton ones, as he is rather hard on them.

Many letters reported that both Albert and Charlie received top grades, and Hebron was proud of their accomplishments and their fine characters. "It is a great comfort to us," he wrote, "to know that they are good and honorable boys and are ambitious to succeed in the work in which they are engaged." Albert wanted to be a doctor, and Charlie wanted to be an engineer. Goodness, character, and honor mattered—and an English education.

At the same time, they noticed how sensitive and lonely Charlie seemed in his letters. Clara wrote to her mother: "I expect Charlie will be rather lonesome with us all so far away this summer. He minds being alone more than Albert does. Just now he is making electrical appliances; he is always experimenting."

Eventually, Albert decided to join the Canadian Air Force at age eighteen in 1916. He was sent to England to train but was kept from the front until he became nineteen. Clara and Hebron wrote to Albert to say they were against his signing up. They did not want Charlie left alone, nor did they want Albert in harm's way. But by the time their letter arrived, he had already joined. It was too late. Charlie became depressed because he was unable to join due to his youth and poor eyesight.

In a letter to his sister, who'd asked if he liked India as well as the homeland, Hebron explained why he had gone back to India:

> I certainly do love this land [Canada] better than I do India and the associations are much holier than the associations are in India. I tell you that it takes pluck to stay out in India and say you like it, and really mean it. But I am going out all the same … to do as much good as possible.

The bedrock of Clara and Hebron's belief was that they were serving their Savior by bringing light into the darkness of India, to the idolaters. Clara exclaimed in one letter, "Why must they keep worshipping idols?" Meanwhile, Albert and Charlie were sent away from home to be educated and to develop good character while receiving an old-school English education rooted in the classics, Western literature, history, mathematics, and biblical studies.

In India, Hebron and the mission matured, establishing more churches and schools in the villages, as well as continuing to build the many institutions. Realizing they needed Indian Christians to carry on the good work, they established a seminary to train Indian Christians to become leaders in the Indian Baptist churches. Their aim was to make the churches self-supporting and self-sustaining, run by Indian Christians.

In 1915, the head of the Bimlipatam station went on furlough, and the board needed Hebron to take over the oversight of Bimlipatam, the district next to Vizianagaram on the Bay of Bengal, as well as to continue running the Vizianagaram station. As noted in *The Enterprise*, "In order to carry on the boy's school, effectively he had to live there." Thus, Clara found herself once again having to move. She wrote to her mother to say they still had their heavy rickshaw for the sixteen-mile trip, which meant a bunch of coolies would pull them and all their belongings the sixteen miles to their new station. Clara also wrote that it would be much harder in Bimlipatam because the railroad did not go there. In order to get supplies, they would have to wait for someone to travel back to Vizianagaram, where the railroad did go. One of the missionaries bought a motorcycle with a sidecar, and transportation became easier. Luckily, though, Hebron had to go back to Vizianagaram for a few days once a month.

Clara found herself enjoying the new station because they had a nice bungalow, and it was cooler due to the ocean breezes, although the area still had its hot season. They could get fresh fish and prawns that tasted to Clara like the lobster back home. Betty seemed to have taken the return to India in stride. In 1916, Clara wrote to her mother,

> Betty grows tall fast, she is well, but is very white, as all English children are in this climate. Her hair grows dark fast and is quite long to what it was when you last saw her. English children in this country wear their hair long, and she is very anxious to have hers grow long. I am in hopes to have her photo taken in another year to send home.

However, they had a season of particularly rampant tropical diseases, and many of the students at the boys' boarding school became sick. Clara wrote in October 1916,

> It certainly was a care with 45 boarding boys on the compound, and the first two weeks of July I got quite tired and anxious as I was here all alone, and two and three boys sometimes more would be ill at a time with bad diarrhea and dysentery. One lot would just get better when some more would be taken, and with people dying in the town as they were, it meant a good deal of responsibility for me. I was glad when Mr. Corey and Miss Woodman returned but the worst was over by then. Fortunately, I had a large bottle of medicine that Dr. Clark had prepared, and I made good use of it, also cornstarch and arrowroot.

During the war, letters took two months to get from the States to India, and they were routinely opened by the censors. Many letters were lost during the war when ships were sunk. Clara explained that the paper had ceased to publish the date of the arrival of the mail steamer, so they no longer knew when to expect mail by the train. According to correspondence from February 14, 1917,

> Mr. Corey is on tour but will return here in a few days and go out the 22nd with Mr. Walker to a village six miles away from here and hold meetings for a week for the new Christians. The two men will live in a tent.

The Coreys no longer went to the hill country every year but planned to go in 1918 to Coonoor, a a city near Ooty in the Nilgiri Hills, to enroll their daughter, Betty, in the only English girls' boarding school in South India. She would be eight and a half at the time she enrolled and had been homeschooled until the decision was made to send her away like her brothers. Clara wrote, "Betty is looking forward to going to school at Coonoor next year. She misses her home playmates and really needs English children for companions." They felt too that their daughter would be safer in the cooler temperatures of the Nilgiri Hills, have English playmates, and receive a fine Christian education.

Cedric, however, would miss her terribly. He had progressed to the point his parents felt he could understand both English and Telugu, even though he could not speak at all and just made certain sounds.

To get Betty ready to go to boarding school, her mother composed a sewing kit with pieces of material, threads, yarns, needles, and a thimble so she could learn to make her own drawers and petticoats and darn her socks and stockings. She had to get a uniform: a navy-blue midi dress with a pleated skirt and a white sailor blouse top with a navy-blue bow. Clara wrote that she had to pay four dollars for a stout pair of boots for Betty, bemoaning that things were so expensive during the war. She wrote to her mother back home to look for stockings for Betty: a pair of white ones for dress and otherwise tan.

The Hebron School in Coonoor was five hundred miles from where Betty's parents were stationed and was accessible only by a five-day train ride with many stops and layovers. Once they reached the bottom of the Nilgiri Hills, they chugged up the mountain to Coonoor on a light blue train known as a cog railway. These steep mountain railroads were equipped with a center rail with cogs. The locomotive had a corresponding cogwheel that engaged with the cogs, which could push the train up the steep grade and hold it back on the downward slope. I took that train when I visited the Hebron School. The old steam engine was on display, but an electric engine had recently been installed. It was thrilling to chug up the mountain on the little blue train, passing villages with swarms of Indian workers crowding into the train to work on the tea plantations farther up. The Nilgiri Hills are among the most beautiful places in India, light blue in color (*Nilgiri* means "blue") and filled with waterfalls, chirping birds, and bright green tea plantations with waving Silver Oak tree branches to keep the sun off the tea.

The Hebron School had a boys' campus and a girls' campus, ten miles apart. Each one looked like a little bit of England amid crowded India. The weather was cool away from the hot plains and their diseases. The Hebron School for girls was run by Christian women from England. Like her brothers at the same age, Betty saw her parents only once a year for two months. During two-week breaks at other times of the year, she was sent to stay with nearby missionary families since home was too far away to go.

Clara toured the school, and she thought the campus was pretty and felt Betty would be happy there. She wrote, "We were so pleased with all the arrangements … and I am so glad there is a good Christian school for her to attend where the teachers are so sympathetic and make a real effort to understand each child." She later wrote,

> Yesterday, the annual prize giving was held. The parents of the pupils were invited to it, also to tea. I enjoyed all the exercises, and was surprised to see Betty in the drill, and doing so well too, for she has been in the school less than two weeks, and it was intricate, and long, but very pretty. The girls were all dressed in white, with their white shoes and stockings, but wore blue sashes and hair ribbons.

Clara's hope for understanding teachers was not realized. Coonoor was not a happy experience for Betty once her mother went back down to the plains. The teachers from England believed in a strict classical education, strict discipline, Bible lessons and worship services for all students, sewing, music, and all the ordinary subjects. They believed that children should be seen and not heard and that sparing the rod spoiled the child.

There were sixty boarding students, all English or American girls. Everything had to be kept neat all the time. Each child had a suitcase in which she kept all her belongings. If they left anything lying around, they were hit on the knuckles with a cane. There was no talking at meals, while they marched two by two from one class to another, or after lights-out in the evening. The school campus had small yellow stucco buildings on a hilly terrain. One can imagine the little girls trudging up the hills in silence. In later years, Betty used to exclaim, "They sure were strict!" and "The monkeys on the paths looked cute but were really nasty, so we learned to stay away from them while walking on the paths!"

The dormitory rooms were spare; each contained five plain, narrow double-decker beds painted a dark brown. There were ten little girls to each modest, Spartan room. How lonely and terrifying it must have been.

Betty knew one girl at her school, whom I will call Mary Miller, from her parents' mission field. Mary's father was a missionary doctor, and he and his wife often shared a house with Clara and Hebron. Betty and Mary found a mangy donkey near the school and snuck out to care for it, including brushing its coat and feeding it scraps from the table. A girl begged to go with them one time, but on the way back, she was so clumsy she was caught. They were all honor-bound to go confess, but Mary tried to make it better for herself by saying the whole idea had been Betty's. The school caned all three of them.

One year, Hebron came to visit Betty, and she burst into tears when she saw him, miserably homesick, but her distress was not her father's top priority. He wrote that the children were being given "a good English/Christian education." The formation of their characters as well as academics were uppermost in Hebron's mind. In contrast, Clara was concerned about Betty's happiness and safety and hoped she was happy with her playmates. Clara was relieved Betty no longer was in the compound with all the boarding Indian boys on the plains. "It was a care, I assure you," Clara wrote, but contrary to her parents' thoughts and wishes, Betty was not happy. She had been sent away at age eight and saw her parents for only two months a year.

She knew grammar, English history, Chaucer, Shakespeare, and the Bible. She became an Anglophile but was miserable so far away from her parents in the overly strict school where teachers caned the students. Betty felt abandoned and was abused but couldn't complain to her parents. She became depressed—the same way I did as a child and the same way all children do who have overly strict parents or who think they must protect their parents and not tell them their true feelings. The cycle continues from generation to generation unless a way is found to break it. In writing up this history, I am trying to understand what happened and what I need to do differently as a mother.

CHAPTER 9

The Faulkner School, 1954-1958

Remember always that you not only have the right to be an
individual, you have an obligation to be one.

Eleanor Roosevelt

During my eighth-grade year at Kenwood Elementary School, I studied to be baptized at Hyde Park Baptist Church, near the University of Chicago, where my parents were members until they moved to Fourth Presbyterian Church. The Baptists subscribe to a doctrine of believer's baptism instead of infant baptism, so baptismal candidates must be of an age at which they are capable of deciding for themselves if they believe the fundamental tenets of the church: that salvation comes through faith alone, not good works, and that scripture alone is the true Word of God. All the young people in the study course said they believed, and I did as well, but I kept trying to imagine how, just by saying, "I believe," I became one of the elect and was saved, whatever that meant. But it was the expected thing for me to do, and I was a compliant child.

The church held Baptism Sunday once a year in the spring for all the people, young and old, who had professed Baptist beliefs in the previous year. Before the regular Sunday service, I was taken to a girls' dressing room in the attached church building by a Sunday school teacher. I took off my Sunday-best clothes, folded them carefully on a chair, and pulled a long white one-piece gown over my head. I was in bare feet. All the boys and girls in our long white gowns lined up excitedly in a hallway behind the main sanctuary, by a door and a red velvet curtain that led into a built-in pool area by the side of the altar.

When my turn came, I walked through the red velvet curtains. In front of me were the many people sitting in the large sanctuary of the church, including Mom, Dad, Johnny, Bobby, and Margie. It was all kind of awe-inspiring. The sanctuary had stained-glass windows and handsome wood carvings. The floor of the baptismal pool, approximately five by ten feet, sloped downward, so one could walk in, and the congregation could watch. Near the side of the pool, which was faced with lovely wood carvings, I came before the minister, Dr. Schloerb, in his black robe. The pool was waist-deep for him, but I was up to my chest in the water. The water was room temperature; I did not feel cold. Dr. Schloerb was a gray-haired older minister I knew, though not well. He was the authority.

After I professed my faith, repeating the words after Dr. Schloerb, he put one arm under my waist and one under my head, leaned me back, and completely immersed me in the water like Christ at the River Jordan. Then Dr. Schloerb lifted me back up so I was once again standing chest-high in the water. I wiped the water off my face, my hair dripped, and I wondered if the congregation could see through that white robe. But something had happened. I felt happy, leading me to the beginning of my long journey.

Several members of the congregation came up to me afterward and made comments such as "You were the only one who looked like you had a true experience. Your face was radiant." My parents congratulated me, and the church gave me my own Bible. I started reading the Bible on my own.

Since I had entered first grade in January of the year I turned six, I would not finish eighth grade until the following December, but Mom thought it would be better if I moved ahead faster and got on a regular school year. Thus, I spent the summer in a public school, finishing the second half of eighth grade in order to enter high school as a freshman in the fall.

I started as a freshman at Hyde Park High School in the fall of 1953. They had placed me in regular math and English, and Mom was horrified. I belonged in honors, she fumed. She did not understand how the school could have misjudged my abilities. She pulled me out after a week and enrolled me at Miss Faulkner's School for Girls. My brothers were left at big, public Hyde Park High School.

Miss Faulkner's must have seemed like Mom's girls' boarding school in India: the students were all girls, we had chapel every morning and small classes, and the students wore uniforms—hunter-green skirts, knee socks, and cardigan sweaters with white blouses. It was primarily a Jewish school and was struggling to survive, a leftover from the glory days of the South Side of Chicago. It eventually moved to the South Shore and then closed.

When I arrived as a freshman, nearly all the girls lived on the South Shore, several miles from Kenwood. I entered a culture of sweet-sixteen parties, bat mitzvahs, and Florida vacations. I did not belong. As a WASP, I was the minority. We did not take Florida vacations. I became the goody-goody. I did all my work; obeyed all the rules; joined the volleyball, basketball, and field hockey teams and the glee club; and spent extra time in the art studio. Soon I was getting mostly straight As and dreaming of when I could go away to college. I was considered an exemplary student and did not rebel as a teenager; I was obedient and easy to raise, but I felt alone and lost.

The school was down the street and around the corner from our house. I got used to walking by all the houses where I no longer knew anyone, past the flower gardens and lawns that were no longer kept up, and past the trash lying in the streets. I just kept walking, carrying my heavy book bag with all my homework. I felt comfortable when walking home during the day, but Mom came to pick me up in the winter, when it was dark after school. "Just don't ever draw attention to yourself by wearing nice coats or jewelry," she said. I wonder if she was thinking of the Indian children in the poor village where she was born who were killed for the gold jewelry they wore.

Mom continued to work diligently as a schoolteacher on the predominantly African American South Side and to give me social contacts with the socially prominent on the North Side. One night, though, Mom didn't want me to go to one of the dances. I had just starred in a one-act play at Faulkner, and Mom had decided what I was to do. She said firmly, "You're tired. You may not go to the dance tonight. You need to go to bed." I was to go upstairs to my lonely, dark, spooky room; put on my pajamas; and go to bed.

But I so wanted to go to the dance that I decided to challenge Mom. I wanted to leave in my light green-and-white plaid organza dress and go to the dance at the Fortnightly Club. "But I'm not tired. I want to go. I've been looking forward to it," I said. "I am not tired, and I want to go to the dance."

"You are tired and need to go up to bed," Mom repeated, immovable. She had lost control over her own life and was determined to exert control over mine.

Images rose up in my mind of the dance, of whirling around with William, my heartthrob from the local parties, in my lovely organza dress. He sometimes even paid some attention to me. "I must! I must go tonight. I have my heart set on it!" I cried.

"You are tired and need to go to bed," Mom said, still immovable.

It slowly dawned on me that I could not win. I was not heard. My wish made no mark. I went limp.

Mom's hand came down, pulled me up to a standing position, and led me to the lonely dark stairs, which I climbed by myself, heavy foot after heavy foot. I took off the organza plaid, threw it onto the floor, and put on old yellowed pajamas. After brushing my teeth, I crawled into bed in the dark and stared wide-eyed at the dark ceiling and saw nothing—no images or pictures, just blankness. I lay there interminably, trying to get through the void, the nothing.

Four years later, Mom decided I should not only be a member of the University of Chicago's Colony Club and the Fortnightly dances but also be on the social list of Chicago so I could be invited to all the debutante parties. She went downtown on the L from the South Side to have an interview with the social secretary of the city newspaper. When she returned, she said, "Betsy, I told her that you come from a very distinguished family in Maine, a long line of shipbuilders. Your great-uncle Albert Bickmore founded the Natural History Museum in New York City, and your great-grandmother was the first woman to graduate from college in the state of Maine." The social secretary seemingly had not noticed that Mom skipped over one hundred years of our family's history, but Mom must have been convincing. I was put on the list, and in due time, the list was published in the papers.

A couple dozen engraved invitations soon arrived, and I was invited to the far reaches of Chicago's wealthy suburbs of Winnetka, Lake Forest, and the Near North Side for the fanciest parties I could ever imagine. Mom took me to Marshall Field's to buy flowered silk party dresses for the spring season and silk taffeta for the winter. Some of the time, I thought the dresses were just like everyone else's, and sometimes I wanted to sink through the floor in mortification because I felt I had on the wrong dress. There were big white tents on enormous lawns of large mansions with piles of food, Lester Lanin playing dance music, and parents and grandparents sitting around the sides, looking on to see who was talking to whom.

I did not know a soul. All the kids knew each other because they had grown up together and attended various boarding schools together. They were simply home on vacation. I was a day student at Miss Faulkner's on the South Side, where no one lived. When asked where I lived, I'd reply, "In Kenwood."

"You live where?" they exclaimed.

"Down near the University of Chicago," I said.

They looked at me strangely. "Oh, way down there? I didn't know anyone lived there."

I felt like a pariah.

Some kids made attempts to be friendly. One tall, lanky sandy-haired boy came over and asked me to dance. "What is your name?"

"Betsy," I replied.

"I mean, what is your whole name?" he asked.

"Elizabeth Bond Hunter,'" I replied reticently.

"Oh, is that the Bond of the Bond Shoe family?" he asked hopefully.

"No," I replied. "It is the Bond from Colonel William Bond of the Revolutionary War."

"Oh," the boy said with disappointment in his voice. He soon excused himself, thanking me for the dance.

Other times, a nice-looking boy or not-so-nice-looking boy would ask me to dance, and that was fun, but mostly, I sat on the sidelines, watching everyone else, or I fled to the ladies' room.

When Dad saw all the parties I was attending in the northern sections of the city, he remarked, "We're not a family of leisure or a golf-playing or fox-hunting family." That was typical of Dad's own form of snobbery, as he'd grown up in western Iowa, where wrestling and boxing were admired. He was digging at Mom again instead of feeling his own sense of inadequacy, but I didn't understand all that at the time. Dad didn't understand that Mom was just trying to find acceptance in her adopted land.

It all seemed perfectly natural to Mom: an island of white people in India and our house in the African American neighborhood of Chicago. Mom continued teaching the King's English, as her father had before her, in the tough local high schools. If she was ever upset about where our family lived, I never heard her express it. Dad continued not to notice, and I continued to hate it, but I did not talk to Mom about how I felt. On a deep level, I continued to sense Mom's hurt and did not want to add to her burden.

When children are afraid to express their own feelings, a sense of alienation or distance develops in the family. They know they are not known and soon do not know themselves, for we know ourselves by having someone mirror us or repeat what we have said in a way we know we have been heard.

* * *

Mom decided to take on a cause of her own. She started a campaign to expose vote fraud in Chicago. She had been volunteering as a poll watcher in elections and complained that she had seen the same person vote twice under different names. She became so fired up that she decided to do something about it. I heard Dad remark one day about Mom's work, "Betty would talk so much about vote fraud that it would drive you crazy." Another dig from Dad at Mom.

When I came home from school, I wanted to spend time with Mom. We sat together at the warn maple kitchen table, but Mom talked politics, and I just listened. "I am particularly upset because I am a naturalized citizen and take this democracy very seriously," Mom told me. "I hate to see people abusing voting rights that I gave up my Canadian citizenship to attain."

I would rather have talked about something else, but I sat there and watched Mom. She had become obsessed. "I feel it is my duty as a citizen to see that the elections are honest," she said. She went on and on in talking politics and wouldn't stop. Feeling defeated about getting close to Mom, I reluctantly gathered my books and went to my third-floor garret room alone to do my homework, determined more than ever to get into a good college far from Chicago.

Mom persisted. She canvassed the precincts with the voter registration rolls, checking to see that the people registered existed. She would be by herself, wearing simple clothes meant not to attract attention, and would knock on doors of apartments and rooming houses to ask who lived there. Elijah Muhammad and Muhammad Ali had moved into Kenwood. They lived on Woodlawn Avenue, just two blocks from our house.

Mom told me she knocked on the door of the mansion belonging to Muhammad Ali, not even knowing who lived there. A guard answered the door, said no white people were allowed, and asked her to leave. The harsh treatment surprised her. She probably did not know about the Nation of Islam.

She took her findings to the *Chicago Daily News*. They were intrigued and published her stories about people on the rolls who were dead or registered from vacant lots.

She continued her work with vote fraud for years and was at the Republican headquarters in Cook County at the time of the 1960 election between Nixon and Kennedy. She knew from her work in the precincts and from watching the numbers that there had been considerable vote fraud in Cook County and called the Nixon headquarters to inform them: "If Nixon will hold off on conceding the election, we can hold a recount and bring in Cook County for Nixon, which will make the difference to his election."

The answer came back from Nixon: "For the good of the country, I am not going to hold up the election result."

Betty felt the fate of the country was on her shoulders that night and felt tremendous personal satisfaction that her work might have made a major contribution to her adopted country.

Decades later, in 2015, while participating in a trip to see the World War II cemetery at Normandy, France, David Eisenhower and Julie Nixon Eisenhower were along as special guest lecturers. I had the chance to talk with Julie Nixon Eisenhower and told her the story about the 1960 election that I had heard from my mother. She looked me right in the eye and replied, "That is exactly what happened." She then explained that her father was always worried after that about the possibility of another election being stolen from him.

When Mom wasn't busy canvassing voters, teaching, and surviving on the tough South Side, she researched her genealogy and found proof of her ancestry for the Mayflower Society, the DAR, the National Society of Colonial Dames, and the Daughters of Cincinnati (descendants of George Washington's Revolutionary War officers). She joined them all and had Margie and me invited as well. She wanted to feel more deeply rooted in America. A friend of Mom's offered to have me proposed for the Chicago Junior League. I was accepted as a provisional. The Junior League planned and sponsored projects to better the community, not unlike some of what my family had done in India in the areas of education and health care.

Mom always felt education and community service were paramount, much as her father before her had in India, but what was missing? Control from without, ideals, obedience, and being good rather than nurturing the inner soul—it was all about what was right and wrong in their terms. It never occurred to them to listen to their children. Their need to control hindered their children from developing their own selves. Our family lived in the midst of the great civil rights revolution but continued to attempt to live the way they had always wished to live.

CHAPTER 10

Wolfville, Nova Scotia, Canada, 1923-1928

The war continued, and as Hebron said, the good work continued in India. When he had time from all his other duties, Hebron went on tour, always pleased when an Indian made the decision to become a Christian and be baptized. Although the new converts had to suffer the condemnation of their own Hindu community, the missionaries seemed blind to the breakup of Hindu families and remarked instead on the Indian Christians' softer, gentler, and more loving spirits.

Clara had no use for the Germans and no sympathy for Gandhi's campaigns of nonviolent civil disobedience and fasting, which had begun in Gujarat in 1915, when he organized laborers and farmers to protest discrimination and high land taxes. Clara called Gandhi's campaigns *uprisings* since her loyalty and sympathy remained with the English. Even her daughter, decades later, frequently extolled the great things the British had brought to India, such as highly organized administration, the court system, the train, education, and the English language.

Clara wrote about her health; her old problem, which she did not explain in her letters but perhaps was nerves; her tiredness; attacks of malaria that came back intermittently; her recipes; sewing; and her longing for the children. She wrote in a letter to her mother, "This would have been dear Harry's birthday." She missed her boys back in Canada tremendously but felt powerless to make any changes, because she accepted the primary importance of the mission.

Meanwhile, their son Albert, back in Canada, fumed that the air force would not send him to the front in France because he was only eighteen. He wanted to resign, go back to college at Acadia University, and reenlist when he was nineteen, but they would not give him permission to go. Like many of his generation, he had not really absorbed the reality of the war. Albert eventually enrolled in courses to become a lieutenant as Clara explained in her letter to her mother in Tenants Harbor:

> Of course, that is rather hard to get, especially as he is young, but hard things are not impossible. Already he had been made an instructor in musketry and was teaching shooting to fifty men ... The sergeant who was the real instructor of the squad had Albert instruct while he sat back and watched. After a while, he commended him on his instructing and in that way [Albert] received his promotion.

In the meantime, mail was not getting through from Canada. One of the large steamers was lost with all the Madras and Bombay mail, so they missed letters from Charlie. They relied on the kindness of relatives and retired missionaries to care for their boys, as Clara explained to her mother in Tenants Harbor:

> If you receive this letter, I wish you would write to Charlie to Wolfville, and find out where he is, for it is such a long time since we have heard from him. Some steamers must have been lost on which his letters were coming, for it is not like him not to write for so long, and we do not even know where he is expected to spend his summer vacation.
> Now we hear that the college may not reopen, as the number of students is so small. If so, I do not know where he will go. Charlie needs some real home life. Maggie and Uncle Richard were very kind to him. He never complains but I can see that he would like a real home.

She confirmed to her mother that all her letters were censored by the British government:

Still, we have so much to be thankful for, I cannot complain, even if we cannot see each other. We have all been spared another year and are in usual health too which is a great blessing, while too many families in the world, it has been a year of hardship and sorrow.

When Albert turned nineteen, he was accepted into training to be a pilot and sent to England for instruction and later to Egypt. Charlie, who wanted to be like Albert, felt even more left behind. His parents, Betty, and Cedric were in India, and Albert was off having what seemed like an exciting and glamorous life as a World War I pilot. Charlie felt lonely by himself and became depressed. He tried to enlist in the military, even though he had fallen from a roof at the school in Bangalore and hit his head, an injury that caused him dizzy spells periodically. During his physical, he was turned in a chair with his eyes closed, stopped, and then told to open his eyes and describe the image in a few seconds. He became dizzy and failed, which disqualified him for the armed services. He tried a second time and again failed.

The rejections devastated him and festered in his lonely mind. In a letter to his parents, he apologized for not writing more often and said, "I have nothing interesting to write about." However, Hebron's cousin, who often invited Charlie to Sunday dinner, wrote to Clara that Charlie had had a profound religious experience and was the deepest young man she had ever known. Charlie's experience, whatever it was, was never explained in Clara's letters.

As Charlie struggled with feelings of loneliness and depression in Canada, his parents in India continued to be proud of his good grades and upstanding character, even though they missed him and were aware he was unhappy. The pictures and reports they received from cousins who saw him all agreed that Charlie continued to be young for his age and very sensitive.

Albert loved flying and did well, becoming an officer and a flying instructor. He flew extensively out of Egypt. When Albert sent Clara a picture of himself in his uniform, Clara wrote to her mother back in Tenants Harbor, "My, how tall and grown-up Albert looks." Albert didn't tell his mother in his letters about all the near misses. After the war was over, he wrote that a boat right next to his had been torpedoed and sunk and that he had been fired upon while flying several times.

In India, the Coreys made the best of things until the war was over. On November 18, 1918, Clara wrote,

> One week ago, today was a day long to be remembered by everybody throughout the civilized world and I suppose eleven will be quite a noted number now. As I saw in a paper, it seemed a strange coincidence that peace should come at the eleventh hour, of the eleventh day, of the eleventh month. God has given us the victory so longed for prayed for and I feel I cannot thank Him enough that He has caused Democracy to triumph. "He maketh wars to cease," is as true now as when it was written.
>
> What a blessing too, that peace has come just at the beginning of another long hard winter, so much unnecessary suffering saved for we in comfortable homes can little realize what life in the trenches is like in the best of weather, and what it is in the storms of winter I do not like to try to fully understand. But the worst is over, and we can all rejoice and trust God to bring good out of all the chaos that is in the world at present. Probably you are glad now that both Albert and Charlie volunteered although under draft age, for it was easier for their father and me to have them willing to help to make the world a safe place for women and children to live in, than to have had them looking out first for their own comfort.

After the war, Clara's spirit lifted, and she could appreciate the beauty of nature around her, such as the waving palm trees and the cool breeze: "India when the moon is full, seems almost like fairyland, the coconut palms in their feathery beauty are especially lovely such nights ... The trees here have put out new leaves and there is a diversity of shades of green all around us." Clara turned her attention to her family in India, Canada, and Tenants Harbor. Tenants Harbor was always the place she called home, even though she hadn't lived there for most of her adult life. Everything happening there was important to her, and she read the local *Maine Gazette* avidly, including the weddings, births, and deaths. She asked about everybody, saying, for example, "How is Maggie, and what was her trouble—a cough or what?"

Charles graduated from Acadia University in Wolfville on May 26, 1920, and was thinking of going on to Harvard, but as Clara wrote, "Whether he will or not I do not know, for he may change his mind by the end of the summer. So far, he has been quite undecided as to his future work."

Albert, despite his three years in the air force, was not far behind Charlie at Acadia. The government gave Albert a three-year grant for education because of his service. He finished at Acadia University in two years and then spent a year at Oxford in England.

Betty's education was a focus of Clara and Hebron's attention both at home and at school. At school, she took all the academic courses and made her own clothes, and at home, she continued to improve herself. Betty wrote to her grandmother in Tenants Harbor in January 1921, "Father hired a piano for my two months' vacation, and I practice every day. This year I am going up for a government exam in music." Betty was always afraid her father would be critical of her, and when she received the results, she felt her father would be disappointed she had not done better. "It is unfair that Dad expects so much of me."

Clara was proud of Betty's other accomplishments. Just twelve years old, Betty had to both enlarge a pattern by ten and cut her own pattern for a princess petticoat. She also enlarged a tiny diagram, cut a pattern, and made a midi suit that was sent to Madras for an exhibition. Clara wrote,

> She is taught all necessary things ... She can do Indian cooking, curry and rice, can clean fish, cut up meat and prepare and do it all herself. Betty's textbooks are far from simple, they are all as hard as those I had as a child, and her history, geography and grammar harder, the latter is altogether too hard for a child. However, one way it is a good thing, for the children must study, in order to know anything about their lessons.

But as suddenly as she had been sent to Hebron School, she was taken away. When she was thirteen and a half, in 1922, her parents took her with them back to North America, to Wolfville and Tenants Harbor. India had taken a toll on the Coreys. Famine and cholera continued to break out, and the people continued to suffer terribly with no way of alleviating their issues, but Clara and Hebron were ready for another furlough. Hebron was sixty years old, and Clara was fifty-four. Hebron was exhausted, and Clara had aged. She wrote to tell her mother not to be too shocked when she saw her.

As usual, Hebron couldn't stay long with Clara, even in his last months in India, since he had to go to Bobbili to start preparing for the opening of the high school, where nearly a thousand students were expected. Clara, left at home with Cedric, was pleased that a friend came for a few days with all his family to visit on their way to the conference at Cocanda. Their daughter had been a dear friend of Betty's at the Hebron School. "They are darling people," Clara wrote.

Betty's schooling during their sabbatical in Canada was very much on Clara's mind.

> At present, we hope to have her attend "The Ladies Seminary" as a day scholar, next winter. The boys went to the Academy. The college, seminary and academy are all on one campus at Wolfville but are quite distinct schools. The Seminary was founded by a graduate of Mt. Holyoke, and is that kind of school, only the girls do not have to work as they do there.

Clara was worried she wouldn't know her boys when she saw them again after seven and a half years. When she last had seen them, Charlie had been fourteen, and Albert had been sixteen. "Albert weighs 175 pounds and is broad-chested now," Clara wrote, wondering if she would recognize him.

They left Cedric behind in India under the care of a kindly missionary.

> Cedric is contented when we are away, though he misses us, and is nearly over-joyed when we return … The lady doctor at Wataire offered to keep him while we were on furlough … When we were down there last week, we saw her, and she showed us the room she planned for him to have. Her offer to keep him is pure kindness on her part, she lives all alone, and it means a good deal to her to have the care of him. The reason she takes him, is because she loves all our missionaries, and is always ready to help,

besides she has always thought a great deal of Cedric, and he is fond of her too. She is a middle-aged woman.

The last letter from Clara in India was written on January 4, 1922. In it, she spoke her mind to her dear mother about her worries about the deterioration of family life due to "two insidious perils in front of us today." One was growing disrespect for the Sabbath, and the other was increasing neglect of the Bible. Though Clara worried that families were deteriorating, she didn't seem to be aware of what was happening to her own family or of the impact Christian conversions had had on Hindu families. Clara's passivity in the face of the long absences from her children seems shocking to me today. She had no awareness of what dark things were in store for her back in Canada.

Clara, Hebron, and Betty left India in the spring of 1922. They left everything behind in India, thinking they were going to return, but they never did. They left their baby Harry's grave and left Cedric with kindly Mrs. Gallisin. They left all their personal household belongings. They took domed trunks filled with clothes for themselves and their extended family back home, their Bibles, and a few Indian trinkets: brass cobra candlesticks, bracelets, and a tarantula in a bottle.

Clara and Hebron had spent twenty-eight years in India and had five children there. The mission for which Hebron had toiled had established hundreds of churches and schools, several orphanages, two leper sanatoriums, and much more. A small Christian community had been created. They had tried to make the Indian Christians self-sufficient, but many still depended on the Western missionaries. They had given the Dalits hope and an education that included English to enable them to have access to government jobs. The few Brahmans who had converted to Christianity carried on the work of the missionaries, running orphanages. Many in India said the missionary schools provided the finest education in India. The missionaries' service took a tremendous toll on both the Hindus and the missionaries' families. The Indian government finally decided the missionaries did more harm than good and made all the foreign missionaries leave in 1970.

The Corey family made the long, arduous trip from India through the Indian Ocean, the Suez Canal, the Mediterranean Sea, and the Atlantic to Southampton in England, where they changed to another steamer to cross the Atlantic back to Boston. Hebron was worn out, and Clara was her usual tired self and a bad sea traveler. Betty, thirteen and a half, looked after them. Bursting with energy and excitement, Betty was glad to be released from the strict and overbearing girls' boarding school and going back to Wolfville to see her brothers after so many years. She had been six when she saw them last and had thought of them often. Charlie, in particular, had faithfully written to her over the many years.

After two and a half months of travel, the ship landed on North American shores on about June 5, 1922. Clara hurried to Tenants Harbor in the hope of seeing her mother, Elizabeth, one last time, having had word that her mother was failing. She did not make it. Clara's mother had died on May 22.

Devastated at having arrived in Tenants Harbor a week after the funeral, they spent time at the cemetery, visiting the fresh grave of Elizabeth Bickmore Long, next to that of her husband, Whitney, who had died an alcoholic two decades earlier. Elizabeth had carried on valiantly as a widow, dying at age seventy-seven.

Hebron, Clara, and their daughter left for Wolfville. They traveled by train up the coast to Bar Harbor, took the ferry to Nova Scotia, and took another train to Wolfville and Acadia University. Their grief followed them.

At Wolfville, Hebron was expected to help raise money and preach during his sabbatical year. It was a charming small town with large, well-kept Victorian houses decorated in pastel colors, groomed lawns, and flower gardens, adjacent to the soft pink sands of the Bay of Fundy, with its twenty-foot tides. Unlike the eastern coast of Nova Scotia, with its rocky gray granite cliffs, Wolfville was surrounded by rich, fertile farmland. In the town park stood a statue of Evangeline, the legendary French Huguenot maiden forced out of her home by the British, as told in Longfellow's poem. In different circumstances, Clara would also be asked to leave Wolfville one day.

The Canadian Baptist Foreign Mission Board arranged for Clara, Hebron, and Betty to live in the parish house of the Baptist church, where Hebron served as pastor. As in India, he was gone from his temporary home most of the time, fundraising for the Telugu churches. Clara continued to mourn for her mother.

Albert came on a visit to Wolfville. He was tall, strong, handsome, and self-confident and had a pretty girl named Inez on his arm. He announced that he planned to wed Inez and move to Massachusetts, where he had been accepted into a master's program at Harvard in history. Clara hardly recognized her own son but was proud of all he had accomplished. She was not sure about Inez.

Charlie also returned to greet his parents and sister. After graduating from Acadia in 1920, he had gone to Babson College and received a master's degree in business. He had been working as a statistician at the Federal Reserve Bank of Boston but had just accepted a job as a banker with Kountze Brothers in New York City. He was tall, lanky, and handsome. His dark brown eyes shone with sadness. He had been left alone too long and still felt badly about his inability to join the military, but he announced that he had saved his money to help send Betty to school. He wanted his little sister to have every opportunity.

Clara and Hebron's hearts filled with joy at seeing their sons after those interminably long seven and a half years. Their sons had fulfilled all their expectations; finished their educations as star students; and, as Hebron put it, remained pure despite all the temptations. Their Baptist evangelical religion remained their guiding light; they relied on their heavenly Father, believing that "all things work together for good to them that love God" (Romans 8:28). That verse was often quoted to me.

Betty dressed like an English colonial schoolgirl in her navy-blue midi suit with white collar, dark stockings, and sensible brown shoes. She wore her hair in a short bob and spoke with an English accent. She was overjoyed to see her brothers but constrained in her ability to show her feelings. She had been taught British reserve well.

Like Odysseus finally coming home from his wanderings, the Coreys had returned, and also like Odysseus, they had not come home to triumph and happiness ever after but to additional challenges. They had all tried hard to live exemplary lives, but the years of separation and loneliness had left many unintended consequences.

The Corey family back from India in Wolfville, Nova Scotia 1924.
Back row: Albert, Betty, Charlie
Front Row: Hebron and Clara

The Coreys expected to return to India, but meanwhile, they wanted to settle down in Wolfville and establish a life like the one they had been living. Hebron would visit Baptist churches to raise money for the missions; Clara would sew, cook, and write letters to missionary friends she had left behind in India as well as to Cedric, whom they'd left under the kindly care of Mrs. Gullison in India.

Hebron was greatly respected for his lifetime service in India and was awarded an honorary doctor of divinity degree in 1923. *The Enterprise* lauded him, saying, "His reliable judgment upon all missionary matters, his industry, and his ability as an educationist, have been duly recognized by Acadia University."

Betty attended the female academy on the campus of Acadia University and found herself a star student, but her classmates stared at her, with her English accent and handmade clothes. Betty was determined to change to fit in with her new surroundings. Her school found her such a good student that they suggested she start Acadia University in the fall, just before her sixteenth birthday.

The girl she had known in India, Mary Miller, was back in Wolfville as well. They both loved learning outdoor winter sports and joined other young people of the town in ice-skating on the local pond. But they didn't get along. Betty was a serious student, and Mary was more interested in having fun and flirting with boys. Betty was taken aback, particularly since she herself had gotten in trouble with her father for just walking home with a boy, something she still resented.

One afternoon, during the first harsh winter the family had experienced in nine years, Betty trudged through the deep, cold snow back to the Victorian parish house and was startled to see two other missionaries on furlough sitting in the living room. "What's happening?" cried Betty. "Where's my mother?"

"Betty," they told her, "your father collapsed at the monthly meeting of the Foreign Mission Board. He was taken to the hospital, and your mother is with him. They asked us to come get you and take you to the hospital."

At the hospital, Betty found her father unconscious and her mother sitting in a chair, distraught. "He had a massive stroke," the doctor said quietly. "We will keep him for a few days to see if he wakes up from his coma." India had taken an enormous toll on his health. Clara and Betty kept vigil at the hospital. Hebron did wake up from the coma, but he could not move. After a few weeks, he was discharged to go home, paralyzed. He remained thus for five years, until he died at the end of the dreary month of March 1928.

During those five years, the family had the sense Hebron could understand what people said to him, even though he could not speak. The expression in his eyes made them think he understood. This minister, missionary, evangelist, builder, and educator who had given nearly thirty years of his life to doing good in India now faced his greatest trial: to lie paralyzed in bed for five years. As his daughter, Betty, said years later, "The rain falls on the just and the unjust alike."

Clara did her best to nurse her husband but became prostrate herself. The strain was too much. Betty, still a slip of a girl, found herself picking up the pieces: keeping house; cooking the meals; and going to school, where she nonetheless still excelled. It is hard to imagine the strain on the family of having Hebron paralyzed at home. Betty, who had already had to cope for so much of her life, now had to again.

Both of her brothers had left Wolfville and gotten on with their lives. Charlie went to New York City but sent money back for Betty's tuition.

Albert married Inez, and after Harvard, he went to teach at Waynesburg College and, a year later, to St. Lawrence University in Canton, New York. He also worked on his PhD at Clark University. After all those years apart, the family remained apart.

Inez, a Unitarian, ridiculed evangelical Christianity. When she came to visit Hebron, she mocked his faith, for it was not making him well. "Once it was told me," she said, "that your faith teaches that you can move mountains. Why are you not healed?" Everyone who saw the exchange thought it appeared Hebron was crying. Clara was so hurt by Inez's cruelty that she threatened to disinherit Albert.

Life splintered in Canada. If India had been hard, Canada was worse. Hebron passed on March 31, 1928. Clara, then sixty was unprepared to be a widow. She had become dependent on Hebron, and the reality of living without him was terrible. She collapsed once again, but her daughter, Betty, carried on, because she knew she had to. There was no one else. Betty was nineteen and graduating from Acadia that spring. She was a theater major and had played Portia in *The Merchant of Venice*.

They had left everything in India when they left, and with Hebron's death, no member of their family ever returned to India. Cedric never saw any of his family again. As time went on, Inez, among others, seemed to think of Cedric as an embarrassment. Years later, a letter arrived from India stating that Cedric had died. He had become an orderly in a hospital and had been greatly loved. The money left from Cedric's care was sent back to Canada and helped to finance Alex, one of Albert's children, through Acadia University, from which she graduated in 1950. What Cedric could not do for himself, his money did for his niece.

Cedric received loving care from the people with whom he was left. I can imagine the mute young man, left in India never to see his family again, mourned his tremendous losses, which freed him to become a loving presence in the hospital to other sick and injured people. I often think of Cedric and wish I could have known him. He would have had much to teach us all.

CHAPTER 11

Vassar, 1958–1962

Mom had been interested not only in her children's social advancement but also in their academic success. She had read to us when we were little, made sure we did our homework, and emphasized the importance of school. The results were impressive. I ended up graduating with the top grades from Miss Faulkner's School. All four children were accepted to quality eastern schools. Mom was tickled all over. Dad would have been just as happy to see us all go to the University of Illinois, but Mom insisted on a different path.

Johnny was not accepted at Yale, and she blamed herself for not knowing to ask powerful friends for help. He went to Trinity College. Two years later, she asked well-connected friends to write letters for Bobby, and he was accepted at Harvard. I was accepted at Vassar, and four years later, Margie was as well. Mom, working at the kitchen sink in her old mended housedress, smiled at the thought of her children going east for college.

Mom didn't buy anything for herself. Her clothes were mostly hand-me-downs from her daughters. She used the money she made teaching to buy good clothes for her children to take to college. I felt guilty that Mom did not do more for herself, but she insisted, "We have skimped a lot, but now it is time to see that you have very nice clothes to wear."

Mom spent the summer getting my trunk ready to send to Vassar for the fall. She sewed a name tag on every piece of clothing, including my wool knee socks and short white gym socks. She hemmed skirts and checked new clothes to be sure they were right. She took me downtown and bought me preppy clothes from Peck and Peck, Brooks Brothers, and Marshall Field and Company: a brown-and-tan tweed suit, a blue-and-green black-watch plaid dress, a simple black dress, Bermuda shorts, button-down shirts, wool cardigans with grosgrain ribbon, woolen knee socks, penny loafers, a camel-hair coat, and black pumps. Mom went all out.

When it came time to put the trunk in the car to take it to the shipping company, I wanted to help and started lifting it into the car. "Don't hurt yourself," Mom said. "You're young, with a life in front of you. When you become an old hag like me and no one wants you anymore, you don't have to be so careful." Mom lifted the trunk into the car. "Take care of yourself, and don't worry about me," she added. I felt terrible watching her.

Mom and Dad took me to the train station in Chicago to catch the train east. I wore my new Peck and Peck tweed suit. We all waved as the train pulled out of the station on its way to Poughkeepsie. I was going to arrive by myself at a school I had never visited. Sitting in the coach, I saw Judy, whom I had met at the Fortnightly dances, and another girl I had never seen before. Both girls also wore tailored suits. I asked if they were also going to Vassar. They were, and we were all glad to find one another.

We shared a taxi from the Poughkeepsie train station to the college. As we drove through the big stone gates, I was in awe at the beautiful campus, with its handsome buildings, great lawns, enormous old trees, and flower gardens. I was thrilled to be away from Chicago and off on my own. It was the fall of 1957.

I was assigned to Noyes, a brand-new dormitory designed by Eero Saarinen. A semicircular building with triangular windows, it sat behind a big circle of flowers in a grand lawn. It was beautiful and safe. After my scary garret room on Chicago's South Side, it was like living in the Magic Kingdom. My assigned roommate was gone a lot. It turned out she was secretly dating a history professor, something against the rules, whom she married the next summer. But the girls on my corridor were around and friendly and invited me to go on walks or go to meals together.

We registered for classes. They took so-called posture pictures, for which we were photographed naked to evaluate our posture. Those who were less than perfect, including myself, had to take a posture class, in which we were taught such things as how to pick up a suitcase by bending one's knees to avoid hurting one's back. Decades after my college years, an article appeared in the *New York Times* about the nude posture pictures at

Vassar and several other elite eastern colleges. Some of the Vassar posture pictures were reportedly stolen and circulated at Skull and Bones at Yale. This practice has long been discontinued.

We had a swim test. I was surprised the instructors didn't like my breaststroke, something I had prided myself on, but nothing really bothered me, because I was free at last. I felt like a butterfly that had finally broken out of its cocoon. Never mind that I found chemistry, French, and English harder than I had expected. I was used to getting all As, and now I was glad when I got a C+. The chemistry professor expected me to know more math than I did, the French teacher expected me to understand more French than I did, and the English teacher expected me to write better papers than I knew how. My Chicago day school had been about memorization and the right answers. Vassar was about thinking, original research, and creativity, but it never occurred to me that I wasn't doing okay.

I had loved chemistry at Faulkner and had entered Vassar thinking I would be a science major, but I quickly gave up that idea when I could barely understand or keep up with freshman chemistry. I liked the ideas in history and English better, although those classes were not easy either.

At the beginning of the year, Miss Sarah Gipson Blanding, the president of Vassar, called the whole school to the chapel for a talk. "You girls can do whatever you like," she said, "but not at Vassar." She meant there were standards that all Vassar girls were to uphold, and the school went to some lengths to see that we did. At the front entrance to the dormitory, a white angel, a lady of mature years in a white uniform, sat at a desk, checking everyone in and out. Curfew was 10:00 p.m. on weeknights and midnight on weekends, as I recall. Boys were not allowed above the first floor, except on Sunday afternoons, but the doors to the dormitory rooms were to remain open, and everyone had to have at least one foot on the floor. They held freshman sex lectures to teach us the ins and outs of the subject. I raised my hand to ask a question; the room laughed. My mother's careful upbringing and protection had had their effect.

My life turned from gray to Technicolor. I was not isolated any more, for I joined a rooming group consisting of Judy and Dana, whom I had met on the train; Leise from Denmark; Marty, Joan, and Pam from New Jersey; and a few others.

One time, I overheard a conversation about me through the radiator to the floor below, in which a girl I will call Pam opined that I was immature and always wanted to join in with everyone else. That disturbed me, but the girls remained friendly, and I continued to join in anyway, with a little sadness. It was Pam who really had the problem, a much bigger problem than I. Her abdomen started getting bigger and bigger. She quietly left Vassar in the middle of the year. Everyone whispered about what the problem might be. She could return the next fall. When Mom heard about Pam, she warned, "Betsy, you are too young to have to handle something so difficult."

No one knew or cared that I came from the South Side of Chicago, although occasionally, I felt like a fraud. But there was something about all of us girls being far from home and wearing the uniform of Bermuda shorts, knee socks, white blouses, and grosgrain-ribbon sweaters that let me be a member of the group at Noyes.

The dorm and college activities delighted me: carving pumpkins and dunking for apples at Halloween, building snowmen in the winter, and attending school mixers with nearby men's colleges and all-school lectures by famous people, such as Governor Nelson Rockefeller's talk on the need for everyone to have a bomb shelter. I was thrilled to go along since I didn't have a vision of my own, like a traveler happy with all the delightful new experiences.

I went skiing for the first time with the ski club during a mixer with Williams College. I didn't have the right clothes, so I just wore a pair of plaid wool slacks. I rented long wooden skis and poles, held on to a rope tow up the icy bunny slope, slipped on the ice, and slid down on my bottom. Everyone laughed, but I didn't care. It was fun. One boy from Williams followed me around until I took off my ski hat, and he saw my hair, which was frizzy from a recent permanent and made frizzier by the moisture. He quickly left.

I went on a blind date to West Point and met a cadet who asked me down again and again to fun dances and football weekends. I wore my trunkful of new clothes and felt stylish. One weekend, when I arrived, he couldn't see me for a few hours, as he was marching around the inner courtyard as a punishment for some infraction of the rules. At the dance, the cadets had a private rating system for their dates. They placed their white gloves in between the brass buttons on their uniforms according to how they rated their dates. Gloves near the waist meant they didn't think much of them. Gloves near the neck meant a high score. I don't know that my cadet played that game, but he did start writing me letters filled with entertaining details of life at West Point. The cadet took me on a walk and gave me a nice, warm kiss under the kissing rock.

Life at Vassar was so busy and happy that I didn't keep in touch well with my parents. Mom wrote me letters and asked me to write back, which I tried to do occasionally. There was a telephone downstairs with the white angel at the door, and occasionally, a telephone call would come in from my parents, but mostly, I was happy to distance myself from everything Chicago, perhaps a little like my mother and grandmother before me.

When school ended for the year in June, I reluctantly returned for the summer to Chicago, where I would be an assistant counselor at a Girl Scout camp and take driving lessons and typing lessons. I was looking forward to returning to Vassar in the fall. My brother Bobby was home for the summer from Harvard, and my West Point cadet sent me letters a couple of times a week.

One day, as the sun rose, I bounded out of bed, excited because I was going off for an overnight camping trip with the Girl Scouts. I went downstairs, where I saw a letter from the dean at Vassar. I couldn't imagine what it was. Standing in our front hall with my brother Bobby, I tore open the envelope. My eyes filled with tears. Bobby stood there trying to understand what was happening, when my mother came downstairs in her housedress. "What's the matter, Betsy?" Mom asked.

The letter from the dean suggested I transfer to another school. My grades were just on the borderline, the letter said, so I could stay. However, if I stayed but my grades didn't improve, I would be asked to leave and not given any assistance in finding another school. If I left immediately, on the other hand, Vassar would help me find a different college.

They wanted me to leave! I put my head on Mom's shoulder. It was one of the warmest moments I can remember, though I was utterly distraught. She pulled away from me a foot and looked me right in the eye. "Well, of course you'll stay," Mom said emphatically. I just looked at her, trying to take in what she had just said. I didn't answer, and she walked on into the kitchen. Bobby stood there and watched the scene but did not offer any advice.

I walked to the living room, sat down on the overstuffed rose-covered sofa, and tried to think. Yes, Mom had spoken, and I was going back, but how in the world could I do it? Failure was unacceptable to Mom, yet how could I possibly succeed? I put my head on my hands and just sat there.

My small high school in Chicago had not provided the background I needed to do the kind of work my fellow classmates, who had mostly attended eastern prep schools, could do easily. Miss Clark, a renowned Vassar history teacher, told me at my twenty-fifth college reunion, "You and one other student had the least self-confidence of anyone who had ever gone through Vassar. I always worried about how you had gotten through life."

I felt tremendous pressure to succeed; I could not disappoint Mom. She had sacrificed so much to get me to Vassar, given up her own life for the sake of her four children, and saved her hard-earned money to buy me all those stylish clothes. It meant so much to her. Her best friend, Jo, had gone to Vassar, as had some of Mom's ancestors. I had always sensed a deep sadness within her, but now I felt her life had some joy, as she was vicariously living through me at Vassar and Bobby at Harvard. I couldn't stand the thought of how unhappy she would be if I left Vassar. I didn't want her angry at me. I liked the thought that I was her angel daughter. Somehow, I had to do it.

My sophomore year, the library became my home. Even the West Point cadet seemed to cooperate by basically going silent, for reasons I never knew. I did nothing but work. "Betsy," I would say to myself, "you have to write this twenty-page paper by tomorrow. Just sit here and keep going." I would sometimes hit my thigh just to make myself continue. Mom called to read me William Ernest Henley's poem "Invictus": "My head is bloody but unbowed ... I am the master of my fate: / I am the captain of my soul."

I spent so much time studying that the material began to seep into me. In nineteenth-century American literature with Mr. Christy, an inspired teacher, we read Emerson, Thoreau, and Whitman. I heard the call to know myself, to be the master of my own life, to be the spider endlessly weaving, as Whitman wrote. These ideas were new to me, and I wondered what was expected of me in life. I listened to great pieces of music many times over and became mesmerized by their passion and beauty. I began to love art. History became fascinating. I loved going back to the primary sources and seeing how people had lived and what they had thought in the past.

Midway through the fall semester of my sophomore year, when I walked into Mr. Christy's class one day, he told me he had received a letter from the dean asking if I was making the grade. He said he was surprised to have received the letter and had replied to the dean, "I am surprised there was any question. She's a solid student."

I looked at Mr. Christy in astonishment, thrilled and grateful. I had made it! I'd never known I could work that hard or become that passionate about what I was learning. I learned that if I put my all into something, it could be enough. From that time through my senior year, when I had to write an original fifty-page thesis, I was okay. I never received another letter from the dean. Mom later had the chance to talk with Miss Blanding, who told her, "It isn't that a Vassar girl does not get into trouble. It's that a Vassar girl works her way out of it." I had earned the appellation *Vassar girl*.

Leise from Denmark and I shared a double room sophomore year. I loved all the modern Danish decorations and our bright red bedspreads. She and I were both taking piano lessons and would walk over together through the Shakespeare Gardens to the castle-like music building. I was learning the Bach inventions—not fast enough to impress my teacher, but I loved the music.

Leise invited me to go with her on some of the fabulous things she did. We spent a winter-break weekend skiing with Tom Watson of IBM, a friend of her father's, at his ski house in Stowe, Vermont. Mrs. Watson saw I could use some warmer ski clothes and gave me a navy-blue cable-knit sweater with a maroon band and a hat to match. I loved it. Sunday morning, I was the only one who wanted to go skiing early other than Mr. Watson. I rode up the lift with him to an intermediate slope, and he showed me how to slalom. I followed along the best I could, and he exclaimed, "You've improved more quickly than any other skier I have taught!" Mr. Watson asked me what my father did, and I replied that he was a lawyer and had run for mayor of Chicago.

"That's impressive," he replied, seeming to me not too impressed. But Mr. Watson and all Leise's friends and family were nice to me even several years later when, on a tour of Europe, her father took us on his 120-foot sailboat around the Danish coast.

I invited Leise to Chicago for Thanksgiving. She met my brother Bobby, and they started to date, but she ended up breaking his heart. Her father wouldn't let her return to Vassar her junior year, for fear she would marry an American. She went to the Sorbonne in Paris and fell out of love, she explained to me years later.

Pam came back to school but went to Cushing, a dorm near Noyes, and back a grade. Our paths didn't cross anymore, which seemed strange since we had been good friends. Our lives had gone in different directions. I loved hearing about outings that Judy and Dana took, such as getting all dressed up in pretty dresses, pumps, and hats and going to New York's Plaza Hotel for tea. We all went to the Metropolitan Museum of Art to see the Greek and Roman galleries and, later, the medieval and Renaissance galleries. Even though Vassar was hard, it was still thrilling to me, but a few of my classmates were in different places in life, feeling Poughkeepsie was too isolated, and they transferred to other colleges or became serious about getting married.

Now that I saw I would be able to get through, I wondered what I would do with my education. I didn't know, despite Mr. Christy's teaching me to be the master of my own fate. After all, Mom had always told me a woman was happiest in being a helpmate to her husband, even though she seldom seemed happy. I had such a habit of complying that I wasn't practiced in self-direction.

Mr. Christy announced one day, "I am not teaching you women to end up as housewives." He expected us all to go out and make contributions to society, but what was I meant to do? How could I live up to the expectations of a Vassar education? I had no idea, but I had to choose a major. What about English? Could I read that much? I had never been a great reader. Should I take history? That too involved a lot of reading. I was in great indecision. What should I do?

One morning during spring vacation in Chicago, I lay down on my brother Johnny's bed, tossing and turning, trying to decide on my own. His room was painted a medium gray with matching gray, red, and black plaid bedspreads and curtains. I kept tossing and turning, trying to see what would come to me. I looked out his windows at the scary house next door and then closed my eyes.

Finally, an idea came: I could major in American history and minor in American literature, and I could teach one day about my own country. *It will be important to teach the young about our country*, I thought. That sounded like a worthy ideal, but it was a choice made with my head rather than my heart.

Junior year seemed easier to me. The terrible pressure had been lifted. I joined the water ballet team and was asked to be head foreign student adviser by the very dean who had written the letter suggesting I leave Vassar. "I think you will be very good working with the foreign students," she wrote. Perhaps she had seen my struggle and success and thought I would be able to empathize with the foreign students from all over the world as they struggled to adjust. I couldn't have been more surprised, but she was right. I loved helping the foreign students and getting to know students from all over the world.

I started a program in which each of the foreign students gave a talk about her country. They were a diverse group from India, Turkey, Iran, Nigeria, Germany, and elsewhere, and the campus newspaper commended me for my work. It was sad for me when a student from India couldn't adjust to Vassar and left. She wore her sari around in the snow, and I can only imagine it was all too difficult.

I found original research in history fascinating and made a trip to Tenants Harbor to study my ancestors' shipbuilding records, which had been left in the sail loft, on a dusty shelf in what we called "the windowless bottle room" on the first floor. There were rows of green-painted boxes stuffed with receipts from the ships the Longs had built and ledgers from the chandlery and from their ships' agents' business. I stayed with my childhood friends across the field, the Bakers, because the sail loft had little heat. Mrs. Baker was the one who had taught me to crochet as a young girl. During the day, I walked back to the sail loft and was able to light the old cream-and-green kerosene stove in the winter kitchen to stay warm. The stove by which I huddled was the same stove my grandmother Clara had used.

I was trying to uncover the history of that old building from those records more than a hundred years old. I tracked the growing success of the business and then its sudden demise. I wrote the research paper to understand what had happened to my great-great-grandfather Deacon Robert Long, who had built the sail loft, and his son, Whitney, who had overseen the bankruptcy of the entire enterprise. My history professor, Carl Degler, known as D-Plus Degler, told me I had done a good job of original historical research and gave me a B+.

Now that I had succeeded at the academic side of the college, a new challenge presented itself. The ideal for many of my fellow classmates at Vassar in the class of 1962 seemed to be a ring on one's finger by graduation. When a classmate was given a ring, she ran down the dormitory corridor, telling everyone and receiving hugs and congratulations. Several classmates left Vassar early to get married. Such a decision was beyond my understanding.

One time, my brother Bobby, a year ahead of me at Harvard, brought William, an old heartthrob from Chicago, to Vassar for a weekend at William's request. He was the same one I had dreamed of dancing with at the Fortnightly dance when my mother instead made me go to bed. I was excited and enjoyed the dances and parties, but the weekend passed quickly, and I did not feel I had gotten to know him any better. A dorm mate, Marilyn, exclaimed, "He's cute! Have you known him long?" He never came back, and I did not hear from him again.

One afternoon, a classmate introduced me to a man I will call Dave, who worked at IBM. He was one of a number of IBMers I met over my years at Vassar. They were ever-present on the Vassar campus since they worked in Poughkeepsie and were often looking for wives, though they were generally not considered as desirable as men at colleges such as Yale or Harvard. Dave certainly lacked the social cachet of my mother's and my fantasy.

I started going around with Dave, even though he scared me because he was older, had already earned his PhD from MIT, and was serious. He had recently broken up with another Vassar girl, and I wondered why. From a distance, the other girl seemed attractive, and I wondered what she'd found out about Dave or what Dave didn't like about her. Would he quickly dump me also? Would he want something from me that I was not ready to give? I was still out for innocent fun. He was brilliant and cute and a good tennis player. He turned out to be a perfect gentleman. I liked him, so I continued seeing him. We played tennis, went on walks, and went out to dinner. He had been accepted at Harvard and would start his MBA in the fall.

There was no fooling around for most of us in those days, including me. There were always chaperones around, and the moral guidelines were clear. I always remembered what President Blanding had said: "You girls can do what you want but not at Vassar." I was also good at protecting myself, and Vassar protected us.

The next Thanksgiving, Dave asked me to go with him to the Harvard versus Yale football game. I told him I'd planned to spend Thanksgiving with my aunt Inez and uncle Albert, my mother's oldest brother, who had left academia and become the state historian of New York. Albert was a dapper gentleman, and he and his wife had a large, gracious country home outside Albany. Dave offered to drive to Albany to pick me up and then drive over to the football game.

Dave was quite a hit. Uncle Albert loved talking with him, and my aunt and uncle were impressed I had such a fine beau. I thought it was fun too. Uncle Albert wrote to Mom to tell her not to interfere with the relationship between Dave and me: "She will never again find anyone so fine and eligible as Dave, with a PhD from MIT and an MBA from Harvard." Mom wrote to tell me what Uncle Albert had written, but she was not too impressed. She was still hoping I would find a socially prominent husband.

In the spring, Dave asked me to drive up to western New York to see his parents. They lived in a tiny house, and it was obvious Dave was the first in his family to attend college. I had the impression I was not the first girlfriend he had dragged up there to meet them. They were polite but not overly friendly, and the weekend was okay but not a big success. I felt awkward with his parents, and they did with me. The weekend made me more conscious that Mom would not be pleased if I decided ever to marry this man, nor did I think I would be happy with his parents as my in-laws. In any case, marriage was not in my thinking then, and it did not occur to me that it might have been on his mind.

Dave and I had a sort of fantasy relationship. He liked the idea I was a Vassar girl, but since I didn't know myself, he couldn't know me, and I didn't have the skill to understand him either. There was a part of me that liked the attention, the activities, and going places, but I was not actively planning my life and pursuing goals, just reacting to what was offered to me. That I was leading him on did not occur to me, all actions and attitudes typical of a pleaser.

My friend Jody said to me many years later, "You had a pretty face and a bright mind but no idea who you were." If I wasn't busy, I still felt empty inside.

That summer, I took courses at Harvard, and Dave was in Cambridge, getting his MBA. He said, "Betsy, let's spend some time together." It meant seeing each another oftener but not anything else. We went on walks along the Charles River and took picnics out in the country. I was happy in his company.

Toward the end of the summer, he put his arms around me tenderly and said in a loving way that he thought we should spend our lives together. I did not know what to do. I was not ready to commit my life to him or even to get married. I turned him down and with the exception of one brief encounter, I never saw him again.

Meanwhile, Mom had been writing to me all summer, having no idea that I had just refused the man her brother thought the perfect husband for me saying: "work on your senior thesis because I know what a procrastinator you are'". Her criticism and control were out of touch with my reality.

I went back to Vassar for my senior year and managed to write the required fifty-page senior thesis. It had to be original research. I wrote it on Booker T. Washington, trying to understand African Americans in the United States and the ones I had lived among but never known. D-Plus Degler gave me a C+, and although my parents were surprised at the low grade, I was relieved. It meant I would graduate.

I met a new beau my senior year at Vassar, Nils. He was another person from IBM, a Norwegian, sent over to America for a year. I had a lot of fun with him and my friends, skiing, dancing, and taking walks, but once again, I was not thinking about marriage. He was around during graduation weekend, and my parents thought it was serious and that Nils wanted to get more involved, but I refused. He couldn't understand my refusal, but I didn't really trust that he would be there for me.

My mind had been opened at Vassar, and my life had tremendously expanded, but I chose to return to my parents' house and pursue a master's degree at the University of Chicago, to keep learning and studying. A therapist helping me analyze the decision later said, "It is hard to get up from the table when you have not been fed." I went back to try to get the love and approval I dearly needed from my parents.

I thought I would have a new kind of relationship with my parents after four such rich years, but instead, it was awful. There I was, staying in Margie's old room since she was away at Vassar, living the same old pattern of wanting to spend time with my parents and being told to go away. My parents seemed no more tuned into me than they had been before I went away. Maybe they had hoped I would be off on my own instead of back under their roof. It upset me terribly. I cried myself to sleep every night.

Dad's political career paid off the year I graduated from Vassar. The Democrats and Mayor Daley made him chief judge of the divorce courts of Cook County, saying what a great family man he was, with his long marriage and four children. He sat in a large, impressive courtroom and had seventeen judges under him. He went around Chicago, giving speeches on marriage and family life and winning accolades for his work.

Dad gave himself a glittering birthday party each September at the Union League Club in downtown Chicago. He enjoyed being the MC, reciting his favorite stories, introducing everyone present, and having his guests give toasts. "Dad, I have written a poem for your birthday," I told him as we all left for downtown. "Please call on me."

I wore a black dress with pearls, hair coiffed, and a gold bracelet, all my best for the glamorous birthday party. Behind me, the mirrors reflected the important people gathered at the downtown men's club. The party and the glitz were exciting. A sleek black satin evening purse hanging on a gold chain from my shoulder contained two folded pieces of white typewriter paper. I had carefully, thoughtfully, and excitedly composed a poem for the occasion and was glowing with excitement about presenting it before the august gathering of Dad's cherished friends.

The shrimp appetizers were served in tall, wide-mouthed crystal champagne glasses, each with a moon-shaped sliver of lemon tucked in at the rim. Dad, still presiding judge of the divorce courts of Cook County, used the time between the shrimp and the filet mignon to take the microphone. His blue eyes sparkled with Irish charm; his hair was thinning but still dark brown and groomed impeccably. He remained a large man and a large presence, the former fullback on the Iowa football team, tough and powerful. His comfort with the deep, rich dark brown suit had originated with the deep, rich dark earth from which he'd sprung out in the Iowa cornfields but had been tailored by the finest in Chicago.

The sizzling filet mignon was served fresh from a red-hot grill with round, plump Portobello mushrooms; sleek, garden-fresh asparagus; roasted tomatoes; and au gratin potatoes, accompanied by good French wines. With his chest expanding, he introduced the seventy-some guests, including Judge Crown, owner of big buildings and big farms; Chief Judge John Boyle; Judge Feldman; the counselors from the conciliation service Dad had started in the courts; Frank Trueblood, an old friend from Iowa, and his girlfriend, Elise, both important lawyers in Chicago; and Jo, Mom's beloved friend, who had flown up from Florida. A high buzz reverberated.

I sat over at a side table, still clutching my sleek black satin purse. Dad introduced me along with all the others but never called on me to speak.

A big chocolate birthday cake was rolled in and lit. All sang. Dad, exhilarated by the attention and the fun of the big party, listened. More champagne and more toasts followed. Eventually, everyone got up to leave. "We had a marvelous time. What a wonderful man you have for a father," the guests told me as they walked out.

"Betsy, I should have called on you to read your poem, but the evening was getting a little long," said Dad when he saw me back at home, taking off my coat.

I smiled with my adoring, questioning, stunned eyes on him and said nothing.

* * *

Every weekend, as he always had done, Dad went to his farm outside Chicago, raised prize Holsteins, and attended cattle shows. Dad started the International Dairy Show in Chicago. He was president of a group called the Chicago Farmers, and he wrote this letter to the membership at Christmas:

> When I was a small boy in Iowa, my grandmother told me that every Christmas Eve at exactly midnight all the animals in the barnyard, and in the fields, and in the woods, faced East. They were suddenly given the power of speech, and they knelt to worship the Christ Child, and to pray to Him. I wondered how my grandfather's old Horny got her halter off and back on again, but I was assured that she did ...
>
> I was at our farm, at midnight, a short time ago. It was cold and the sky was clear. The stars shone with a blue-white brilliance that they have only on frosty nights during the Christmas season. In the east was a low-hung, very bright but reddish star that made me think of the shepherds on the hills, the Star of Bethlehem. I went into the barn. It was warm in there, the calves and the heifers and the cows were all lying down chewing their cuds. The bull banged his door and bellowed low so that I wouldn't forget who was boss around there. I opened the door and scratched his head. He gingerly edged sideways so that I could scratch an itchy spot on his back. The children's pony, in the other end of the barn, whinnied for a little attention. I was glad that I could be on a farm at the Christmas season. I was glad that we had a farm where our children could learn to love animals and to work with

them, and to see things grow, and to learn to toil, and to sweat and to use their hands. We had wanted them to learn the good sense that farm folks have, the tolerance and the patient faith that they must live by.

In this Christmas spirit, your officers, your directors and your office secretary send you their sincere and hearty greetings. We wish you all a peaceful and joyous Christmas.

Dad continued to put a lot of his earnings into his farm, and Mom continued to defend him, saying, "This will be good for you four children eventually because you each should inherit some money from the farm." Mom continued to live on very little, wearing secondhand clothes and driving her children's cast-off cars. She lived on the reflected glory of her children whom she continued to devote herself to helping, the satisfaction she felt from teaching, and the pleasure of attending lectures at the North Side women's club. I could feel the strains between Mom and Dad.

I persevered and received an MA in history and international relations, a high school teaching certification and qualified for a PhD, all from the University of Chicago. I didn't have the languages required to be accepted as a PhD candidate, so I taught history at the University of Chicago Laboratory School, but I was once again eager to get away from Chicago.

In the meantime, Bobby received both his MD and his PhD from the University of Chicago, receiving the two impressive degrees on the same day. He had lived at home during his medical school years, and Mom had spent many an evening, particularly in his first year of medical school, sitting with Bobby and helping him master the enormous quantity of material.

Bobby was seeing a Mount Holyoke girl, Becky, a girl from the North Side, whom I had met at one of the Fortnightly dances. I had introduced the two of them, and I had had a wonderful summer trip with Becky, seeing Europe. We were great traveling companions and friends.

Becky and Bobby were married the day after Bobby graduated with his two advanced degrees. My brother John, also back in Chicago, worked in real estate management, earned his MBA from the University of Chicago, and married a girl he had met at the Christian fellowship. Both my brothers moved ahead in their lives. I felt left behind.

Our family was an unusual family where fine educations were ultimately not enough to ensure the success of the generations of children. Nurturing of the inner self needed to go hand in hand with education and that was lacking, with dire consequences.

CHAPTER 12

Charlie: Wolfville, Nova Scotia 1928

Charlie and Albert came to Wolfville for their father's funeral and were both able to take off some time to help their mother cope with the death of their father and all that entailed. Albert was busy in his life at the time, with a full-time teaching position at St. Lawrence University, a wife and children, and ongoing work toward his PhD at Clark University.

Although Charlie had a good job as a banker in New York City, he felt lonely in New York. He decided to spend more time with his mother and sister to grieve with them over the great loss of his father. He had a girl he was sweet on in Wolfville and longed to see her. Clara and Betty were thrilled to have Charlie around for a few weeks, particularly Betty, who had always adored her older brother.

Clara with her Son Charlie, Nova Scotia, circa 1926.

One day Charlie came over to talk and sat down in the kitchen with his sister and mother. To his surprise, Betty bitterly complained about her father. "I am sorry he's gone, but Dad was so rigid and judgmental. He was so wrong about a lot of things," Betty said bitterly.

"Oh, now, Betty, don't talk that way. You don't mean it," Clara said.

"I do mean it," Betty said firmly.

"Betty, you must stop talking that way," Clara said.

"No, Mother, let Betty talk," Charlie said. "It's important that she has a chance to speak her mind." Turning to his younger sister, he asked kindly, "Why are you so angry? What happened? Please tell us."

Betty turned to her brother with enormous surprise and appreciation. No one had ever asked her what she thought. She took a deep breath, looked at her mother and then back to Charlie, and slowly said, "Father accused me of immoral behavior, but really, I just took a walk. He blamed me for being improper with a boy, when we just talked and walked. Also, I did the best I could on the state music exam in India, but Father was angry I had not done better. He expected more of me than I could do." She put her head in her hands and muttered, "So critical and judgmental."

Clara was horrified. "No, darling, he didn't think you were impure with that boy. But the school had a rule that boys and girls were not to walk together after a certain time at night, and you broke the rule. He just thought you should follow the rules. As to the exam, he thought you were really too young to be taking it and was actually impressed you performed as well as you did."

Betty burst into tears, suddenly realizing at age nineteen that she had misinterpreted her father, and now it was too late to ever straighten out anything with him. At the same time, she felt grateful to Charlie for helping her to speak. Although not all her wounds were healed, her burden felt lighter. Charlie smiled sweetly and then said he had to be off. They wondered if he was off to see his girl and wished they knew more about what was going on.

Two and a half weeks later, on an April evening at six o'clock, Betty was preparing to give her senior recital at Acadia. She looked at the clock and had a terrifying premonition: "Something has happened to Charlie." She just knew via a sixth sense that something horrible had happened to him. She shivered all over. Then, by dint of long training and sheer determination, she forced herself to relax enough to get through her recital.

Betty's premonition was correct: Charlie had disappeared. Hikers reported finding him on Cape Split, about a forty-minute drive from Wolfville. Albert was called to be part of the rescue party, and they drove to the cape and then walked the two-and-a-half-hour hike through the woods to Cape Split, overlooking the Bay of Fundy. They found him there on the spectacular, high, dangerous plateau jutting out into the bay. He was nearly dead from a gunshot wound. A .22 rifle lay nearby. They brought him down. He was delirious.

Albert knew about Betty's recital and withheld the terrible news until she had finished. He sent a telegram to his mother: "Charlie gravely ill."

Charlie did not last the night. Albert, horrified and grief-stricken, sent a second telegram to Clara: "Charlie is deceased."

Betty's world collapsed. Her best friend in the world, the person who had always been kindest to her, her dear brother, had taken his own life just as she was about to give her senior recital at Acadia. How could he?

Why? She was shocked and horrified at the violence—the sin of it and the sadness. Her worst possible nightmare could not equal it. Betty was devastated beyond her ability to cope.

Albert took over doing what was necessary. He had to talk with the magistrates of the town, who needed to investigate and make a report. He had to talk with the morgue and arrange for Charlie's remains to be taken to the funeral home. He had to secure a plot in the cemetery. Because it was a suicide, they were not allowed to erect a headstone. He had a terribly difficult time in finding a minister willing to give a graveside service for the suicide. Charlie was laid in the unmarked grave near where his father had been buried a little more than two weeks earlier.

Everything in the family's world was desolation. Letters came pouring into Clara and Betty from Hebron's relatives in Canada, who had helped to take care of Charlie all the years he was left in Canada alone, and from the missionaries still in India:

> To my very dear Mrs. Corey,
>
> Charlie was so good, so true, so thoughtful, so needed it seems to us. I can only pray God to give you strength to bear up under this heavy burden. It is hard to reach up to the hand which seems so heavily laid upon you dear, but it is the only thing we can do, my heart aches for you and Betty.
>
> Well dear, I am not able to write more now, tears fill my eyes as I think of you both.
>
> My dear little Betty:
>
> I don't know what to say. I only know I love you all and I grieve with you in this trial. You dear girl, you sure have had your share of burdens, but I see you with that wonderful disposition rising above it all for your dear mother's sake. Be strong. God cares and will not fail you now dear.
>
> My heart is so full of sorrow that I can hardly think of anything but you, know how deeply I feel for you, Albert and Betty and wish I might help in some way.

How little we know when one's work is finished.

Not only is his going a loss to his family but to the world at large for I was always sure he would make a name for himself.

Am so glad the recital was such a success but was very sure it would be.

The dear boy, how my heart aches for you all and especially for Betty whom he loved so much and did so much for. He used to speak of her in his letters to me and I still have them. I could never destroy any one of them. They were so intensely interesting and so different from anyone else, so frank and innocent.

The following came from a missionary worker in India:

I think just the day before this sad news reached me, I took a book down to read and in that found a picture of Charlie taken while he was in Kimedi I think. He had on a little plaid dress. It was so like Charlie as I knew him best … Then came the shocking news simply telling that Albert had sent you one telegram saying he was ill and another saying he had gone.

No particulars had here … I wonder if you remember that night I taught Charlie to take his first steps. He was a tiny babe when I went to Doty that Aug. and Sept. in 1904. Then he and Albert used to come in and breakfast with me at times. My table was so tiny I could only have one at a time and the other one would likely perhaps finish his meal and perhaps bring us in some special dish or else stand and look in.

It seems hard to realize they are men and that one has finished his earthly course. You remember your writing desk that I took over. I am sitting writing at it now. Behind it was the corner where sometimes Charlie was punished. Do you remember the day when he knew he had been naughty and when you looked at him he ran and bumped his head on this table, in his haste to get to his corner even though you had not told him to go.

It seems as if the Lord must be preparing you for
some special service as he has led you through some dark
shadows. I remember once you said you could thank God
in all things, but not for all things. May he give you peace
and comfort according to your great need at this time and
make the dark shadows light with his presence.

How strange it is that you, Clara, with the delicate
health should be the one to outlive these two strong men,
Charlie and Mr. Corey.

* * *

Clara couldn't stay in Wolfville, because the parish house was needed
for the incoming minister, nor did she want to. The shame of having one's
son commit suicide made her a bit of a pariah in Wolfville.

Although she had spent most of her life in India, with furloughs in
Wolfville, Tenants Harbor was home, and it beckoned. She wanted to be
near her sisters and cousins, her beloved Baptist church with the white
steeple shining high in the sky, the home where she had grown up, and
the blue and gold of the harbor. She had never liked being on the water
but never tired of looking at it, with its ever-changing light and moods.

Clara returned thirty-four years after she'd left on the steamer as
everyone waved handkerchiefs to wish her well in her new life with Hebron
in India. She returned afflicted and in mourning, all in black, a widow and
deeply bereaved mother after the loss of three sons: one injured and left
in India, one dead and buried in India, and the third dead by suicide and
buried in Wolfville. Out of her five children, only Albert and her daughter,
Betty, were left.

O Beulah Land, sweet Beulah Land,
As on thy highest mount I stand,
I look away across the sea,
Where mansions are prepared for me,
And view the shining glory shore,
My heaven, my home forevermore.

Clara had nearly another twenty years to live, but the spirit had gone
out of her. Albert went back to his family, his teaching, and his studies

a changed man. The shock, tragedy, and catastrophe of Charlie's suicide moved him to leave the Baptists for the Unitarian church. He no longer was an evangelical. He no longer thought one should try to change another's religion.

Betty, age nineteen, heartbroken and crushed, was left to take care of her mother and pick up the pieces of her own life. She packed her mother's few clothes and household belongings in big domed trunks and shipped them to Tenants Harbor. She packed her own trunks, including the trunk of things she would need at Northwestern University, where she was enrolled in the School of Speech starting in the fall. The rest was sent for storage in the attic of the old sail loft in Tenants Harbor.

When they left Wolfville, their fellow missionary families on furlough, the missionary board, and the townspeople did not know quite what to say. What had happened to Charlie was a disgrace, shocking and shameful. People avoided talking with Clara and even Betty. They were relieved the Coreys were leaving. In years to come, they would think up their own stories or, better yet, forget about it. Betty helped her mother leave quietly and quickly.

The two took a train down to Yarmouth, Nova Scotia, and caught the ferry to Bar Harbor. From there, they traveled by motor coach down the coast to Thomaston and then by taxi to Tenants Harbor.

Though Clara and Betty considered Tenants Harbor their true home, they were barely known there or not known at all. The villagers of Tenants Harbor considered the pair a bit odd: Clara, all in black, and her beautiful daughter, Betty, planning to begin graduate studies in Illinois and leave her mother alone in Tenants Harbor with a companion.

Betty and Clara's stay with Clara's sisters on High Street in the old family home, the small white clapboard Cape with green shutters and attached woodshed and barn, did not go well. Clara had been away too long. Betty arranged for an apartment to be made for her mother above the old store at the sail loft, the building all four sisters owned in common on the shore, built by their great-grandfather in the heyday of the wooden ships.

Clara's sister Alice and her husband, Charles, still ran a grocery store in the old ship's chandlery on the first floor and lived in a small apartment on the south side of the second floor, but there was space on the north side of the second floor, enough for Clara to have an apartment. That space formerly had been the village school, and a large central room, the former classroom, became the front parlor and Clara's bedroom in one. Space left over was divided into a winter kitchen and a summer kitchen. A small room that had been the cloakroom became the yellow room, Betty's bedroom when she visited. Later, another bedroom was added, as well as a bathroom for indoor plumbing.

Betty found a town carpenter to build walls. A green-and-cream kerosene stove was ordered from Sears for cooking and keeping warm in the winter. Betty found a mismatched table and chairs in an old storeroom and painted them cream and green to make a matching set. She had learned the skill of fixing up things from her theater studies at Acadia.

In a corner of the summer kitchen on the second floor, she found an old cabinet. She cut out a hole and placed a kitchen sink in it. A barrel at the end of the summer kitchen was used to store kerosene for the stove. She found an extra oak icebox and put it in the summer kitchen too. Cream-and-green-checked linoleum was ordered for both kitchens. There was an outhouse outside, and there was a cistern in the basement, with a hand pump on the old wooden sink, where they could get water. Betty felt gratified in being able to put together an apartment for her mother out of the old things she found around the sail loft.

The front parlor, which also served as Clara's bedroom, had a piece of furniture that served as a couch in the day and a bed at night. They found a Victorian settee for the parlor, a wing chair, a wooden secretary with a glass front, and patterned carpeting. On the walls, they hung favorite prints of flowers, English architecture, and beloved verses of scripture. They hung a small, round mirror over the settee, and against the far wall, they put one of the store display cases with shelves. Clara filled the case with her Bibles and Betty's favorite English poetry books. In the closet, Clara hung her black velvet coat handmade in India—a beautifully tailored coat with a fitted waist and careful pleating.

Clara and Betty unpacked the trunks, and Betty set out vases of fresh flowers she picked from the field out back: black-eyed Susan, Queen Anne's lace, and goldenrod. The apartment became cozy and comfortable. A woman named Rhodie Hart was hired to live with Clara as a companion. Rhodie was a local lady around Clara's age who had never married and had lived a simple life as a housekeeper. She was glad to have a home and happily slept on a small daybed underneath the window in the winter kitchen. She was short, with a big pockmarked nose. Kind and gentle, Rhodie was an easy companion and helper for Clara. Goods were regularly delivered to their sail loft apartment home in Tenants Harbor—ice for the icebox, milk, eggs, bread, and whatever else Clara needed.

After Betty arranged everything for her mother by the middle of summer, she left for Chicago to find an apartment and get settled for the fall semester at Northwestern.

Clara settled uneasily into the routine of Tenants Harbor: attending services at the Baptist church on Sundays and Wednesdays, joining the sewing circle at the church to make handmade goods for the yearly church bazaar, and visiting with her sisters and cousins. It was not easy without Hebron, and she remained devastated about Charlie, but she managed to get through the days with Rhodie's care.

About four months after Charlie died, a young woman made the trip across Nova Scotia, the ferry ride to Bar Harbor, and the drive down the coast to Tenants Harbor. She rang the bell and slowly walked up the steps to where Clara was sitting in her rocking chair overlooking the harbor.

"Good afternoon, Mrs. Corey. I have come all this way to ask for help. I am pregnant with Charlie's child. I need money. I have no place to turn but to you. I cannot turn to my parents."

Clara, shocked and furious, cried, "How can you say this? Charlie would never have done such a thing. I don't believe you."

The young woman pleaded. "But, Mrs. Corey, I need help. Please help me. Please accept me and my baby-to-be. I was so young; I am still too young. I did not know I was pregnant. I am desperate," she sobbed.

"I will not add shame to the terrible tragedies that have befallen my family. Charlie being gone is the greatest sorrow I can bear. The pain and grief I will carry to my grave. Don't ask me to do more," replied Clara. "Besides, I do not believe you."

"Mrs. Corey, please, please help."

"What you are accusing Charlie of doing is a sin, a moral outrage, a shameful act, a disgrace. How could you have done such a thing with your upbringing? Nor will I ever believe this about my Charlie," said Clara.

"Mrs. Corey, I have no place to turn," the young woman whimpered.

Clara hesitated. "All right. I will give you the little money I have. I do not do it gladly, but I think it is the right thing for me to do." Even though her heart was broken, duty once more called. Clara continued. "You have disgraced us. I won't allow your shame to ruin our family name."

"No! The mistake I made was in not realizing how much I loved Charlie and not accepting his proposal!" the young woman exclaimed.

"You have brought disgrace to my family's name. I want never to see or hear from you again," said Clara, and her heart banged shut.

"It is all terrible—a nightmare!" wailed the young woman.

"I have nothing more to say," said Clara, now in control of herself.

"I must have the money to have the child," the woman said.

"I will give you the money I have on one condition: you will go and never tell anyone. Don't ever say again that Charlie was the father of your child, and never contact any of us ever again. I am going to have a contract drawn up that you will sign to accept my terms," said Clara stonily. "Furthermore, I am going to have all the dates changed so it will be impossible for anyone to ever say this was Charlie's child. I still do not believe Charlie would ever do such a thing, and I am going to make sure no one in the future can ever trace your child to Charlie."

Clara had the contract drawn up, and the young woman signed, vowing eternal silence in exchange for Clara's meager savings. The woman made her way to Washington, DC, where she had her baby. She subsequently returned to Wolfville and married. The story in town was that the baby's father had died before the baby girl was born, and that man was not Charlie Corey.

Nearly sixty years later, I made a trip to Wolfville and met with Albert's oldest daughter, Alex, who had a home in Wolfville. She was obsessed with the story of her uncle Charlie because there was a lovely family in Wolfville in which the grandmother and her daughter looked just like Charlie Corey. She was sure they were her first cousins and wished to know them but never had had the nerve to go look them up.

I decided to contact the family and met a young woman who said her grandfather had died before her mother was born, about the same time Charlie had died. She said that her grandfather was not Charlie and that three young men had committed suicide around that same time in Wolfville. It is unclear what could have caused three young men to commit suicide around 1928.

She added, "Even if Charlie were my grandfather, I don't want to know it—or you. We've all lived our lives with another story and don't want to change it now." That was the end of my contact with them. Clara had made the young woman agree that she would never associate her baby with Charlie Corey. She had kept her promise and made up a whole new life.

On that same trip to Wolfville, Alex told me something else that opened up a new avenue for understanding Betty, my mother, and the effect of Charlie's suicide on the rest of her life and on me. Alex said the young woman who was the mother of Charlie's baby was Mary Miller, Betty's best friend from the Hebron School of India and Acadia University. I do not know for sure if Alex was right, but that was the same family of the young woman I met, whose family members looked like Coreys but denied the connection.

Betty too spent the rest of her life covering up the story of Charlie. She never returned to Wolfville, where many friends and relatives lived, except to attend Albert's funeral decades later. She did not even have any contact with any of her fathers' many relatives or any of her college friends. She never talked about the suicide until near the end of her life and never even whispered that the woman was her best friend. The one time she mentioned that a girl had come to see Clara, she called her "some woman." She once mentioned she had changed the date of Charlie's death to 1929 when, years later, she had a tombstone erected for Charlie in the cemetery. She said, "Some things are better left alone." In fact, exactly what happened remained such a mystery that no one could quite come to terms with it; therefore, it has drawn people back to try to find out the truth. For Betty, it was just too painful to ever revisit again. Betty ran away to Chicago to hide from it all, but of course, one cannot bury the past forever. It pops out in unexpected ways.

Thus, Betty's and Clara's coping mechanisms were similar. Clara ran away from Tenants Harbor to India to get away from her family's bankruptcy and her father's drinking. All the time she was in India, she kept longing for her mother and remained sickly in bed instead of insisting on being with her own children. She sent her own children away, and they were left lonely like their mother. Likewise, Betty ran away from the terrible tragedy, shame, and loss of Charlie's suicide and possible his baby out of wedlock. She left everything and everyone she had ever known in Wolfville and went to Northwestern University, where she met Jo and my father and decided to start a whole new life. But when one runs away, the past follows.

In writing this book, I have come to see that Mom didn't want us children to know about Charlie, for she couldn't handle it herself. She believed she was protecting us out of concern that telling us about Charlie might give us ideas to do the same thing, but secrets in a family keep people apart. One cannot have true intimacy when there are secrets.

Mom always used to say, "One never knows what one's child is thinking." Her parents had no idea what she thought; my parents had no idea what I thought; and for many years, I had no idea what my own children thought. It does not have to be that way. My life's quest became how to become connected to the people in my life. I did not understand how I pushed my own children away.

PART 2

Part 2

CHAPTER 13

Marriage to Bob, Chicago, 1968

If you don't love yourself, you'll not feel okay inside. *You will criticize others.*

During my college years, I had had many beaux and took none of them seriously. I just wanted to have fun. However, once I began working, having accepted a teaching job in Dover, Delaware, I had little opportunity to meet people. I was lonely and felt I was getting old. I didn't deeply love teaching and kept wondering what other opportunities might be open to me.

Out of the blue, I got a call from Dave, who had moved to the West Coast. He had come east on business, and he decided to take the afternoon off to drive down to see me. I couldn't wait to see him and would have gone with him anywhere. But he didn't stay long, and as he was leaving, he said, "My life is elsewhere now, and I'm going back to California." He had someone else he was contemplating marrying and just wanted to see his old girlfriend one last time to be sure he wasn't making a mistake. That was the last I ever heard from him, and it was painful.

A Vassar friend introduced me to Bob Jacks, a New York businessman fifteen years older than I. He had been raised in New Orleans and was brilliant, a devout Catholic, and an old bachelor. He had been the first person in his family to go to college and had a master's in engineering from MIT. He had been told Harvard Business School would give him an MBA in just one year after his graduate work at MIT, but he'd thought he needed to go start earning money and accepted a job at Exxon.

Bob Jacks came to see me in Dover and invited me to New York for weekends. I always stayed at the Barbizon Hotel for Women. Everyone kept telling me he was too old for me and too set in his ways. Whenever I was with him on a weekend, we attended a Catholic mass. He kept telling me how important I was becoming to him, and he began soothing a deep void within me. Although older, he had a certain strength, purity, and integrity I admired and trusted. Still, I was not convinced he was right for me.

* * *

"Betsy," he said, and the word went right to my heart. Amid the euphoria of time spent with old Vassar friends, the sparkling lights of the Christmas season of 1967, and the exciting people at a fun reception in New York City, the exhilaration of it all was pricked by Bob's exasperated and wounded voice on the phone. "Why haven't you come downstairs to meet me? You're very late. I've been waiting for you in the lobby of the hotel," he said pleadingly.

"I'm coming down right away," I said, feeling mixed up, torn yet obedient to Bob's voice, not wanting to hurt him and not wanting to leave him but not wanting to go downstairs to meet him.

I knew what was about to happen. He had a big, beautiful, expensive diamond ring in his pocket, and he intended to give it to me that night. I knew that this time, I was not going to say no, even though I knew I did not love him the way he wanted to be loved. He idealized me, thinking he had finally found the girl of his dreams after being a bachelor until age forty-three. Here is how he wrote to a friend: "She has light brown hair, beautiful blue eyes, and a radiant smile." He was five years older than my father had been when he married my mother. I was twenty-seven, Mom's age when she married

I got my coat and pushed the elevator button to go downstairs, thinking, *He doesn't know me. How could he? I've never been honest with him about the way I feel. He's living in a world of dreams, and that scares me. I'm living in a world of insecurity, looking for someone I can trust not to abandon me.* Despite my worries, I decided to go down to him.

"Betsy, I almost left," he said with tremendous hurt in his voice as I stepped out of the elevator in the lobby of the hotel. "I almost put my coat back on. I was thinking about going back out into the cold and ending it all—you kept me waiting too long. But I decided to wait because you are my beloved Elizabeth"—his name of endearment—"whom I have been looking for all my life." This standard speech of his both pleased and scared me. I didn't know what to make of it. I felt like an object he had suddenly found that did not have much to do with me. On the other hand, I wanted a father like person, and maybe he could be one.

Bob put his arm around me, and together we walked two blocks through the crowded, dark New York Streets to an elegant old New York restaurant, La Grenouille. We were seated at a quiet back table, as he requested, and ordered champagne. We enjoyed gourmet dishes under a vase of magnificent fresh flowers. I started enjoying myself, basking in the attention I had always craved.

"Betsy, I want to devote the rest of my life to making you happy," Bob said, smiling warmly, having already forgotten how long he had been kept waiting. I thought that no one could do that, but the sentiment was music to my ears. He said unequivocally he adored me.

Bob took a black velvet box out of his side pocket of his dark brown business suit. When I opened the tiny box, there before my eyes was the prettiest diamond ring I had ever seen. Bob reached over, took my hand in his, and put the ring on my finger. I did not say anything. It made me happy, and at the same time, I wondered if I could or should go through with it.

"Bob, it is absolutely a beautiful ring," I said, looking into his radiant eyes, which made me feel both happy and conflicted because I didn't know what to do. "You are very, very nice."

"Very, very nice," he repeated, "but are you going to marry me?"

"Can you give me some time?" I asked plaintively.

I returned to Chicago after the weekend, as I had decided to accept a teaching position at New Trier High School, a prestigious school in the northern suburbs of Chicago. I stewed over what to do about Bob. Mom told me, "Better to marry Bob than to struggle on alone in life."

My mother's words resonated with my own growing fears about my future. Even though I had secured an excellent job at New Trier, I knew I didn't want to teach high school history for the rest of my life, and the idea of a career was not part of my vision for myself. I didn't know all the other things I could have done, particularly with another graduate degree in either law or business, but it was not how I understood myself at the time.

A fellow teacher noticed how anxious I looked and suggested I consult a counselor.

"You are ambivalent," the counselor said.

"What is love?" I asked.

The counselor replied, "It is wishing the very best for someone else."

I contemplated what the counselor had said. Certainly I wished the best for Bob, but was that enough to marry him? When Bob had met me in Chicago three years earlier, it had been like Dante seeing Beatrice. He instantly had formed a romanticized vision of me, and I enjoyed being admired but did not have the kind of attraction for him that he had for me.

Bob had been providing an apartment for himself and his mother in New York City ever since his father died and left his wife in New Orleans without means nearly fifteen years ago. There was a story that the railroad for which his father had worked as a salesman was supposed to leave his widow a pension, but the agreement was not in writing, and the pension never materialized. Bob took his mother in, took care of her, and even built up a portfolio for her. His mother, in turn, took care of Bob and the house. They even traveled together. Everyone worried that he was too attached to his mother.

I lay down again on my brother Johnny's bed in Chicago by myself and wrestled with the question. I looked at the faded gray, black, and red plaid curtain and the beat-up brown furniture and pondered what was right for me to do. Finally, a conviction came to me that it was right to marry Bob—that even God wanted me to do it. Obeying the inner sense gave me a clear course to move ahead. I had made the decision, but it was not from my heart.

Before we were married, Bob took me before the chapel at St. Patrick's Cathedral in New York City and asked God and the Blessed Virgin to bless our marriage and use it to His purposes. Bob told me that I would be his life and that he would devote himself to my happiness. I told Bob I would be his wife and would be faithful to him always.

* * *

My father had wanted to cancel his wedding to Mom in 1936 the night before the wedding so he wouldn't be tied down. Thirty-two years later, married and with four children, he had managed not to be tied down much or often and had ample time for his politicking, farming, civic organizations, and work.

In 1968, I decided to marry Bob Jacks partly because he was offering me the kind of love and acceptance my own father did not know how to show: delighting in my presence, wanting to be with me, and wanting to make me happy. In other words, he would be like the father I had always wanted.

But as my wedding approached, my real father continued to make it clear he was not happy about my marrying Bob Jacks. My father admired big, strong he-men who didn't let women impose on them. Bob Jacks was the opposite. He promised to always stay close to me to make me happy. Since his father's death some years before, he had lived with his mother to help take care of her. My father thought he was a mother's boy, didn't understand him, and didn't like him.

My mother also continued to be against my marrying Bob Jacks. During the thirty-two years of her marriage, she had worked hard to lift me up socially so I would never have to start over the way she had had to do. Bob Jacks did not fit her idea of the socially elite. He did not make her feel better about her life, but my needs were different.

Confronted with both my parents fretting over my coming marriage, I decided to stay on course—to go off and start a new life. I liked it when Bob was around. He felt like my solid rock. But I also sometimes wondered if I was doing the right thing, knowing I was not deeply in love with him.

However, in marrying Bob Jacks and going to New York City despite my parents' objections, I was following in the footsteps of a long line of women before me. Clarissa had fled her parents by eloping. Clara had left her mother and gone to India. Betty had left Wolfville and gone to Chicago. In their cases, however, these women had intended to create in the new places lives not unlike the ones they fled. In like manner, I planned to flee Chicago to start a new life in New York. Could I break the cycle and create a new and healthier life in New York?

The conflict in Mom between not wanting to interfere and wanting something better for her daughter intensified as the wedding approached, because of her increasing concerns about both Bob and his mother. Nana, as everyone called Bob's mother, insisted on wearing a long gold-brocaded dress, completely inappropriate for an afternoon June wedding. "It is some old thing she already owned that she had cleaned," Mom complained. "Well, we'll just have to go through with it, but if I had known ahead of time and you'd still insisted on marrying Bob Jacks, we would just have had a small, private wedding"—meaning she would not have risked inviting all her fancy friends and being embarrassed.

Despite her reservations, Mom took her teaching money and went downtown to Marshall Field's to order monogrammed linens for me with my new initials: cocktail napkins, guest hand towels, and regular towels. She helped me with the bridal registry and saw that I had a set of Gorham sterling silver, Wedgewood table settings, and Baccarat crystal goblets. My parents' friends sent silver: Revere bowls, silver casserole dishes, trays of all sizes, two silver tea sets, silver candelabra, gravy boats, and water pitchers. There were so many silver gifts that tables were put up in my old third-floor bedroom to display the gifts for friends to come see. It looked like a silver store.

Nana Jacks chose the upstairs room of a Swedish restaurant for the rehearsal dinner. Mom thought it was not up to snuff, but there was nothing to do about it. At the rehearsal dinner, Bob first toasted me, saying I was the love of his life. Then he toasted his mother: "Mother, I have always loved you, and never worry: I am not leaving you. I will always be there for you."

Everyone gasped. I could almost hear the guests think, *Poor Betsy. It's painful to marry a man who is so attached to his mother.*

I winced at the toast but had little understanding of what it would mean to me.

Bob and I were married at the golden-domed Byzantine church on Chicago's North Side on June 15, 1968. My sister sang "Ave Maria," sounding like an angel come down from the heavens. There were five bridesmaids in pale sky blue, and I radiated light. The groom was handsome in his afternoon formal wear. Both a priest and a minister officiated, and I promised to teach my children about both Catholicism and Protestantism. It was a perfect service, except I was not Catholic and thus not allowed to have communion, and we said our vows at the lower level rather than the high altar. These were big sacrifices for Bob. I accepted the rituals of the Catholic church but loved having my Protestant minister who gave a blessing and a heartfelt sermon on marriage.

The reception was held at the Fortnightly Club of Chicago, an elegant women's club on the Near North Side. Mom had arranged an elaborate party and was upset that Bob Jacks seemed more interested in getting his new bride on the plane for the honeymoon than appreciating all the effort she had gone to and all the expense. On that point, Betty was right. Her new son-in-law could barely wait to sweep away his new bride instead of standing around making polite conversation to all of Mom's friends.

Finally, we caught a plane to California and landed in time to board a ship to Hawaii. Bob was forty-four, and I was twenty-seven. I felt secure and happy. We had promised we would remain faithful to each other till death did us part. I believed him.

We stayed first at a romantic beach resort on Oahu, where we had our own thatched-roof cottage. There were long beaches to walk and dancing under the stars at night. I wore a stylish and colorful Hawaiian muumuu. We visited a volcano and flew to the Big Island of Hawaii, where we stayed at another resort and experienced a traditional pig roast and Hawaiian hula dancing. I would have been just as happy to stay in one place, but Bob wanted to sightsee and experience more of Hawaii. I went along.

My marriage, like the marriages in the generations before me, was more about getting away from an untenable situation than thoroughly planning for the new. Thus, without knowing it, each generation re-created what they had known. It was all they knew.

CHAPTER 14

Peter Cooper Village, New York, 1969

When we returned from our Hawaiian honeymoon, we moved into an apartment at Peter Cooper Village in New York City, a post–World War II housing development owned by Metropolitan Life. Originally built for returning veterans, it stretched between Twentieth and Twenty-Third Streets along the East River in Manhattan. It had twenty-one redbrick buildings set among playgrounds and parklands, a private security force, and large rooms, many with views of the river or the gardens. It was considered a well-run, desirable housing enclave. Bob had been living there in a two-bedroom apartment with his mother for the last fifteen years. Before our marriage, Nana had moved across the courtyard to a one-bedroom apartment from which, if she looked up to our seventh-floor apartment, she could see her son's living room window. Bob's mother had never before lived alone, and Bob was concerned about her. At the same time, my parents were concerned about me and afraid I would have to live with Nana. When Dad heard she had moved, he exclaimed, "That's one hundred percent better!"

When we came into the apartment, it was empty except for a nice suite of bedroom furniture that had been Bob's for a long time, with the bed nicely made for us to sleep in the first night. We set out together to furnish the apartment.

I had to become a housewife, which included the matter of getting dinner on the table. I had never cooked before but decided to just open a cookbook Mom had given me and follow a recipe. In fact, I had a lot of recipes from which to choose, because at a bridal shower, everyone had been asked to write down a favorite recipe. I chose a chicken dish and was surprised how easy it was. I was even more surprised when Bob exclaimed at the end of the first dinner, "I have a chef for a wife!"

My parents packed up all the wedding presents in Chicago and drove them across the country to New York City, planning to drop them off on their way to Maine. I was thrilled they were coming and made a dessert for them. I felt sheepish that I didn't have the ingredients on hand to make something better, but I managed to make a blueberry crumble by topping canned blueberry pie filling with a mixture of brown sugar, butter, flour, and walnuts. I baked it and planned to serve it with vanilla ice cream.

I was eager to see them but fearful to confront their criticism again. On some level, I felt bad that I had not lived up to what they wanted me to be, but I had married Bob to find the approval they had not been able to give me.

They stopped at a telephone to let me know they would be at our apartment in about fifteen minutes and told me they would not come up but would just drop off the boxes and go. I did not know where they planned to leave the boxes since there was no place but the sidewalk, but it was clear they had been so hurt by Bob's lack of appreciation for all they had done that they didn't even plan to come up to see where the two of us were living. It was a Saturday, and Bob was home.

When I went downstairs to greet my parents, I was upset to see Mom's hurt face. "Mom, you have to come up. I just made a dessert for you."

"Well, since you have made dessert, we'll come up," said Mom, and we all carried as many of the boxes as we could up to the seventh floor.

"What a nice apartment!" Dad exclaimed as he walked into the living room. We sat at our newly purchased Baker Queen Anne table, which I had carefully set with my best dishes from the wedding.

"Why, Betsy, this is quite nice. You should be comfortable here," Mom said with evident relief in her voice. My parents had worked themselves into a frenzy about Bob, but for some unexplainable reason, their worry was somewhat dispelled when they saw I was living in an airy, spacious, and comfortable apartment in a complex of buildings surrounded by well-kept lawns, with Bob playing the part of gracious host.

To my surprise, my parents slowly changed their minds about Bob, and months later, they wrote me a letter saying, "Bob and you are doing so nicely together that we now understand what a fine man he is." In a few months, we found we were expecting a child around the time of our first anniversary, and Mom started sending me things for the baby and knitting sweaters.

Nana, however, was not happy that her son had married me and kept telling me how lucky I was to have married brilliant, successful, and good Bob. She told me the same stories over and over: he had always been first in all his classes at school, college, and graduate school at MIT, and he had won all kinds of awards and scholarships because of his brilliance. In addition, she was never quite satisfied with my appearance. One day she brought over a hairnet and tried to put it on me, saying it would be a way to keep my hair in place. I was horrified at the ugly, old-fashioned hairnet and took it off as soon as I dared.

On another day, Nana brought out photographs of one of Bob's old girlfriends, who had neatly groomed blonde hair, to show me what she liked. Evidently, Nana had been good friends with the former girlfriend and was still sorry Bob had not married her. In showing this to me, Nana didn't hurt me as much as stun me. I was surprised both that she would show it to me at all and that she would care so much about the details of appearance. It showed me clearly that we did not share any interests other than Bob. I had a master's degree in history from the University of Chicago, as well as my Vassar degree. Nana had just a high school education. There was little I could talk to her about. We just didn't care about the same things.

"I don't want any wife of mine to work!" exclaimed Bob. I did not fight him, even though I had worked hard at my teaching and done well. I was told by the Head of the History Department at New Trier West that some of the seniors had told him I was the only history teacher who had ever taught them anything. taught her anything. Even so, I had never envisioned a substantial career for myself or even taken great pride in my work, though I had taught at one of the best public high schools in the country. I didn't try to get another teaching job in New York and instead started doing volunteer work. I wanted to make some friends.

I don't think many young women would do today as I did and just give up without a thought careers they had worked for years to establish, but it was what my mother and grandmother before me. It was what many women did at the time.

My mother's hard work to give me social contacts in Chicago was useful in New York. I transferred my membership in the Junior League and several other societies. Mrs. Nichols, a wise and gracious lady whom my mother had accidentally met at my brother's graduation from Harvard, was related to my great-uncle's wife, Lottie Bruce, whose husband, Albert Bickmore, was the scientist born in Tenants Harbor who'd helped found the American Museum of Natural History in New York City. Mrs. Nichols took me under her wing and introduced me to another Vassar graduate, who became a good friend. She also took me to the Natural History Museum and put me on the women's committee, which raised funds for the museum. When I started giving tours, the thought crossed my mind that I was well qualified to be head of the whole volunteer teaching department rather than just giving a few tours, but no one inquired about my background. In addition, I was beginning to feel sick every morning.

A year after the big wedding, my lovely daughter appeared: Elizabeth Bond Jacks, nicknamed Betsy-Bond, another in the long line of Elizabeth Bonds going back to the daughter of Colonel William Bond of the Revolutionary War.

My mother came out to help me with the new baby, but once again, she got mad at Bob Jacks. "He acts so helpless around the baby and in the kitchen," she said. The truth was that he had never been around either before. His mother had always done all the cooking and housekeeping, and he was an only child.

Despite Mom's annoyance, both Bob and I were enraptured with our baby girl. I fell into all the same patterns as my mother and her mother before her. We devoted ourselves to our babies and continued in volunteer work. Like my grandmother in India and my mother in Chicago, I too was distant from family and friends.

However, life becomes complicated with a triangle, and I lived with one: my husband, myself, and Nana. Bob continued to be concerned about his mother's living alone after so many years with him. He checked on her frequently and asked her over for dinner often. She was high-strung and very thin, and as the daughter of a seamstress, she took great care with her clothes and appearance.

Once her granddaughter arrived, she made beautiful clothes for her, many with charming embroidered decorations. Betsy-Bond was given handmade lace bonnets trimmed with pink ribbons, a pink wool coat and bonnet set, and a yellow smocked dress. For her christening, Betsy-Bond wore a handmade lace dress that had been made for her father as a baby.

Nana became the babysitter, and she doted on her granddaughter. Nana was so infatuated with Betsy-Bond that it began to seem she felt my daughter was the daughter she'd never had. When Nana came for a visit, she brought crumb cakes for Betsy-Bond but hid them since she knew I disapproved. When I was gone for an afternoon, Nana would come straighten up my closets, not liking to see things out of place. It felt to me like an invasion of my space.

The more Nana took over Betsy-Bond's care, the more I resented it, feeling left out. I experienced strong feelings that I didn't understand. I tried talking to Bob about it, but he couldn't understand either. He was so concerned about his mother's feelings that I became upset. I needed my husband's full support. Finally, I tried to tell Nana how I felt. We were sitting at lunch one summer day at the Scarsdale Country Club, and we started talking about my daughter. "Nana," I said, "I am glad you love darling Betsy-Bond, but please try to remember that I am the mother."

"Why, Bob," Nana complained to her son, "Betsy is trying to take my living doll away from me." I felt such a bond between Bob and his mother and between his mother and my baby that I felt I wasn't getting the support I had so counted on when I married him. The triangle was awakening all the old painful feelings of my childhood.

Without being aware of it, I had brought into my new marriage all the hurt feelings of the little girl who'd felt left out and been told to go away. Bob had likewise brought into the marriage all his complicated emotions about taking care of his dependent mother. These emotions were played out over our baby daughter. A marriage needs to be rock solid to protect one's children.

However, our regular church attendance together did a great deal to bind us together and keep us on course. Bob would never miss a Sunday mass but quickly liberalized to be willing to attend Protestant services with me at the Fifth Avenue Presbyterian Church. We started alternating Sundays, going one week to the Presbyterian services and the next to the Catholic mass. Nana went to her own services at a different Catholic church, so Sunday services were times just for the two of us.

In the late spring, with the grass bright green and Betsy-Bond nearing a year old, I sat in the rocking chair in our bedroom while our daughter slept for her morning nap in the crib in the next room. I could see the lovely blues of the East River and watched the barges going back and forth, carrying cargo from countries all over the world.

The rocking chair in which I sat had been made in India of intricately designed reeds, and I had brought it down from Maine the previous summer. It had originally belonged to Clara, and she had placed it in front of the window in her bedroom at the sail loft, looking out at the lovely blues of Tenants Harbor. I imagined she also had read her Bible in the morning while sitting in the rocker. I liked the idea of generations of women in my family reading their Bibles in the morning as a source of faith and hope.

I opened the Bible and read a few verses, as I did most mornings. I had long read the Bible as a guide and inspiration for my life. I attended weekly Bible classes at an apartment in Peter Cooper, led by an Intervarsity Christian Fellowship worker. The scriptures helped me gain strength to keep myself going on the path I had chosen—being a wife and mother— even though it was often lonely. I felt housebound without being away at work, as I had been before I was married, but I was determined to find a way to make a success of the life I had chosen. Besides, I adored my daughter and didn't want to leave her to go to work.

I had latched on to the household codes in the Bible: "A husband should love his wife like Christ His church and a wife should obey her husband; then the children will rise up and call their mother blessed." (Ephesians 5:21 – 6:9). I meditated on these verses, and they brought me a sense of purpose and calm.

That morning, I started reading Job, and a particular verse kept sticking in my mind: "The Lord knows the Way that I take and when I have been tried, I shall come forth as gold." (Job 23:10) The verse reassured me. It felt like a message: I was following a good path, and it would be a blessing. I wanted to share this belief with Bob.

I decided to call Bob at work and read the verse to him, something I had never done before. I dialed from the rocking chair in our bedroom overlooking the East River, and he answered the phone himself. "Bob, I feel a little foolish, but I have this urge to read you this Bible verse that has struck me so forcibly this morning."

"Go ahead," he said. "I have a minute."

After I finished reading, he exclaimed, "That is amazing, Betsy, because a pink slip has just been handed to me! The company is being moved to the South, and I am not being invited to go with them." Bob's voice sounded wounded, like that of a trusting animal that had been shot. The firing came completely out of the blue. We had heard nothing about the M. W. Kellogg Company's plan to move. There had never been a question about Bob's quality of work.

"That's awful, Bob, and astounding. I'm terribly sorry," I replied. I looked out at the East River, not comprehending what this would mean to us.

After I hung up the phone, I continued to sit in the rocking chair and look out at the river. I thought of my great-grandmother Elizabeth Long, Clara's mother, up in Tenants Harbor a hundred years ago in 1870, when her husband no longer had work once the shipbuilding company went bankrupt. She had soldiered on for many years, and I vowed I would do the same.

Bob was forty-six at the time, a couple of years away from being vested. By firing him, the company would never have to pay him a pension, which saved it a lot of money but was devastating to us. To lose the possibility of a pension and be out of work in one's midforties with a young family was an enormous blow to Bob's ego and pocketbook. Luckily, Bob had savings and a stock portfolio from all those years he'd spent as a bachelor. (Rules were later changed so companies would no longer be able to dispense with all their pension obligations when they fired people.)

Having a hard time was something I understood, and I just kept encouraging Bob and lived economically. I would bake a whole chicken, use the leftovers in a casserole the next night, and make a big kettle of chicken soup the next night that would last a few more days. I was good at spaghetti and meatballs, macaroni and cheese, tuna and noodle casserole, and meat loaf. There was a babysitting group at Peter Cooper in which mothers took turns watching the children at the playground or babysitting in the evenings. My mom was concerned and frequently sent me money out of her teaching salary. When one of her hundred-dollar checks arrived, I would hurry to the grocery store to fill up our pantry and refrigerator. I repeated the verse from Job often to reassure both of us that something would work out. That verse was like a bulwark, keeping up our hope and faith.

Bob started a massive campaign to get another job, but the interviews were few, and none resulted in a job offer. Looking for a job was like a roller coaster. He would get a lead, follow it up, and wait for calls that did not come. He was a brilliant chemical engineering manager and disciplined, but he was not getting anywhere. The economy was slow at the time, and companies were not hiring. Also, his age made it harder. He tried to take on some consulting work. He applied for unemployment insurance, joined a self-help support group called the Forty-Plus Club, and enrolled in an MBA night school program at Baruch College.

After two years of enormous frustration, he was offered a job with a small environmental engineering company, Teller Environmental Systems. One day, sitting at his new office after hours, he received a call from someone wanting to sell the stock they held in the company. Bob bought it, and his boss got mad at him for buying it. I suppose he had wanted it himself. Eventually, that stock provided the down payment on a co-op apartment. In the 1970s, apartments were at the bottom of the market, and it turned out to be the perfect time to buy.

The job at Teller Environmental Systems lasted two years, until once again, he was out of work. The head of the firm got mad at Bob when he didn't volunteer to fly out to California on a weekend. The boss said he wasn't a team player. He was let go.

After another few agonizing months, Bob was offered a job at Union Carbide, the big chemical company.

After a year at Union Carbide, he once again made some people mad at him, for putting a chart up on the wall that showed the shortcomings of some of his fellow engineers. A brilliant engineer, Bob was not much of a people person, but this time, a secretary saved him. The secretary went to her boss and said, "You can't fire Bob. He has a young family." I had gone in one day and met the secretary and had Betsy-Bond with me.

Union Carbide consented and moved him to a different department. They sent him to a Dale Carnegie course and gave him an executive coach to soften the sharp edges of his personality. The executive coach met with him weekly to go over incidents at the company, explaining how he could handle fellow employees differently. He ended up being much more sensitive to people and keeping his job at Union Carbide.

Without my understanding it, the Bible verse given to me that day in my grandmother's Indian rocking chair had come true. I don't pretend to understand the mystery except to call it grace.

Without realizing it, I was following the same pattern the long line of women before me had followed. Would the result be the same for my daughter?

*   *   *

One day I made a conscious choice to change a little. Sitting on the floor of her sunny Peter Cooper bedroom, my young daughter put on her shoes to go out, only I had asked her to put on the sturdy oxfords, and she was putting on her pretty party shoes, ignoring me and what I had asked her to do. I looked at this young child with a steel will of her own and thought I could either break this child's will or let her have her own will. Even though something inside me was angry that she was ignoring me and I could have given her a spanking, I did not. I made the conscious decision to let this darling daughter of mine be. I was not going to force my will on her. After that, she began to speak up more.

On another day, we were out taking a walk, when I said to her, "I'm cold. Please put on your sweater." She went on running ahead of me. I pleaded with her again to put on her sweater.

"But I'm not cold," said my little daughter, skipping away.

"But it's getting chilly, and I don't want you to get sick," I said.

"But, Mom, I'm not cold. You're the one who's cold. You put on your sweater," said my daughter.

The incident surprised me because I had not realized what I was doing. I was also surprised my little daughter could speak up to me, something I never did with my mother. I made a conscious decision then to let her make some decisions and not force my will on her the way my mother's will had been forced on me. Even so, years later, Betsy-Bond would say that I had never listened to her. I had listened more than my mother had but not enough to satisfy my children's need to be heard. I continued to arrange things for them, thinking I knew best, as my mother had, and they longed for more of a say in their own lives. Although I had changed a little, I continued to do things for my children just as my mother had before me.

It would take years of hard work to change the pattern from doing to listening, and to nurturing the inner growth of my children.

Our goal as parents is to raise our children in such a manner that they are enabled to have their own voice with confidence.

CHAPTER 15

Mother, Daughter, and Son, New York, 1972

It was June 6, 1972. My daughter was soon to be three, and a second child was about to be born. I had a set date with the doctor to enter the hospital on June 7 to have my labor induced. I was looking forward to having my mother come out to help me once again. I called her up to make final plans, but instead, she gave me terrible news: she had to go into the hospital for an operation. I was shocked. She hadn't told me she had any health concerns.

I slept fitfully with the new baby pressing upon my vital organs and moving around during the night. My mind was just as active, trying to take in the news from Mom, replaying the conversation in my head. "Betsy, dear, I won't be there to help when the new baby arrives, because the biopsy just came back," Mom had said.

"What biopsy?" I'd asked in disbelief. "What is it, Mother?"

"They tell me it's a lymphoma cancer," she'd said matter-of-factly. "They took the biopsy from my neck, where there was a secondary malignant tumor. The primary cancer is in my abdomen."

"Mom, this is terrible. I didn't know any of this," I'd said, trying hard to take in what she was saying.

She'd continued calmly. "I am to go into the hospital tomorrow. I cannot come out to New York, as I had promised. I have to have the operation." The way she'd said it made me sense she was more worried

---

153

about not being with me for the birth than about the impending operation. I kept trying to absorb what it all meant.

The timing was uncanny: a new life and new, terrible cancer. How like my mother to be concerned with me rather than herself. She didn't want me fussing over her. It made her uncomfortable. I shook my head. I would not be able to go be with Mom with a new baby. Two women, mother and daughter, because of distance and circumstance, were unable to be with each other in a time of need. My concern was with Mom, and hers was with me.

The next day, I was in the hospital, in the labor room, having contractions monitored by the hospital staff. My doctor came to check on me periodically. Then a nurse whose name I'd never heard saw some bleeding that alarmed her. She called my doctor, who decided to take me into the operating room and hook up a monitor on my abdomen that would broadcast the fetal heartbeat to everyone in the operating room. He assured me it was just a precaution. Listening to the baby's heartbeat, I heard nothing alarming.

All of a sudden, everyone went into action upon recognizing a change in the heartbeat that I could not hear. The fetus's heartbeat was in trouble. A young resident doctor in hospital green pushed a button that made a sound like a series of warning buzzers. Staff people came running down the hall into the operating room, putting on their masks and gloves as they ran.

Evidently, the placenta had left the uterine wall too soon and cut off the fetus's oxygen. They had just four minutes to save the baby from severe brain damage or a stillbirth. A nurse in white climbed onto the gurney and straddled me the way one rides a horse. "This will hurt," she warned, "but it's necessary." She pushed on my stomach hard with both hands. I felt the pressure, but it did not hurt much, or maybe I was just too much caught up in the drama to be aware. Instead, I watched her two hands, their fingers spread wide, push on the huge hump of my abdomen. The nurse was straining with all her might. She pushed twice and pushed out the baby. I was just far enough into labor; otherwise, they would have performed an emergency C-section. It all took less than a minute.

"Doctor, is my baby okay?" I asked with enormous concern. I watched the doctor hold up my new son and inspect all seven pounds of him: tiny, vulnerable, and innocent.

"He is ninety-nine percent. Only my babies get a perfect score," he joked.

I was in a state of shock and enormous relief. My tiny son had been almost lost but miraculously saved just in the nick of time by an unnamed nurse and a well-trained emergency team at New York Hospital. What a difference a minute out of a whole lifetime can make.

A little later, lying on a bed in the recovery room with the door open to the hallway, I saw a nurse skip down the corridor in glee. "I saved a life," I heard her say. "I saved a life." I still don't know that nurse's name, but it but it made me think of something I once heard: "You can accomplish a lot in this life if you don't care who gets the credit." Her reward was knowing she had saved a life.

Bob came in to see me. He had been kept in a waiting room the whole time. He had missed it all. I tried to explain to him the immense drama that had just taken place. He listened but couldn't take it in, as he was so excited about having a son that he could barely contain himself. When he left the hospital after the visit, he took pictures of New York City so his son one day could know what the city had been like the day he was born. "I have a son. I have a son," he kept repeating, handing out cigars to all kinds of people.

The tiny boy was named after his proud and happy father: Robert LeRoy Jacks Jr. I was so traumatized by the near miss that I became overly protective of my new son—so much so that my lovely daughter thought I was unfair to her. It was a tale of unintended consequences—the same way my mother had become overprotective of my brother Bobby, who had a stutter and had had a near miss. Had I been in India like Grandmother Clara, my son would probably have died or at least been hurt, as Cedric had been.

The same day the new baby was saved, Mom's operation took place in Chicago. The news was not good. The cancer had already spread throughout her body. Markers were placed on the tumors in her abdomen to enable the doctors to track the progress of the disease with x-rays. Bobby was with her as one of the young resident doctors in the hospital. Margie, Dad, and John came to see her.

While she was still in the hospital, Mom called me. She had heard from Margie about my son's birth. "Betsy, dear, now that I have heard of the saving of your son and that you have been spared the agony of a stillborn child or one with cerebral palsy, it doesn't matter what happens to me. I'm just so grateful you were spared the heartache of what I saw my mother and father go through." She thought and then added, "The baby being saved this way must mean he is destined to do some important things in life."

Mom's self-sacrificing love and devotion made me weep. There was a true missionary spirit in the missionary's daughter. Even far away from the land of her youth and facing her own mortality in a big Chicago hospital, she could think of me and my son. I wept for my mom.

In due course, I took my son, whom I called Bob-Roy, home. Mom was released from the hospital after a week. I was consumed with caring for the new baby and my daughter. My sister, Margie, came out toward the end of the month from Chicago and did what I most wanted: she put on a birthday party for my daughter, Betsy-Bond, who was turning three. She made a cake; bought ice cream, birthday hats, and napkins; and entertained a group of ten little girls with balloons, food, and games around the Peter Cooper flagpole. Betsy-Bond wore the yellow dress handmade by Nana with dotted Swiss and white lace.

Over the course of the next year and a half, my new baby boy grew rapidly into a healthy, happy toddler. Mom endured two courses of radiation and chemotherapy, each of which took away more of her vigor. During that year and a half, I managed to see Mom only three times.

The first time, over Easter, I flew to Chicago. Mom looked thin but had a good level of energy and was nearly her old self. She fixed a big Easter feast and gave everyone several presents. She had gone to the toy store and picked out an appropriate present for each grandchild. She gave Bob-Roy, who was nearly ten months and just learning to walk, a plastic roller toy with bells that played as he pulled it behind him. Betsy-Bond received a big, fluffy white toy Easter bunny that she loved.

When I complimented Mom on the generosity of her presents, she replied, "I can't take it with me."

I appreciated Mom's generosity, which showed how much she cared about us, but I was overcome by the matter-of-fact way she acknowledged what was happening to her and that she was not going to be long with us. She seemed to accept her future in a way that none of the rest of us were able to do. Everyone else seemed to be playacting his or her traditional role, not knowing how to talk about Mom.

The second time I saw Mom in person was the following summer. The children and I managed to travel to Maine to be with Mom at the sail loft, the place where this long family story began with Deacon Robert Long and his then thriving shipbuilding business.

I thought about Deacon Long's son speculating in ships and bankrupting the company. I thought about Clara leaving for India in her handsome handmade gray dress with matching shawl and handmade lace. I thought about her returning in black as a widow. I thought about Mom visiting as a girl, visiting as a college graduate and discussing the terrible news about Charlie, and visiting her mother with her own young children. I thought about myself coming as a child and having a wonderful time playing on the rocks and swimming in the ocean. There I was again, having once again traveled to Maine, with my own children to see and talk with my mother as she struggled with lymphoma. Mom had grown very thin and was weaker that summer, taking frequent rests.

One day we were sitting around the cream-and-apple-green kitchen table, the one she had painted for her mother, Clara, when Clara returned from India and needed a place to live. Bob-Roy was in a playpen in the kitchen, wearing a bright yellow jumpsuit, happily playing with his many toys. Betsy-Bond was sitting at the table, making a painting. Mom and I chatted, happy to see each other. "Mother, I so appreciate your coming all the way to Maine to see us," I said.

"Do you think I would miss seeing your children?" exclaimed Mom. She now kept a bottle of water with a straw close by. The radiation had burned her throat, and she kept drinking the cool water to lessen the burn.

I tried to take in what was happening, but Mom was thinking ahead and wanted to talk to me seriously about some of what was to come. At nighttime, after the children were in bed and we were in our twin beds in the room off the living room, the one with gray wallpaper and a pattern of pink roses, she began to talk. The windows with white lace curtains looked out over the harbor; there was no moonlight, just the twinkling of the stars.

Mom and I sat in the dark. "Betsy, I need to talk with you and share with you about your sister, Margie, because Margie is going to need a friend, and I won't be here," Mom said.

I could tell this was hard for her. She didn't like to talk about one of her children to another. She had always prided herself on her wisdom and control. She had never wanted my help, which always made me feel pushed away, but tonight she was asking for me to help; even more, she was turning over to me the job of taking care of Margie and, by implication, the whole family. She no longer would be here to have control and to provide answers.

"Margie's marriage is in trouble," Mom said. "Her husband, the man I thought was perfect for her and even urged her to marry, is not the man I thought. He has betrayed Margie many times in a number of ways."

It flashed through my mind that Margie's husband, had had all the outward trappings that Mom, the daughter of a missionary and herself a United States immigrant, had sought in order to feel accepted in her new country: he was an eastern prep school and Ivy League college graduate, a young investment manager, but he lacked character. In contrast, my husband, Bob, did not have all the outward trappings, and Mom had been against my marrying him. However, over time, to give her credit, she saw his character and realized her mistake.

"Although I don't believe in divorce, I support Margie in whatever she chooses for her life, because in this case, I don't know," Mom said thoughtfully.

Lying there in my twin bed next to Mom's bed, I was stunned. I listened to Mom's confiding in me and passing the torch to me: her worry and love for Margie; her acknowledgment that her judgment had been wrong and that she no longer had all the answers; her helplessness to take charge or even to be there for Margie because she was dying; her steadfast love and concern; and her confidence in me—the child who had been made to feel helpless and hopeless and told to go out and play and not help—to be there in her stead to carry on her love. At that moment, I listened intently. She had confidence in me and my ability to lead. She wanted me to carry on in her stead to help the family. I didn't want to think of her not being there, but she was clearly thinking of a future without her.

After our late-night talk, it was soon time to return to our homes. Mom went back to Chicago, and I went back to New York.

The third visit took place the following October. I flew out to be with Mom in Chicago. The cancer treatment was failing badly. Despite all the painful treatments, the cancer had metastasized. I continued to struggle with what that meant, but Mom knew clearly. She had come to terms with her impending death.

I tried to take care of Mom personally, but Mom resisted becoming the one in need. When I drove her to the University of Chicago Hospital for another radiation treatment, I pleaded, "Let me come in with you."

"No, I'm okay," she said. "You just take care of yourself."

"No, Mom, I really want to be with you in this ordeal," I said again.

"No, Betsy," she said with finality. "I am okay on my own. I've gone through so many of these treatments that I am not even modest anymore when I have to lie naked on the floor. I want you not to worry about me but to go on with your own life."

I felt once again deeply rejected and began to wonder why my dying mother would send me away.

She had been on her own all her life and could not bring herself to change it now, even with her daughter's pleading. Little did she know how much her daughter longed to be with her or how much time I would spend over the rest of her life worrying about her, but her lifelong unconscious reaction meant keeping me away. She rationalized it was to protect me— the same way she had rationalized she was protecting me when she told me as a little girl to go play instead of being with her in the kitchen, saying she did not want me burdened the way she had been burdened as a child by her mother. Mom couldn't bear to have me with her. Had she never trusted that she was truly loved, even by her own daughter?

I have come to theorize that when my dying mother said to me, "Don't worry about me; go on with your life," her words represented a deep emotional block stemming from her painful childhood in India. Mom had experienced deep neglect by her sickly, helpless mother and absent father; abuse and neglect at her boarding school; and abandonment by her brother's suicide. Like all neglected and abused children, she turned against herself unconsciously, decided she was not worthy, and developed deeply negative self-esteem. It was an unconscious, unexplored feeling that dominated her life. She'd decided she was not worthy enough for her own daughter to spend time with her on some of her last days on earth.

A thought suddenly flashed into my mind: in that way, my mother and I were alike. She had turned against herself the way I had turned against myself as a child, thinking something was wrong with her. It is called the cycle of abuse. Could I learn to be different to free my children, to break the cycle?

I reluctantly obeyed and watched Mom get out of the old beat-up red car, which she had been driving until recently, and walk down the long sidewalk to the door of the hospital treatment center. She had grown thin and wore a knee-length black coat with a fitted waist. She walked haltingly and grabbed the bannister to climb the few steps up to the door alone.

I stayed and watched until she was gone, feeling helpless and sad.

Being alone was all she could tolerate; it was what she had known for a good part of her life. She had been sent away alone to school as a child in India at age eight, alone to Chicago, and alone through much of her marriage and was alone in her final days of treatment. I wanted to disobey her and go with her anyway, but old habit made me obey again. I felt terrible. I will never forget the image of her black coat hugging her thin, frail figure as she walked haltingly into that hospital alone.

The next morning, after breakfast, the sun was shining, and Mom showed me another side of herself. My sixty-four-year-old mother and I, her thirty-three-year-old daughter, sat down across from each other in the TV room and library of our old South Side family home. She was unusually quiet and looked right at me. The rose-covered couch I had curled up on as a small child when feeling alone was still there, but now my mother was there with me, present to me, and dying. I did not have to hide. Something had dramatically shifted in her during the night, through all her suffering.

"Betsy, dear," Mom said.

Her calling me "Betsy, dear" got my attention and made me weep. She was not judging me. She was not controlling me. She was just loving me. It was as though she saw me for the first time.

"You know we are all spirits, and the only thing important in this world is love. To the extent I loved those children I taught at school, to that extent it was important." Though Mom spoke of her students, I think she meant me, since she was looking right at me—to the extent she loved me, it was important. She was giving me the love I had longed for all my life. Her face shone with radiance.

I sat there looking into her sweet face. We had a connection that would last me a lifetime. "Betsy, dear" was what I had always wanted to hear. I breathed deeply and sat quietly. There was peace in that room.

She went on to talk about her faith. She quoted the Bible: "In my father's house are many mansions. If it were not so, I would have told you. I go to prepare a place for you." (John 14:2) She was preparing herself to go on to the next world, where she had confidence a place was prepared for her. She was espousing the same faith her mother before her had when she had to face the deaths of her own children: "In this world, there is suffering, but in the next world, there is joy."

We sat there for a long time. I looked at my mother across the room and felt a deep bond, a deep looking. We were completely open to each other. I wanted to just stay there. My longing was fulfilled.

How grateful I was for those few moments.

Finally, it was time. I flew back to New York with my son. I talked by telephone with Bobby, who was a resident doctor at the University of Chicago Hospitals and was assisting in Mom's care. "I've been talking with Mom, and she has been crying," he told me. "She's realizing she is not going to beat this thing. She said, 'My father died, my mother died, my brothers died, and I will die too.' Also, she is wrestling with her feelings about Uncle Charlie."

Bobby told me that Mom had said, "You know, Son, something I never told you, but my brother Charlie committed suicide when he was twenty-seven years old up in Wolfville. It was a sin that he committed suicide, yet I have missed him so all my life." Bobby had never heard about the suicide before and felt she was struggling with the conflict between her great love for her brother and his abandonment of her through suicide. It was one of the knots that had tied up so much of her life: Mom's conflict between the law of God and her love for her brother.

John came to see Mom, and Margie spent a great deal of time with Mom in the hospital. She kept remarking to me how much Mom had softened. Dad was there sporadically but also said he had to go on with all his responsibilities to the court and the farm. I was thinking of flying out to Chicago again and called Mom in the hospital. She said, "Oh, Betsy, I am so glad to hear from you." That was all she could say, but it was all she needed to say to stay with me forever.

On November 4, I received the dreaded call from Chicago. My wonderfully healthy son was playing happily in the living room with his sister, Betsy-Bond. I collapsed onto the floor. The loss of Mom was unimaginable. I would have to accept it.

I flew out to the funeral in Chicago, bringing Bob-Roy with me, while Betsy-Bond stayed home with her father. The large Fourth Presbyterian Church on the Near North Side overflowed with people. Even Mayor Daley came, saying to each one of us, "I am sorry." Many of the children Mom had taught in that tough South Side school came. They told us they had dedicated their school yearbook to Mom as Outstanding Teacher of the Year. There was a beautiful picture of her in the yearbook.

Jo was there with her husband, Ted, and told us how much she had valued our mother's friendship.

Dad planned to bury Mom in Mapleton, Iowa, his hometown, far away from Mom's mother in Seaside Cemetery in Tenants Harbor. When it was time for us to leave, Dad said gruffly, "Leave that baby in Chicago. We can't deal with it." I was so used to obeying that booming voice that I left Bob-Roy in the care of Margie's husband, who was taking care of his own two-year-old son.

On the way to western Iowa, through the fields of corn and soybeans, Dad cried several times. "Your mother was the finest Christian woman I have ever known. I was mean to her a few times, but she always bounced back."

At the cemetery next to the cornfields, the family gathered for the burial. There was a moment when everyone was gathered on one side of the cemetery, and the casket was over on the other side. I walked over to the casket and raised the lid, wanting to look at Mom one last time. What I saw amazed me: a radiant face. I thought the sweetheart roses on the casket were common and ordinary in comparison to the beauty and shining light coming out from Mom's face. It made me think of my mother's story of seeing her own mother dead. Mom had said her mother must have seen something when she died that made her very happy. My mother must have seen the same. I closed the casket, knowing I had seen my mother for the last time, but the shine imprinted on her face when her spirit left her body showed she had met great joy and radiant love. All her earthly trials and tribulations were over. It was my turn to carry on.

Dad buried Mom near his parents, where he would one day be buried. In death, he kept her near him. From the grave, one had a long view over Iowa cornfields. He had planned a simple graveside service. Sweetheart roses were laid on the grave. Afterward, Dad arranged a big roast beef dinner at a local restaurant for all who had come to the grave. I could barely swallow.

Back in Chicago, when I went to get my son, Bob-Roy ran the other way and hid under a bed as soon as he saw me. I knelt down on the floor and stretched out my hand to him under the bed but could not reach him. He refused to budge. I stayed there, kneeling and reaching, and said, "Bob-Roy, I have missed you terribly, and I love you with all my heart. I had to go out and bury my mother and was forbidden to take you with me. Please forgive me."

It took a long time, but eventually, Bob-Roy trusted me enough to come over to me. I held him tightly and realized I never should have listened to Dad. I packed up and left Chicago as quickly as I could.

In New York, I received a copy of the yearbook dedicated to Mom: "Upon her untimely death, to our outstanding teacher of the year." I recalled her words: "The only thing important in life is how much you love. To the extent I loved the children I taught, that was what was important." Her suffering had softened her spirit and, in turn, transformed the legacy she left me and her grandchildren. I had hurt my son, but I fervently hoped it would not do permanent damage. I remembered something else she had said that afternoon: "It is the overall pattern that counts, and a single incident can be overcome with a long pattern of love."

I called Margie in Chicago and repeated to her what Mom had said to me in Maine: "Margie will need a friend, and I won't be here."

At the time, Margie was lying on her bed, crying, feeling desolate and alone, and saying to herself, "I want my mother." I called at ten thirty in the morning, which was unusual for me because the cost of long-distance calling was high during the day. Margie told me later how my call had affected her: "I had gotten my wish. My mother had come back to me through your call, and somehow, it made life a little bit easier. It was a holy mystery I cannot explain. It increased my faith that at the exact moment I needed Mom the most, Mom was alive through Betsy."

Through passing on the torch to me, through me, Mom would still be there. Margie was not alone. I was there. It was a first step in repairing the family.

That a holy mystery came through me to start the healing in my sister's life left me in humble awe.

CHAPTER 16

Life and Death, New York, 1974

Everything worth having costs something, and the price of true love is self-knowledge.

Multiple Sources

When I came back to New York City after the summer in Maine as the new owner of the sail loft, I knew I had to tackle the tension I felt in my marriage, the tension beneath the surface. I felt like an imposter playing the roles of wife and mother with Bob seeming so in love with me and doing so much for me. I was glad he seemed happy, but I wasn't happy. I wanted more than a father. I wanted a husband. I had changed, and I was afraid to express my true feelings. In fact, I was afraid of my own feelings of anger and need. I was missing a deep connection. I felt alone and unknown. I dreaded deeply what I thought I had to do. I felt trapped in the marriage but agreed with Bob and the Catholic church that divorce was out of the question. I was just looking for a way to have a real marriage with this man I had married. I was afraid the truth of who I was and why I had married him would break my husband's heart, but I felt I had to do something.

I had heard of the Catholic church's Marriage Encounter weekends and signed us up. Marriage Encounter was started in 1952 in Spain by Father Gabriel Calvo, who developed weekends for married couples and explained he wanted to help them develop an open and honest relationship within marriage and "to learn to live out a sacramental relationship in the service of others." The brochure explained the weekend would be a time to be together away from all distractions and to concentrate on communicating with each other "to make good marriages great."

As the Encounter weekend approached, I envisioned every step of it: we would drop off our two beautiful children with a babysitter, pack our bags, and drive to Marymount College, a Catholic women's college then located just north of New York City. We would check in, sleep in the same bed, go down to breakfast together, and listen to the presenters talk about marriage. We would be told to start writing letters to each other in which we told the truth. We would be told to listen to each other. When the weekend ended, we would pack our bags and drive back to New York, but I imagined we would be living in a totally changed relationship. I feared Bob would be deeply hurt by what I intended to write. I feared I would have to sleep on the sofa in the living room, and my husband would get up early and go to the office after grabbing breakfast at the corner. The thought occurred to me that I should warn Bob before we went for the weekend, but I even feared speaking to him without the structure of the letters and the community which the weekend would provide.

I was a needy and scared, but I couldn't go on living in a make-believe world. After this weekend, he would know me. We would be two people who knew each other for I planned to take off my mask.

I went into our kitchen and fixed dinner, as I did every night. Our daughter was sitting on the floor at my feet, playing with the covers from the pots and pans. Our son was in his bouncy chair in the living room, watching *Sesame Street*. I needed to hurry to fix their dinner of chicken and vegetables, or they would both get fussy from hunger.

I was afraid I was going to take away the innocence of our family.

Both children were wearing white cable-knit sweaters that my mother had knitted while sick before she died. Betsy-Bond wore a hunter-plaid skirt, and Bob-Roy wore matching pants. As I put the chicken in the frying pan, I heard the doorknob turn. I froze with trepidation.

"Hi! Daddy's home!" Bob came into the front hall, removed his chocolate-colored overcoat, hung it up, and opened his arms to catch the two children, who ran to meet him.

"Daddy's home!" they squealed.

During the last week, I had been trying to convince myself that telling the truth was a good thing to do. It didn't have to be a tragedy. If I never told the truth, I could never have a true relationship. We would always be strangers. Breaking someone's heart, pricking his fantasy, had to be for the better. It was a positive act that would bring a better future. I kept trying to convince myself.

When I was growing up, my parents seldom, if ever, spoke the truth to each other. We lived in a shaky world made up of fantasies. Appearance was what mattered, not truth. My mother felt a terrible shame all her life about her brother's suicide, but she only got around to sharing the secret on her deathbed. There was an elegant strange lady sitting in our living room all by herself when I came home from school one fall day. After peering in on her, I walked through the house to the kitchen where Mom was in her usual light turquoise house dress washing dishes and asked: "Who is that lady in our living room sitting there all by herself"? Mom replied: "That is a friend of your father's". That one comment ended the conversation. Sometime later when Mom and I were walking down the street, Mom suddenly, out of the blue, said to me: "You must be myopic and never see if you ever have a husband that strays, don't see. Women who make a fuss lose their homes. Much better not to see and keep your home". Again, that was all Mom said, and we never discussed that strange lady sitting in our living room all alone. We didn't talk things over in my house growing-up but I had to try with my husband.

Bob was in the kitchen now. He said, "Mmm, it smells good. When will it be ready?"

"Soon, dear. Why don't you relax in your easy chair for just a few minutes until I finish?"

"Thank you, sweetheart." He smiled. "You are so lovely to come home to."

I thought how hard it was to be home tending to small children and being a housewife all the time. I wished I could trade roles for a while and be the one who went to work. I needed to find more to do.

I heard Bob get angry with the children in the living room: "Why haven't you picked up your toys and put them away?" I wished he wouldn't expect a perfect house when he came home. Couldn't he understand that children needed to play?

Finally, dinner was finished. Afterward, I bathed the children, Bob read his newspaper, and I read the children stories. He came in to kiss the children good night, but they didn't want to go to sleep. They wanted to play some more. Bob came back into their room, and they dove for the covers. Finally, all was quiet, and we started getting ready for bed ourselves.

He seemed content to be going off for the weekend with me but had no idea what it was about.

The next morning, as planned, we found ourselves at Marymount in the rolling hills of Westchester, listening to a panel of couples talk about how they made their marriages great. "Feelings are who you are at any given moment," one said, "but they are neither bad nor good; they just are. It is what you do with them that is your responsibility."

That made me feel better. All my angry, stuck feelings didn't make me a bad person. Feelings were okay. It was the actions based on those feelings on which one could be judged. I followed the procedure and wrote a letter pouring out how I felt, but I was scared. We were told to write our letters separately and then take turns reading them to each other while the other person listened. Then each would write another letter in reaction to the letter he or she had just heard.

Bob read his letter to me first. "My beloved Elizabeth, you are the love of my life. You make me so happy and so proud." He went on for several pages, telling me how happy he was.

Then it was my turn to read my letter to him. I was terrified. I was sitting alone in a small college dormitory room with matching chintz curtains and bedspread and dark paneling on the walls, writing what I had never dared to speak. How could I speak to someone living in a dream? He had been an old bachelor when I met him. He'd told me I was the one he had been looking for all his life. He had been living in a fantasy.

Dear Bob,

I do not feel inside to be the perfect paragon of the beautiful, dutiful mother and wife. In fact, Bob, I have never been what you think I am. I married you for you to be my rock in this world. Someone I could count on, not because I was madly in love with you.

It has bothered me for so long that when I married you, I thought I was ambivalent toward you. I knew I cared desperately about what happened to you, but I also knew that I was not overwhelmed with joy in thinking I had found my one true love. But I felt God wanted me to marry you, that it was right. What I have learned is that I didn't understand anything when I married you. It was not that I was ambivalent but that I was not honest with you about all I felt. Therefore, I didn't really feel loved by you. You were not honest and open about all you felt, so I couldn't find you.

But if I tell you now and if you will not wallow in your own hurt but look at me, our marriage will be healed. Please understand how hurt I have been that I could never tell you how I felt. I felt so abandoned, so lacking in self-worth. If you leave me now, I will feel truly lost and lacking in all worthiness to be loved, but if you will turn to me and see the frightened thing that I am, then I will feel joy in being loved.

I am counting on you. This is the real reason I married you. I finally found someone I could believe and trust. I so much needed to be loved that I did not know how to love in return.

I went on for a number of pages, but unfortunately, the booklets in which we wrote our letters to each other have been lost. When we finished reading our letters to each other, it was nighttime, and we tried to get some sleep, so emotionally exhausted that we couldn't do any more that night.

The next morning, I wrote a new letter, and Bob did the same. We read them to each other. I wrote,

I am so sorry that I had to hurt you, but I just couldn't reach you. I didn't trust your love because I knew you didn't know me, yet I knew you were dependent on me. You felt so vulnerable. You kept telling me if I didn't love you, you wouldn't have anything to live for—but you wouldn't let me see you so I could love you. You wouldn't let me reveal me—the frightened, doubting, confused person I was.

Bob wrote that he was devastated by my letter. He told me he contemplated giving it all up and had had a terrible night. I was terribly upset to be upsetting him but started writing the prescribed next letter.

"As awful as I feel, I will never leave you," I wrote to Bob. "Rather, I will spend my life finding you and me." I told him I would never give up on trying to listen to him, know him, and love him. The panel had told us that two people could love each other as long as they listened fully to themselves and each other.

> Now I think I am going to continue finding more and more of you.
>
> You have to teach me and show me that you really love me. I have not felt truly loved and accepted by you, but I believe you are going to reach out to me in a way no one has ever done before.
>
> I see in you now a real person I can love. When I looked into your eyes, I was so excited that you and I could know the love that you and I have always dreamed about in each other.
>
> I feel at peace now. I pray that you do also.

Bob read my letter and then wrote back to me,

> My dear Elizabeth, you broke my heart. I did not want to go on living. Then I remembered the way you said you would never leave me, and I decided to go on. This morning, I have hope.
>
> I want to go on living this morning too, darling, because of how you looked at me. The words you said were there too, but somehow, all I remember about them was your telling me that I was more important to you than what I did. No, it wasn't the words that made the difference but the love in your eyes and on your face that I remember and will remember forever.

These were Bob's words, and they were moving to me.

I started shaking. This was harder than I had feared. I had been right to be scared of how Bob would react. I had sensed that he had a vulnerable, fragile side. My image of his feelings was of a beautiful cut-crystal box that could shatter. I, on the other hand, started looking into his eyes and felt a sense of connection. I felt a mutual honesty there for the first time. His hurt eyes made me sad, but there was more—his total presence.

We took a walk into the hills, and the red, yellow, and orange fall leaves were startlingly beautiful. We held hands. We stopped and looked at each other. I saw his piercing, radiant blue eyes looking right into me. I was surprised at my light and free feelings. My hand felt warm, safe, and happy in his hand. I felt deeply connected to him. He was there with me, and I was there with him. We were learning to love one another.

My marrying a man I didn't know how to love had been a mean thing for us both. We do mean things when we are not in touch with ourselves. Underneath, I had thought something was wrong with me, unlovable, and thus, I'd married someone who would be like a father to me, but he had wanted a wife.

Breaking with the way I was brought up and speaking my feelings to Bob was harsh for Bob since I had not spoken up for so long, but in the controlled environment of the Marriage Encounter weekend, we managed to be okay. People remain apart and disconnected when they don't know their own feelings and don't share their feelings with their mates.

My risk paid off, for Bob did come around and enter a new kind of relationship with me. Here was the dream come true. We became happier and more open with each other, and the weekend set the stage for a renaissance in our lives. We were enabled to move to a new neighborhood filled with a community of friends and fine schools for the children. We had a Camelot period for eight years.

However, all this did not stop me from feeling terribly guilty for what I had done, until one day I had the sense that he had seen me with compassion, seen the troubled young woman that I had been, and forgiven me. I have slowly been able to forgive myself and will be ever grateful.

I realized there were ramifications for my children of my deeply ambivalent feelings. They sensed their father's frustration and tended to side with their father. I understood that the more I reconciled with their father in my heart, the more I would be united with my children.

At the same time, my journey was not over. Life comes together, falls apart, and comes together again like the ebb and flow of the tides. But the tides are predictable, and life doesn't seem that way when you're living through it. It never occurred to me that in a few years, Bob would leave me forever.

CHAPTER 17

Tragedy Connecticut and New York 1983

Just as we all settled into our fruitful lives in New York City, a bombshell hit: Union Carbide, the company where Bob worked, announced they were moving their headquarters to Danbury, Connecticut. It was too far for Bob to commute every day. After a lot of turmoil, we decided to move to Middlebury, Connecticut, which was within commuting distance of the new Union Carbide headquarters. Our family could be together, and we could have a nice house on a pretty piece of land near some good schools for the children. We simply tore out everything we had built up in New York City and went to a place where we hardly knew anyone. But we would be together.

Bob bought a sports car, which he had always wanted, to commute to work, and we bought the children a springer spaniel puppy. I felt distant from my New York friends, but a welcoming group in Middlebury invited us to join the local country club and meet many local families. I took a part-time job at Westover School, a girls' boarding school, teaching history, though I was rusty, having not taught for a decade.

I tried to hold on to my ties in New York City and decided to drive the children there for monthly ballroom dancing classes, two hours each way. My son, Bob, told me years later he'd felt like a pariah at those New York City dances I dragged him to. I realized then, much later, that I had done exactly as my mother had done to me when she dragged me to the North Side for dancing classes, where I'd always felt out of place. At the time they were young, I was unaware of my children's feelings. When my daughter, Betsy-Bond, was an adult, she told me, "You never listened to us"—the exact complaint I'd had about my parents.

I worked tirelessly to care for my children, always making them my top priority, just as my mother had done before me, but that did not mean I was loving. The just doing can be cold and harsh if one doesn't listen to one's children.

For reasons I did not understand, once we'd moved to Connecticut, Bob seemed concerned with what might happen to us all if he were suddenly gone. He understood better than I how dependent the three of us were on his care. He announced one day he was relieved to have secured mortgage insurance, so if anything ever happened to him, the mortgage would be paid off, and we could stay in our home. I wondered why he was so concerned. He also pored over his investments every day, keeping careful graphs and records, building up his portfolio.

The second Christmas we were in Connecticut, two local families approached us, suggesting we all rent a ski chalet over New Year's in Quechee, Vermont, a few hours north of Middlebury. The children and I enjoyed skiing. Bob did not ski, but he agreed to go because he thought a short break in Vermont and the camaraderie with the other families would be fun.

We piled into our car with skis, boots, and jackets and headed north. It was a small ski area but fun. I skied with the two children, enjoying the fresh air and exercise. Bob came over to the ski lodge for lunch and stood at the bottom of the hill, watching us all come down. I thought to myself how out of place he looked in his old chocolate-brown gabardine overcoat and fedora. Why couldn't he have found a ski jacket to put on? It brought back my old ambivalent feelings of both how old and fatherly he looked and, at the same time, how much I depended on him.

Bob might have been having similar feelings of disappointment in me. As he stood at the bottom of the hill, watching me struggle to control my skis on the ice, he said critically, "You used to be a good skier. What happened?"

I got angry, feeling that he didn't understand how hard it was to ski on an icy hill or how hard I was working to soldier on. "It's ice out there," I fumed. "Why don't you try it?" Little did I know what I was saying, for as it turned out, he unexpectedly and tragically met with ice just a little later.

He finished his hamburger and soda and said he was going back to the chalet to read the newspaper and would see us after our afternoon skiing. We had all planned a dinner together for New Year's Eve.

That afternoon, when I drove up to our chalet, I jumped a foot when I saw that Bob's car was not there. It was three o'clock in the afternoon, and he had said he was going right back to the ski house to read the newspaper and would be there when we arrived back at three o'clock. Bob was always where he said he would be. I could always count on Bob. Everyone else said not to worry, but I was nervous. Within twenty minutes, I called the police. When I asked if they knew anything about Robert Jacks, the voice on the other end of the line said, "I will have someone call you."

I hung up and waited. I assumed I had called the emergency line and they wanted to free the line and to talk to me on a regular line to say they knew nothing but would fill out a standard form in case they heard anything.

Not long after, the phone rang. "You are the lady looking for a Robert Jacks," a man's voice said. "I have a Robert Jacks here, and he has expired." That was the way I was given this terrible news—no buildup, no preliminaries.

"What!" I yelled into the phone. "Who are you to tell me a thing like this? Who are you? How dare you?"

"The body is at the morgue, and we need you to come over to identify it. There was a terrible accident. It took two hours to clean up."

Stunned, I simply asked where to go. Turning around to the children, I said, "This person on the phone said your dad has died." Betsy and Bob jumped into the laps of the other mothers and began to scream. The women held them tightly. "Will you children come with me?"

"No," they said.

"I'll come with you," one of the fathers said.

We drove in silence to the police department. I walked into an antiseptic brown-tiled room where a man sat behind an empty brown wooden desk. "He's in there," he said, pointing to a second little white-tiled room separated by a curtain.

I went in. Bob was lying on a narrow stretcher, with no marks apparent on him. He looked asleep.

I went over to him, kissed him, hugged him, and clung to him. I did not want to let go. I was numb, but I wanted to know more. I gently used my thumb and index finger to open his eyes. The most happy and beautiful expression was there, as though he had seen something amazingly wonderful. "Oh, sweetie," I whispered. "What have you seen? What has happened to you?" He had been a man of enormous faith, a true follower of the Catholic church, a faithful and pure soul. What did it mean, his lying there asleep forever? I had no idea.

I closed his eyes and stayed there with my head on his chest, not wanting him to leave me, not able to take in what had happened to him, to us, to our children.

Then the man from behind the desk came in, gently took me by the arm, and led me back to the outer room with the brown wooden desk. "Since this is a fatality on a state road, the state needs to carry out an investigation." He asked me if there was anyone I wanted to call.

I could think of only one person: my father. I picked up the phone and called. "Dad, Bob has been killed in an automobile accident. What do I do?"

"Oh, that's too bad." Dad's voice was warm but also matter of fact. "Call a priest and a lawyer."

I did not talk to Dad long but instead immediately asked the attendant at the morgue if I could have a priest.

In came an old and tired priest who looked as if he were called every day. He gave Bob last rites, almost winking at me to let me know he knew Bob was already dead. I managed to thank him and to give him a donation. I knew Bob would have wanted those last rites.

Somehow, I decided to have Bob's body sent to the Middlebury funeral home, but first, the state said they had to do an autopsy and file many reports. I told the police I wanted to be taken to the scene of the accident and wanted to see the car before I left Vermont. They were reluctant to show me anything but agreed to pick me up the next day.

When I saw the spot on the snowy road where the accident had occurred, there was nothing to see, just a pretty Vermont winter scene. They told me his car had slipped on the icy road into ongoing traffic. Strange, Bob had always been afraid of driving on the ice. Having grown up in the warmth of New Orleans, he had never gotten used to the ice.

When they showed me the car, which had been towed behind a garage, I held my head in horror. It was awful. The driver's side had been pushed all the way over into the passenger seat. He had been hit right where he sat. The autopsy later showed that six ribs had been broken, and one had severed his aorta, killing him instantly. He had died so quickly that they said he never knew what had happened. A violent, terrible moment ended the life of a peaceful, good man. Random violence had taken away goodness, destroying lives and a family, out of the blue, with no warning, no preparation, no explanation, and no way to integrate it into our view of the world.

There was nothing else for me to do in Vermont but to pack up and return to Connecticut. I called Bob's boss, my family, and a few close friends. The next morning, my children and I squeezed into the car of one of the other families, and they drove us back to Middlebury. We arrived at an empty house overflowing with flowers, casseroles, hams, and messages. The postman handed me bags of mail.

We had made it, I thought. We had managed to make a solid family and a big, broad community of friends. It had been unlikely that someone as scared as I and someone as old and set in his ways as Bob would make a success of it, but we had.

I decided I wanted to honor Bob and give him a great tribute at the old stone Catholic church on the Green in Middlebury, Connecticut. I called my minister and the Catholic church and arranged a joint funeral in the Catholic church. To my amazement, the church was filled to overflowing.

I don't remember any of the ceremony, except the Protestant minister gave a beautiful tribute to a fine man, and the Catholic priest performed a traditional funeral mass. I felt the eyes of all my friends from New York City, my family from Chicago, and my new friends from Middlebury. Bob had had a wide circle of business and professional friends, and they were all there as well. I walked out of the old stone church behind the polished wooden casket ornamented with a huge spray of sweetheart roses, similar to what my father had had placed on my mother's coffin. I held my children's hands. My friend Jody said no one would ever forget the sweet look on my face as I held my children's hands while walking behind the casket.

I had had the minister invite everyone to our pretty home, with its floor-to-ceiling windows overlooking a winter scene of gardens, fields, and woods. The townspeople brought an abundance of food of all kinds. My dear friends from New York City came out to help with all the details. My sister, Margie, had flown in right away, and my father and all my Chicago family were there. I greeted everyone with my children in front of our newly installed white marble mantel. Flowers were everywhere. I was overwhelmed by the turnout.

My son, Bob, age eleven, came in from playing in the snow outside and said, "Okay, it's time for all this to stop and for Daddy to come home."

Betsy-Bond, age fourteen, said, "We prayed to God to protect Daddy, and he didn't."

One of Bob's business associates said I acted as though I did not know what had happened to me, to us. He was right.

My sister-in-law Becky, my brother Bobby's wife, came out to help. Many friends stayed close to me. Susie kept calling to see if I was okay. John and Jody invited us to be with them many times. Marianne and Dyke helped us in many ways.

My father wrote me a beautiful letter: "Bob's death is like a great oak tree falling in the forest. Bob was a man of integrity and caring who had a great faith and lived it. He did the work of three men at his office. What a shame when everyone in a family is working together that it is torn apart." I received more than one hundred letters.

We could not bury Bob because the ground was frozen. We had to wait till spring. I arranged to buy a large gray granite stone, and in addition to his name and dates, I had the following verse engraved: "The Lord knows the way that we take and when we have been tried, we shall come forth as gold" (Job 23:10). It was the verse that had kept us going through so many years, believing things could work out for us. They had—until now. I thought about Bob's taking me to St. Patrick's before we were married and asking the Mother Mary to bless us. She had but no longer.

A couple from our group at St. Thomas's Church in New York, Diana and Joe, arranged for a private mass for Bob with our friends a couple of months later. I sat in the pew with my children on either side of me, holding their small, vulnerable hands. We looked at each other and shivered, wondering how we would get through the sad ceremony and beyond.

Bob's professional organization, the American Institute of Chemical Engineers, held a luncheon in his memory and announced they were going to initiate two annual awards in his memory. They gave me a handsome hand-engraved memorial in a gold frame. I thought at the time I shouldn't take the children out of school and drag them down to New York City for a luncheon, but maybe I should have had them with me.

The devastation slowly crept deeper and deeper within me, past all the surface annoyances, until it hit the umbilical cord that had grown between Bob and me throughout our fifteen and a half years of devotion to each other. Now the cord was severed. We had become more a part of each other than I had known.

I was terribly concerned for my children and wanted them to go right back to school. I did not want them to miss a beat or fall behind. I wanted to assure them their lives would go on. They needed a strong mother to reassure them. It scared them when I cried. They both soldiered on. I did as well.

At the reception at our home after the funeral, my husband's boss at Union Carbide handed me an envelope with a letter he had found in Bob's desk. On the outside, Bob had written, "For my wife in the event of my death."

My dearest Elizabeth,

Since you will read this letter only in the circumstances that I am no longer with you, it has a sadness connected to it—but please, darling, try to think of it as I am doing right now—as just sort of an insurance policy for you and the children. I do not write it with any feeling that there is an urgent need for it and, in fact, feel great right now and expect to be "husband and daddy" for a long time yet. But we do not know God's plan for us so I am writing down some facts and information that would, I think, help you with those things you would have to face if I were suddenly to no longer be here with you.

I will try to write these notes in two parts, the first being this "cover letter" that is meant for you alone. All the really personal things I will try to write down here. Then I will "attach" a second part that will cover non-personal things. That way, you can use the second part openly with those to whom you would turn—your father, brothers, lawyer, etc.

First of all, my dearest love, know forever that I have loved you completely and deeply all those years—those wonderful years—we had together. You were, as I said to you on the eve of our wedding, my life. Through all the troubles we faced, in all those happy successes we had and always in the day-to-day progress we made together along life's path, you were my staff and strength—my beloved Elizabeth. No one can ever take that gift from God away from either of us. Thank you, my darling, for *all of that* and for your love.

Second, darling, I would like to ask that you try as best you can to convey to dear Betsy-Bond and precious Bob-Roy that their Daddy loved them very dearly and wishes he could live to see *all* of their lives—but that God knows best for us all and wanted it another way.

They both brought such great quantities of sunshine and pride into my life. If you can, dear, try to bring into their minds memories of me they can keep and cherish; as I have done with my Mother and Father. We have lots of pictures—and even movies—of happy times together. Make up a set for each of them to remember me as much as they can.

Thirdly, sweetheart, please know that I want you to go out from our life and do what is most necessary—make a new life of happiness for you and the children. This includes finding, as you should, another man to whom you can give love and from whom you can receive it. If that comes, we both know it is God's way.

It will be very hard for you for a while darling, but our dear Lord will help you and I have tried to ease the burden financially at least. *Go slowly*—take your time. Keep a stability in your home and relationships until a rational stability replaces the emotion of the initial moments. Then your good judgment will take care of you.

All My Love—Always,
"Your Robert"

I clung to that letter as to a lifeline. *Don't do anything quickly. Keep stability in your home and in your relationships.* I would eventually find my way. That letter eased the terror of being on my own.

Bob was wrong about a few things, one being that I should keep all my relationships the same. Every relationship instantly changed. No one treated me as the person I had been before. I had to begin to forge a different identity, because I was no longer a married woman. I was that scary word: *widow*.

I was forty-three years old, with an eleven-year-old son and a fourteen-year-old daughter, living in a new community with no family around and little anywhere else. My dear mother was gone, and Nana Jacks had died. I would have adored her help, but I was grateful she had not lived to see her only son killed. I was well educated but had no career, having given up working when I married and became a mother. My husband had left me comfortable but not wealthy, and I wondered where to start. I cried out for help in the dark.

Betsy and her two children as a recent widow, 1984.

CHAPTER 18

A Cork in the Ocean Tenants Harbor and New York 1984-1989

In Tenants Harbor, Maine, the inhabitants get on edge when a northeaster is coming. The sky darkens, the waves grow, the wind howls, and everyone heads for shelter. Storms out of the northeast are powerful and violent. The lobstermen and sailors pull in their boats or move them to a safer harbor and secure them. Boats left in the harbor can be pulled off their moorings and sent adrift, possibly to smash on the rocks.

A northeaster had hit our family so suddenly there had been no time to head for shelter. The car had crashed and instantly ended Bob's life, smashing our family in the aftermath. The carefully constructed life we had built together had toppled like a house of cards.

The letter Bob had left for me with his boss to be given to me in the event of his death became my mooring in a storm. It told me he loved me unconditionally and advised me not to make any hasty decisions, to keep everything the same for at least a year, and to care for the children.

He needn't have worried about my caring for our children. They returned to their schools the day they reopened after the holidays, and I tirelessly drove them to sports, play practice, 6:00 a.m. ice hockey, tennis lessons, playdates, doctor's appointments—everything and anything I could think of. Maybe I didn't want to leave empty time.

When the children were in school, I tackled the mound of legal and financial issues and papers presented to me. I was the executor of Bob's estate and had to pull together all the information, the insurance, the cases involving the automobile accident, the investments, and much more. Since the cause of death was an automobile accident, there were suits and countersuits filed that went on for years. A sheriff had come to our house and handed me a suit from the people in the other car in the crash, who had barely been hurt. My son exclaimed, "That's not fair!" He was right, but it was reality.

Bob had always managed the finances of the family. Suddenly, I was on my own. I did not know what to do, and nothing had been arranged. It had all been too sudden.

Bob had handled many things around the house: fixing the cars, paying the bills, shoveling the walks, and paying the taxes. Everything became my responsibility. I needed to find a team of professionals to help me. I had to figure it out. The local doctor said, "I don't know what keeps you going, but you are a good woman." What kept me going was that I wanted to survive, and more importantly, I wanted my children to continue to thrive.

The first weeks were awful. I knew I needed to stay in the small Connecticut community to find some stable ground before thinking of doing anything else. I sought help from a local minister, who said, "If I were free, I would come camp on your doorstep." I never went to see him again. Even ministers have trouble in knowing what to say to a young widow.

Like a cork in the sea, I was having trouble finding a firm mooring. Once, at a cocktail party, when I started a simple and innocent conversation with one of the men there, his wife came right over and took him away. I had not the slightest interest in my head about the man; I was just trying to make a conversation so I was not standing there alone. Such things had never happened to me before. Was I really such a seductive beauty? Then I had to go home alone in the dark.

One night, after the children were finally asleep, I sat down in the living room, knowing I had to do something. The loneliness and emptiness were unbearable. What did I want to do? I remembered I had always wanted to understand and know more about my missionary grandparents, so I decided to enroll at Yale Divinity School and take a course on missionaries. The mystery of what had happened in India intrigued me, and having my past to investigate felt like a rope line of help in the storm, a way forward.

However, I had to get there, and the drive was about forty-five minutes by car. After what had happened to Bob, I was afraid to drive alone at night, so starting in late January, just a month after Bob had been killed,

I hired a local police officer to drive me back and forth in his off-hours. I sat in the backseat and felt safe. It was a job for the police officer, who was professional and polite. I felt lucky to find someone willing to help me. The course at Yale Divinity School about the history of missionaries was dull, talking about the devolution of leadership in the missionary movements in China and India, but going to classes provided a much-needed structure for my days.

I also took a course called Ethics of Commitment, which covered commitment, loyalty, honesty, faithfulness, purity, and time. I ended up writing a history of my marriage, so at least I would better understand where I had been. The essay, for Margaret Farley, a renowned professor of social ethics in the Yale Divinity School, turned out to be both helpful and reassuring: Bob and I had been committed and faithful, which had given us time to build a strong, if imperfect, relationship. Fifteen and a half years had knitted us together in deeper ways than I had understood. After writing that history, I could appreciate even more deeply why I was torn apart.

"What are you doing writing a history of your marriage now?" asked an old friend. "Why aren't you looking for a job and maybe a new husband?" She didn't understand that I needed to heal and that it would take time. It made me feel alone that even a good friend didn't understand. If you don't have a firm connection to anything, you can't go on.

At the end of the school year, faced with the summer, I sent both children away to camp. Yes, I continued sending my children away. I was lonely without them but afraid that if I kept them home, there would not be enough for them to do. I decided camp would be healthier for them. Worried about their welfare, I continually told them what to do instead of listening to them, which would have brought us closer together. I didn't know better.

In the middle of August, after camp, we three made the trek to Maine with our dog, Pepper, in a cage; our cat, Mittens, lying on the seat beside us; and luggage tied to the top of the car. I felt like a pioneer woman. I wasn't used to being in the driver's seat, but I had to do it.

Since I had placed a copy of Bob's obituary in the local Maine paper, the *Courier Gazette*, people would know before I arrived what had happened. Old family friends Ellen and Jack had called at the time, and dear Everett, our caretaker, had gotten the water turned on and found a woman to clean the house and make up our beds.

The harbor was again blue, lavender and gold, but the old sail loft, our family summer home, looked abandoned. The paint was peeling, and the steps were rickety. Inside, the wallpaper was spotted and water-stained. The roof and plumbing leaked. Everything still needed fixing—us and the house.

Our refuge was June and Everett's home, where we visited daily. June was Everett's childhood sweetheart and longtime wife and the lighthouse keeper's daughter from Southern Island, where Jamie Wyeth now resided. June had sore hips, which she refused to get replaced, so she was lame and always in the rocking chair on their sunporch, where she primarily lived with her seven cats, their food and litter boxes, stacks of old newspapers and magazines, and all the attendant smells. The house was small, crowded, and a mess, but we were happy there. June was always welcoming and busy, making things for us, such as stationery made with pussy willows glued to pieces of paper or cartoons cut from the paper. She listened to us, providing what we didn't have at home.

Everett watched over us. Once, the owner of a bed-and-breakfast up the street tried to come calling on me, saying that although he was still married, he was estranged and would be interested in courting. Everett swept him out of the house, even though he never threw anything else away.

The town manager came over to say he was sorry about Mr. Jacks and then asked, "Are you ever going to spend more than two weeks a year in Tenants Harbor? You know, this town needs to be for the people who are living here now." It rankled him that I owned the sail loft and seldom used it. I didn't know how to convey how much his little village meant to me and my family—even though we were seldom there physically, an essential part of our spirits had been there for generations.

To keep the children busy, I found a sailing program for them in a nearby town. I went to the courthouse in Rockland to research all that had gone on in Tenants Harbor with my family, understand the old deeds that would explain the complications with the road and the rest of the boundaries, and look into the old wills. I wanted to understand for myself the fight of the previous generation.

At the sail loft, I went to work in trying to paint and scrape the parts of the outside I could reach, just as I was trying to fix the parts of my life I could begin to touch. I wanted everything to look better. Both children joined in to help when not sailing. We painted and scraped some of the peeling paint on the inside. None of us wanted to think or feel too much.

We kept trying to live each day the way we always had. The children enjoyed playing on the rocks down by the water, picking apples to make apple pies, and playing baseball out back, but it wasn't enough.

"Mom, it's no fun around here without lots of people," Bob-Roy complained. I think he was saying it was terrible without Dad, but he never said the word *Dad*. Betsy-Bond tried to plant a garden. She wanted something new to grow, something beautiful. Enough of so much sadness. A garden would be beautiful. I kept trying to be both parents, but I couldn't.

We invited up a family from Middlebury, and we took them to the abandoned granite quarry filled with fresh water for a swim. My son showed them how he could jump off the highest cliffs of the quarry into the water. "Oh, I get it," said the lady from Middlebury. "The worst has already happened, so one might as well jump off the cliffs."

The tensions with the town left over from my mother's fight with her cousin and the disputed ownership of Front Street surfaced before we left for the summer. I became angry and frustrated from dealing with the undefined boundaries, the double ownership of the ball field, and the road that was ours but used by the town, but then summer was over, and we packed up and returned to Connecticut. Everett turned off the water and closed up the house for us for another year.

It was important that the old building stood. Even though we were going away again, just as Clara, my grandmother, and Betty, my mother, had left long ago, it was a connection to our past, and it was part of us. It had withstood many northeasters, and even though it needed repair, it was still standing strong. Clara, Betty, and I all clung to that old building as a lifeline, a connection, for generations. However, everything would have to wait for another summer, with nothing settled in Maine and everything unsettled in our lives: the estate, the management of our funds, and where we should live.

In the fall, both children went off to boarding school. They didn't go across the ocean, as my uncles Charlie and Albert had from their home in India, or five hundred miles away, as their grandmother had, but they went away just the same. They went to Taft, a boarding school a little more than six miles from Middlebury, in Watertown, Connecticut. Taft promised to give them an excellent education and to take care of them.

It turned out Taft gave them that excellent education, but the children were hurting and needed something more. Their first priority was survival, and Taft provided the framework. They also needed to mourn, but healing came only slowly, with time. No one knew how to mourn.

With the children away, I was alone in the beautiful but isolated and lonely house in Connecticut. I hated coming into that house at night—it was dark, silent, and empty. I stood there and shivered in the dark. I had to do something. I returned to New York City and sublet a one-bedroom apartment on the Upper East Side for the school year. I switched from Yale Divinity School to Union Theological Seminary on Manhattan's Upper West Side, hoping to find my way. Union had told me I would have to prove myself as a student before I could matriculate, but I could start by taking some courses.

On an early September day a year and a half after that icy road in Vermont, I walked up to an imposing Gothic gray stone building, a formidable and forbidding structure. I wore a pretty cotton summer dress with heels and pearls, my standard Connecticut housewife's outfit. I was greeted by an array of students in jeans and T-shirts who were ten to twenty years younger than I. I walked down the long halls lined with wooden and glass doors, looking for room 203. It turned out to be the largest classroom.

Everyone else was seated when I walked in, and I saw only their backs. I surveyed the room and saw one back with a tweed sports jacket next to an empty seat, somehow a kind of familiar mooring in the sea of the strange and unknown. I sat there. The tweed jacket turned out to be a lawyer in the middle of a messy divorce, also searching, who became the friend I needed for a while, though ultimately, he had a different set of values, and I had to flee out into the loneliness once more.

That first day, the professor spoke about the study of the scriptures. "All of you will have your cherished beliefs questioned by the findings of the academic examination of the scriptures. When you come to understand such findings as who wrote the Old and the New Testaments, under what circumstances, in what context, and with what intent, the meaning changes. You will confront what you have always thought and believed. You might be shaken for a while, but finally, you'll be more deeply grounded. The old saying that an unexamined life is not worth living can be turned to say the same thing about an unexamined belief system."

I listened to the distinguished professor and knew I had to be one of those who stayed with the process until I could find something new. My carefully constructed life had been blown apart and toppled. I had clung to the household codes in the biblical texts as a guide during all the years of my marriage that said wives should be faithful and husbands should love their wives. Yes, we had indeed prospered despite all our shortcomings. But it had all been smashed; none of it applied any longer. I had no one to be faithful to. I was filled with pain.

I met Cardinal Koenig of Austria at a conference, and he and I had a heart-to-heart. I told him, "I still have faith that there is something left for me in this life as a single woman, but I have no idea what it is."

"My dear," he answered, "that is your mission". I did hear later that only when there is a fire in the forest can new growth appear.

I started doing the assignments at Union but was rusty. I had not been a student for more than twenty-five years, and I feared I couldn't do it anymore. The Old Testament teacher assigned a twenty-five-page paper analyzing one of the chapters. I was paralyzed. A friend, the one I had to run away from later, sat with me and took me through the assignment step by step just to get it done. "Since I don't want you to leave," he said with a smile, "I will help you." The paper was acceptable, and my confidence began to build.

I practically lived in the library, the way I had done at Vassar, and loved learning again. The Psychology and Religion course helped me articulate things about my life. I had believed that by my being good, life would go well for me. From the time I was a small child, I had looked around to see what the people in my life expected of me and tried to comply. I'd tried to be good. It was the way to be loved: to be a pleaser. I wondered if Uncle Charlie, my mother's brother who had committed suicide, had been a pleaser too. Everyone said how good he had been, but something deep had been missing inside. I felt something missing deep inside me. Being good was not enough.

My theology professor asked me to write a paper describing where I found God in my life. I realized that God had been in the scriptures. My authority was the Word of God in the scripture, and it had seemingly worked—but no longer. I kept asking how an all-powerful God could allow my good, innocent husband to be killed. My mind couldn't make sense of what had happened.

The halls of Union Seminary were filled with young students wanting to be ministers, and I just wanted to heal. Several of the students tried to minister to me, asking what was wrong and how they could help. I decided I would humble myself and take comfort from whomever offered it. My professor for Psychology and Religion said, "Pick up the crumbs, and they will feed you." I picked up the offerings and often felt a little better.

At the end of my first year at Union, I sublet a two-bedroom apartment on a high floor with views and a fireplace at Manhattan House on Sixty-Sixth Street on the Upper East Side. Both children preferred staying in Manhattan, where they had friends, to the house in Connecticut. They took part-time jobs as mothers' helpers or in offices in New York for the first part of the summer. Toward the end of the summer, we went to Maine. My son asked me why I was studying theology rather than getting a job, and my daughter went more and more off on her own, but I had to find my own way. I was too upset to be able to get a job.

I signed up to take CPE, clinical pastoral education, during the summer, a program that trains seminary students to be hospital chaplains. I was in a small group led by a Union professor and pastoral counselor named Dr. Russell Davis. The group included a Franciscan monk, a Jesuit priest, and a Catholic priest. We spent each morning discussing how to be of comfort to the people in the hospital we were assigned and spent each afternoon in the hospital, talking with patients on the wards or just being with them as they talked. I found myself clinging to the Franciscan monk for comfort. He was a light-brown-haired Polish monk about fifteen years my junior but happily became my support. As part of our training, we were asked to watch open-heart surgery. Draped in a surgical cover-up, I held his hand tightly just to get strength to watch.

One morning, it was my turn to have a private supervisory hour with the leader, Dr. Davis. We sat down across from each other in a small yellow room. I was startled to see tears running down his face. He looked at me with great compassion and said, "You are an abandoned woman, and it is very sad."

I stared at him.

"I have been thinking not only about your late husband but also your father."

I continued to look at him in silence. This was the unmentionable thing I had never wanted to feel. I sat there and said nothing. He continued as a presence with me in great compassion.

We sat in silence for a long time, and finally, I said thank you and left. I walked around the hospital that afternoon and began to feel lighter. Naming the unmentionable had made me feel better.

That afternoon, I visited patients struggling with enormously difficult diseases, such as a middle-aged lady with multiple amputations caused by diabetes. I found myself able to quietly sit with her and hold her hand. She told me how happy she was that I was there.

My children returned to school in the fall, and I returned to Union. In another two years, I completed the master of divinity degree. In those remaining two years, I continued to heal. I sought out counseling and, for the first time, began to confront and to feel my feelings. A PhD student needed a counselee, and I volunteered. Every week, I went and cried in her office, telling her how scared, lonely, and overwhelmed I felt. She listened. I had a new idea: I would become a counselor myself, so I could help others the way she was helping me. She told me once, "Do you know how moving it is to me to listen to you every week?"

I was beginning to heal by thinking new thoughts inspired by the great thinkers who had grappled with the same questions I had, such as why an omnipotent God would allow a good man, such as Bob Jacks, to be killed. I came to see that no one had ever had a satisfactory answer to that question. The great Dr. Morris, professor of church history at Union Seminary, said, "You are called to withstand, not understand." The religious leaders who found peace and joy entered into a spiritual practice, a daily practice of prayer, meditation, and readings.

In the handsomely paneled, tall-ceilinged reading room of the Union Seminary library, I studied the great philosopher Kierkegaard, who theorized that people pass from a rigid belief system and a strict morality to self-giving love through a long process of development, pushed by periods of disruption and anxiety. It was a description of my life: a progression from finding authority outside myself to finding it inside myself. I was being beaconed to a freer life of joy. We are called not so much to be good, which is someone else's definition of life, as to love, which is an act of giving.

The dark waters were providing a passage to a more grounded life. My hope began to reemerge as I turned to a daily practice of attending worship service. I remembered the verse in the window in Maine about the living water. I sat and listened, cried, prayed, and found comfort, but I still went home every night to my lonely apartment. Often, I would have dinner at a cafeteria nearby and stay in the library late, delaying going home as long as possible. One time, I decided to drive out of town to my house in Connecticut by myself, leaving at ten o'clock at night. An old friend exclaimed, "You can't do that! What would Bob have thought?"

"But he is not here," I answered.

One noontime, I was coming out of a Good Friday worship service at Union's chapel, in which the preacher had spoken about Christ on the cross: "My God, my God, why have you abandoned me?" The great pastor and my professor of preaching at Union, Dr. James Forbes, an African American who soon was to be appointed pastor of the famous Riverside Church, tapped me on the shoulder and said, "I know you know what they are talking about in there, and you know things that others would like to know, but it has been too hard on you—you can't take any pride in it." Dr. Forbes, with his loving and understanding spirit, had seen into the depths of my pain in the abandonment that was widowhood. He had seen me. He understood that I understood the Good Friday gospel to a degree my fellow students would perhaps have liked to understand it.

I looked at him in stunned silence. My whole body went into shock. I froze and then ran through the dining room, trying to find a place to gather myself. A couple of people asked what was the matter, but I just kept running. A stairway at the end of the dining hall led down to a small empty chapel. I entered the chapel, closed the door, and lay down on the floor. I tried to grasp what I was experiencing. I was in shock but wide open to the experience of the moment. Dr. Forbes's words had pierced all my layers of armor, right to my most inner self.

I was in a daze, and then I began to sense another presence with me. I wondered if I was hallucinating. There was no one else in the chapel. Was this the Holy Spirit with me? I had read accounts by medieval mystics of feeling the presence of the Holy Spirit, but this was the first time anything like this had ever happened to me. It was unmistakable. I was surrounded by a loving presence. I was not alone. I had the sense the presence knew me and accepted me completely. I trusted that spirit and was open with it. I had the feeling I knew the presence as well. I had hidden all my life, but here was total openness, a loving presence with me. Joy spread through my body and soul. My life, broken apart, had found a new kind of unity.

I thought again of the Tenants Harbor church window. A loving presence had found me. I was in awe. I was experiencing something that didn't make rational sense but was so real that I knew I was forever changed, joyful and free. I felt the spiritual union often sung about. I was no longer alone. I was no longer abandoned.

After that mystical experience, I was filled with smiles. I had been so needy that people ran from me. Now I met people, and they were drawn to me. I was amazed at the change both within me and without. "Betsy, you are radiant. What has happened to you?" friends would ask. Old friends from my married community began to introduce me to their widower friends. My phone began to ring with people asking me to dinner, the theater, and concerts. It continued to amaze me that life could be so changed.

In my heart, I knew I had to write about my healing journey for my master of divinity degree. I researched mystical experience through the ages in the church and found various theorists, such as William James, who, in *The Nature of Religious Experience*, described what I had experienced. He said mystical experience had been known through the ages: it was not explainable, it was always a surprise, it was powerful, it was life-transforming, it could not be brought on at will, and it could not be repeated.

I looked into psychological writings to try to explain how my personality had changed when I transitioned from following an authority outside myself to having my own inner voice to follow. I found the process of writing grueling. I had to do it, but I didn't know if I could. I just kept going, trying, writing, sweating, and pounding away at my typewriter. I sought the great hope sung by the psalmists:

Thou has turned for me my mourning into dancing.
Thou hast loosed my sackcloth and girded me with gladness,
That my soul may praise thee and not be silent. (Psalm 30:11)

I kept thinking of the people who had gone before me who had not been healed: Clarissa, who had died of pneumonia when her parents forbid to marry; Great-Grandfather Whitney Long, who had died an alcoholic; and Uncle Charlie, who had committed suicide. Had Charlie felt as I had felt when he was left in Canada for nine years without seeing his parents, with Albert gone to war, and perhaps with a girl saying she never wanted to see him again? Had my mother felt abandoned as an eight-year-old girl left at boarding school for ten months at a time without seeing her parents? Was this how she had felt when Dad said he wanted to call off the wedding? Was this how I had felt all my life? Always told by my father to go away. Always told by my mother to go play so she could work. *Abandoned*—what a word! The great tragedy of Bob's being killed was abandonment.

I dared to hope that my healing was for them all. They had not had all the help I was given: the wisdom of ages at the seminary, the skillful counselors and pastors, and the mystical experience. I knew I was called to share what I had learned and experienced. It was not just for me; I also thought of my mother, whose spirit had been transformed in the end.

My master's thesis received honors. I could hardly believe it. The journey had taken me far in mind, heart, and spirit. I could choose what I wanted to do, and I chose to be trained as a counselor to work with others through their trials. In freedom, I could fall in love.

My son and daughter came to my Union Theological Seminary graduation, which was held in Union's handsome Gothic courtyard filled with spring flowers on a warm and sunny June day. My children snapped pictures the way I had at my daughter's 1984 Taft graduation and 1989 Duke graduation and my son's 1988 Taft graduation (and the way I eventually would at my son's 1992 Duke graduation). We all three were honor students. What a triumph!

Still, I felt lonely and terrible about not being in close communication with my children. Like Clara before me with her children or Betty with her children, I knew about academic excellence but not enough about connection. I did not know how to close the gaping hole in our relationships. When I heard them talk about me, it was mostly "My silly mother." Sometimes my son would say, "Mother, I am your son." I would always look at him with confusion, because I kept doing everything I knew to do for him, yet he did not feel connected to me. I would never give up. I would keep trying.

CHAPTER 19

Marriage to Al, Maine, 1991

After graduating from Duke with degrees in painting and art history, my daughter, Betsy, came back to New York City and tried several careers involving art, including working at a gallery, interior decorating, and full-time painting. She soon realized she needed more education and took an MBA in marketing at Kellogg's School of Business at Northwestern University. She became the director of marketing at the Whitney Museum and later the executive director of the Thomas Cole National Historic Site in Catskill, New York, where she has been able to use her love of art to guide the development of a museum.

My son, Bob, graduated from Duke in engineering; received a master's in engineering management from Stanford University; and, after working for a few years, received an MBA from Columbia University. He entered the pharmaceutical industry, working for Pfizer, and after a few years, he left Pfizer and became president of a small start-up biotech company, where he has gained immense satisfaction.

The children were going on in their lives beautifully—college, graduate school, good jobs—but the distance in our relationships bothered me enormously. I wanted to find a way to be close to them and be connected, as well as to be full and happy within myself. Despite the healing of my grief, I knew I still had more of a journey to finally be fully healed from all the things I had experienced as a child.

I wanted to move on with my life. I decided I would become a therapist to work with others struggling as I had struggled. I would be a wounded healer. Needing a state license in order to be a therapist and see patients in a private office, I enrolled in Hunter College's School of Social Work. At the same time, to my amazement, my social life began to pick up.

My social life was like the marine world of Tenants Harbor. For months, the harbor was empty. Then the mackerel ran, and they came in abundance. When the mackerel were in, one just had to put a shiny hook in the water, and four or five mackerel would swirl about. That seemed to be what was happening to me. Friends introduced me to their widowed or divorced friends, who would call the next day to ask me to dinner. Just a few years before, people had swum the other way. Going through grief had freed me to have something to give to another person.

One of the widowers was Al, introduced to me by my loyal friend Susie in New York City. I was immediately attracted to him, like one of those mackerel and the shiny hook. Al was ten years older than I and a recent widower when I met him. It was too soon for him to want to know anyone else, so it was three years before I started to see him. He had two children a bit older than mine, to whom he was devoted. He was a lawyer who had gone into business and become an entrepreneur. He had started an investment bank in New York and a company that rented and sold big equipment in the South. He was a tall, handsome gentleman with warm blue eyes, and he was conservative and creative, with a deep kindness and compassion in his soul. He loved antiques, his farm in the country, and the natural world. My children liked him right away.

When we finally started seeing each other, he took me to dinner at the Carlyle Hotel, an elegant restaurant, where we sat on a banquette under big arrangements of fresh flowers, and to the antiques show at the Armory on Park Avenue. Later, we often went to dinner and dancing at Doubles, a private nightclub in the lower level of the Sherry Netherlands Hotel in Manhattan. More than once, we shut it down at two o'clock in the morning.

After we dated for a couple of years, Al said he wanted to show me his farm in Columbia County, New York. It had lovely rolling hills and beautiful views of the Catskill Mountains. It was springtime, and there was a full moon. We took a walk along his roadway, and he said, "Betsy, I think we should get married. Will you marry me?"

I didn't answer him immediately. It was a big step. He had taken a long time in coming to that decision, and I decided to take my time. However, I didn't need much. Before the weekend was over, I told him, "I would love to marry you." Al was older, as Bob had been, and had a farm, as my father did, but he was different from them both. We set the wedding for August 24, 1991, in Tenants Harbor. We wanted our four children to be our attendants. I wanted to celebrate the beginning of a new life on the old sail loft property, and Al agreed.

I was required to go to the town office in Tenants Harbor for a wedding license thirty days in advance. I was almost afraid to walk in, with all the history of animosity, but I went with hat in hand to follow the law. I wanted to be married in Tenants Harbor despite what anyone from the town might think. It was my emotional home. Love won out.

Al had two requests if we were to be married at the old sail loft: "Please take the bathroom out of the hallway, and buy a dishwasher." The building had not been changed since my grandmother Clara had lived there as a widow huddled around her cream-and-apple-green cookstove. It was time to put the past behind and reconfigure the sail loft for our new life together. I lifted Clara's handmade black silk coat from India out of the closet and brought it to New York. I would find a new use for it. I moved the cookstove to the kitchen.

My daughter, Betsy, joined in the celebration to make the old building sparkle. On the dining room wall, she painted a mural of her favorite buildings in the area, including the Marshall Point Lighthouse. That was like a beacon for the new marriage, with the breezy apple trees on our front lawn forming a canopy over the village houses like the new canopy over our lives. She scraped off the old, peeling wallpaper and painted the walls a pure white. She sent the antique couch out to have its ripped orange upholstery recovered in new white fabric. Carpenters made the two apartments on the second floor into one comfortable apartment.

In the woods on Long Cove, above Tenants Harbor, stood an unpainted wooden chapel with a steeple bell tower where Episcopalian priests visiting during the summer gave services. When jammed to capacity, it held eighty people. I used to attend the sweet chapel with my parents and, later, my children. I wished to be married there.

The senior warden, the layperson in the Episcopal church who is in charge, was Forrester Smith, a Smith from across the harbor, the old-line summer community who traditionally had nothing to do with the people living on my side of the harbor, the townies. When I told him I would like to get married in the Long Cove Chapel, he replied, "We welcome weddings, but I cannot be present because I'm so busy." I thought to myself that he wasn't sure he wanted to know us.

We asked Al's brother-in-law, an Episcopalian priest, to officiate. Al's wife, Anne, had died five years previously from cancer, and it had been terrible, but all her relatives were coming to the wedding. It was hard for Al's daughter, Carolyn, to see her father remarry, and she ended up crying at the wedding, but her sadness could not dampen the joyous occasion for Al and me. Local cooks made their favorite fish casseroles, poached salmon came from the lobster wharf next door, and a local baker made three large wedding cakes—blueberry, bourbon, and carrot. The baker poured extra bourbon onto the large yellow sponge cake, and people still remember it today. Our matchmaker, Susie, came and brought a brass band with her as a wedding present to play at our rehearsal dinner, a lobster bake on the shore.

Another local lady picked armfuls of wildflowers—Queen Anne's lace, black-eyed Susan, yellow yarrow, and goldenrod—and decorated the church and the sail loft. My sister-in-law Becky picked heather off the shore and made boutonnieres for the groom and the best men—our two sons—and wildflower bouquets for our bridesmaids—our two daughters, who wore white dresses. I wore a white silk dress covered with spring flowers.

When I contacted a local photographer, he asked who was getting married, and I replied, "I am," not realizing it is not every day that a fifty-year-old mother marries a sixty-year-old father with such fanfare.

"What a handsome, kind, distinguished, dapper man!" he exclaimed when I showed him Al's picture.

The wedding plans were coming together, when the news announced that Hurricane Bob was on its way. When the hurricane tore through the area a few days before the wedding, we all took cover from the winds and storm. The town docks were torn from their moorings and landed on our rocky beach. Boats not taken out of the water broke from their moorings and floated loose. When the winds were sixty miles an hour, we went outside and leaned into the wind. It held us up. We held each other and crawled back inside. What did it mean that a hurricane preceded our wedding? We wondered if this terrific storm was cleaning out all the old air the way my life had now been cleaned out.

The hurricane winds and rain indeed cleared out the air and watered the ground. Fresh, clear weather arrived in time for the wedding weekend, plus a full moon. One hundred people came, including my ninety-four-year-old father from Chicago, who walked me down the aisle. My sister made a wedding quilt, and my two brothers were the ushers. Our four children, their friends, my friends, Al's friends, local friends, out-of-towners, and even Forrester Smith joined the celebration. Forrester ended up finding some people he knew and stayed the whole time, deciding we were acceptable after all. He even began to introduce us to his family and friends on the other side of the harbor, as well as others from around the area. The harbor, the house, the two of us—all were becoming united. Within a few years of Al's and my wedding, all four of the children were married in lovely ceremonies of their own.

We had champagne on our front lawn and a band for dancing. "Won't some of the locals be upset with me about all the noise?" I asked one of the grandmotherly local cooks in her white shirt, black pants, and frilly flowered apron.

"Don't worry about that," she replied.

Everett, our beloved caretaker, had spent the summer making us a flagpole as a wedding present. He'd cut down a spruce sapling in the woods, scraped the bark by hand, let it dry, and strung it with a rope. He set it up on that clear August day. The Stars and Stripes waved for the first time at the now shined-up summer home. June, Everett's wife, dug deep into her trunk and gave us a great treasure: a cream-colored popcorn bedspread that she, the daughter of the lighthouse keeper, had crocheted during the long winters on Southern Island. I was overwhelmed with the love that poured forth from Everett and June. Their material goods were meager, but their lives were deep and abundant. Their love had done so much to pull us through.

I married Al with great joy and overflowing happiness. The blues and golds of the glowing harbor had beaconed me on and brought me to a place of renewal. The tides had gone out and now had come back in. I had no idea the tide would go out again. I had no inkling how much more I had to learn, with more healing to endure, another long journey to take, and mountains to climb.

CHAPTER 20

Early Years of New Marriage
New York 1996

*You must love yourself before you love another. By accepting
yourself and fully being what you are, your simple presence can
make others happy.*

Anonymous

As newlyweds, we spent weekends up at Al's farm in the Hudson
Valley, which he owned with his sister, and weekdays in New York City,
living in an apartment where he had lived with his deceased wife and raised
his two children. I felt there was no room for me. I was used to having my
own home, and now I was crowded into someone else's home. Despite my
being happy with Al and keeping myself busy with finishing a social work
degree, I started going into what Al affectionately called a *funk*. It was as
if a switch I couldn't control or get rid of went off inside me. "Excuse me,
but I am going for a walk," I would say to Al.

As I walked around the block, wandered into Central Park, sat on a
bench, or just kept walking, my thoughts went haywire: *Al hasn't really
married me; he is still emotionally married to his first wife. I should leave.* Anger
boiled up and spilled over. I couldn't repress the anger and put on a smile,
as I had as a child. My system wouldn't let me. It was as if a steam kettle
lid kept on tightly burst open as the pressure inside became too much.

The anger would last for a couple of days but would finally subside,
and I would go on with our life together until it happened again. I had a

complex—a walled-off or unconscious set of emotions and thoughts inside that, with the right stimulus or button, erupted into consciousness.

With all the tension I was feeling in trying to adjust to my new marriage, I enrolled in Hunter College's postgraduate family therapy training program, a part-time program that met weekly with required clinical work. Finding it hard to navigate our new blended family, I went back to school to find some new ideas, new theories, and people to talk to. It seemed my way. When I found myself in a situation I couldn't handle, I hoped new information would show me a new path.

The first night of class in a neon-lit classroom at the Hunter School of Social Work on East Seventy-Ninth Street in Manhattan, I raised my hand and said, "I am in a stepfamily, and I am finding my husband is more connected to his sister and the rest of his family than he is to me."

"Of course he is," replied the teacher. "He has known his sister all his life and you for just a few years. What do you expect?"

"But I wanted him to be more for me," I replied.

"A stepfamily, by its very nature, has a divided loyalty. Of course he is more connected to his own family than to you, his new wife. It will take time to build your new marriage."

I could understand the teacher's point intellectually, but it was hard to navigate emotionally. It slowly dawned on me the family therapy theories were not going to cure me. They helped me to understand the new situation I had entered in my life. We needed to take some action.

I talked with Al, and he lovingly agreed we needed to make space for our new marriage. He said he was willing to sell his family apartment and buy a new one, and we could buy a new farm together. We decorated the new apartment with a combination of furnishings from both our pasts, with fresh new colors and fabrics. It was thrilling to have a new space to organize our new life together.

We were able to buy a farm across the road from the old family farm, which seemed a great solution. We divided the ownership equally between our two families so it could serve as a project for our new marriage. "I am delighted we were able to buy this farm together, and I love our new apartment," said Al. We made sure we had space for all our children to visit.

As Al had done so much to accommodate his new wife, what happened next deeply surprised me. One weekend, my daughter and Al's son were visiting us in the Hudson Valley at our new farm, and Al wanted us to all go have dinner with his sister. That sounded like a reasonable request, but it hit a button in me that I didn't expect and didn't understand. I didn't want to be with his sister again. I suddenly came apart. I wanted to be loved alone, not part of a big family with his sister a frequent presence. I started to cry and went into the bedroom and curled up into a ball. My daughter came in.

"Mother, everyone is waiting for you."

"Al is always putting his sister's wishes first, and I think he needs to stop," I sniffed.

"Mother, you are the one who is wrong, not Al. You look ridiculous," said my daughter. She then left the room and went back to join the others.

I curled into a ball even tighter. How could my daughter say such a thing to me? I had tried so hard, but this from my daughter was unbearable. I'd thought she would take my side. With all the pain I was feeling, my daughter was telling me I was the one who was wrong! I never had thought I would hear such a thing. How could I be the one wrong? I knew better than to lash out. A part of my brain did not want to say anything I would later regret. Instead, I just stayed curled up. My daughter was saying I was wrong. Something was wrong with me. She was saying I was the one who needed fixing. It was a terrible blow. It was as if she had hit me, but she hadn't. She was telling me the truth I had to hear.

She left the bedroom, and I stayed curled up. Maybe this was the truth I had to hear to start on the journey of creating true loving relationships in my life—with my children, with Al, and with my new stepfamily. Was my daughter trying to find a way to reach out to me? My daughter had told me recently she was now going to tell me every time I made her mad. Although it hurt, I knew she was really trying.

A few minutes later, Al came in. "Everyone is waiting for us. Won't you please get up and come with us all to dinner at Bonnie's?" I let him pull me up. Something in me decided to get up, wash my face, put on some makeup, and go to dinner. Once there, my emotions calmed down, and I tolerated the evening.

I realized I had to be psychoanalyzed. What inside of me made it so hard to tolerate the complicated blended family? I knew that failure of my marriage was not an option, so I had to change. I was not going to run away and escape. Something was wrong with me. I had spent many years studying my grandparents in India and my parents, but I hadn't studied me. Al had made significant changes. Now it was up to me.

I enrolled in the Object Relations Psychoanalytic Training Institute, a six-year program in which one learned theory, saw patients, and had to be psychoanalyzed oneself. Object relations is a school of psychoanalysis, a variant of Freudian theory, developed largely in England by Donald Winnicott and Melanie Klein. *Object* is another word for "person," and the school studied how the relationships with significant people in one's life develop one's personality, especially the relationship between mother and baby. It examined how the nature of that attachment influences the emotional development of the baby. Winnicott talked about the true self and the false self. I had developed a false self and now had the possibility to develop a true self if I could stand the pain. Analysis meant going through more deep waters if I ever wanted to feel truly okay in this world.

I wanted to work with others but couldn't go on profound journeys with others and really be there in their pain, as Dr. Davis and Dr. Forbes had done with me, unless I went there first myself.

I found analysis excruciating. To talk about myself and my feelings was the opposite of what I had been taught as a child. I had been told to obey without asking questions and taught that other people had the answers. I always studied other people to see what to do. Now I had to get to know myself. Analysis was not something one did in a family such as mine. Even my name signified a different path: as the descendant of Colonel William Bond of the American Revolutionary War, who had died while fighting for his country at Bunker Hill, I was to value duty, honor, and obedience and maintain a stiff upper lip. Analysis was unfamiliar, and it felt humiliating, but I went ahead with it because I knew I had to in the hope that I would finally understand my emotions. I needed to learn not to have such overpowering reactions to certain situations, and I desperately wanted to have closer relationships with my children and not to ruin my relationship with Al.

I had faith that there was an answer if I searched hard enough.

Susan Kavaler-Adler, the founder of the institute, became not only my teacher but also my analyst. I started the process at about sixty years of age; Susan was in her fifties and a hard driver proud of the books she had written and the institute she had started. I wondered how interested she would be in someone like me, but she was an experienced analyst, so I put myself in her hands with deep trepidation.

Susan asked me to lie down on her couch in a small white-walled office while she sat behind my head so I couldn't see her. I hated it but felt I had to see it through to the end. My sister kept asking me, "Why are you doing something you hate so much that makes you feel even worse?" I was compelled to go forward.

I had to confront my enormous anxiety, anger, and shame at last. As a child, I had willingly and quickly turned against myself as a way to make sense of my father's and mother's constantly sending me away. In analysis, I had to face my feeling that neither had seemed to want me around, with Mom telling me to go play and Dad telling me he had other more important things to do.

My inner response to my parents was that something was fundamentally wrong with me. Shame and anxiety filled my soul. Blaming myself made the world seem safer and more predictable—the classic childhood defense of neglected or abused children. It is far scarier for children to think something is wrong with their parents than to think something is wrong with themselves. In children's minds, if something is wrong with themselves, they can fix it. But if the problem is with the parents, then the world is out of their control and terrifying. It became clear to me that my own inner world of anxiety and shame made it hard to be connected to my own children and to their father years before. I had not broken the cycle of dysfunctional parenting but was carrying on like Clara and Betty, filled with shame, projecting my feelings onto others. I had tried controlling my children the way my mother had controlled me. I was critical of my children, seeing them as extensions of myself, and since I wouldn't do, they wouldn't do.

I had worn the shame like a heavy weight on my back. I had studied other people to see what I had to do to make them love me. As a child, I had tried to hide or to please others. When I'd met people, I'd had the sickly feeling that something was wrong with me. In high school, a referee had had to stop me from raising my hand to take responsibility for committing a foul in basketball even before it was called. In college, I had expected my papers would come back Ds and had been surprised when they came back Bs. I always had thought I would not make the grade, whatever I was doing. Worse, I always had felt overall that I wouldn't do, as though there were fundamentally something wrong with me. All of this I had come to know about myself, but there was more. I still had to feel the feelings.

"Betsy, what are you feeling?" Susan asked one day.

"I feel alone, helpless, and something more—rotten all over," I answered.

"Can you picture where you are right now?" asked Susan.

"I feel very young. I sense I am in a dark place; I can sense barriers on either side of me, as though I am trapped and can't get out. Is it possible I have gone all the way back to my crib?"

"Yes, you have gone back. You know, our minds forget, but our bodies remember everything," said Susan.

"I want my mother, but she doesn't hear me. I start to cry hysterically."

"What's happening?" Susan said softly.

I suddenly stopped crying. "The thought flashed through my head that if I were better, my mother would come. I wasn't good enough for my mother to come."

"Betsy, breathe. Just tolerate how it feels, this shame."

Feelings I never wanted to feel came pouring forth. I turned against the wall and tried to hold myself for comfort. These feelings I'd felt as an infant had until now been trapped within me. I had never dreamed these intolerable feelings were lurking inside me all these years. They were worse than anything I had ever imagined. I had projected these feelings of self-hatred and shame onto my children, criticizing them the way my parents had criticized me.

Then suddenly the terribly painful feelings evaporated.

"Good work, Betsy," Susan said with compassion. "You were at the bottom of your darkness."

I breathed. Nothing more was said. I sat up and walked out of the office into the open air. I walked through Central Park, upset by all the painful emotions.

Such sessions went on for some time, but finally, spring came. New leaves, frilly and light green, budded on the old oaks above daffodils and bluebells. It was a long, slow process as Susan peeled away the layers, helping me go way back into my life and feel who I really was. Slowly, those primitive, terrifying feelings of fear, anger, and depression began to enter my conscious mind. In the evenings, back at my apartment, I ruminated. The feelings of shame did not go away completely, but they did lose their tight grip on me.

I had been learning a new place to go back to whenever I was filled with shame: to remember and know in my heart that I had been just an innocent child with an overburdened, overworked, lonely, depressed mother filled with her own secret shame and anxieties who had also turned on herself. She had spent her energy covering up her past of deep neglect from her own sickly, overburdened mother. When she had been sent to boarding school all alone at age eight, the experience had compounded the pain. The betrayal and shame of her brother Charlie's suicide had shut her down for life.

These patterns of neglect and feelings of shame had passed down through the generations from grandmother to mother to daughter. It was my cross to feel these intolerable feelings, bring them into the air, and digest them so the next generations could be free. I hoped my own children had been spared, not burdened with the same feelings. I came to understand those buried intolerable feelings had turned me into a narcissist. Feeling the intolerable had rooted me in my soul.

When I graduated from the Object Relations Institute, my son was out of town, but my daughter came. I told her, "I've gone through this institute so I can have a better relationship with you, your brother, and Al."

"That is really nice," said my daughter. In retrospect, I realized my daughter also kept trying. My son, three years younger, had been more affected by my moods and criticism, but he had always kept going.

It is difficult to break the cycles of dysfunctionality in a family. I had known something was deeply wrong, and I went on a great search to understand what was wrong. I wanted to be different, but that was not enough. Until one is aware and feels those painful feelings that have been covered up over and over, then one cannot change. Those buried feelings control a person. They are unconscious, and one is not aware one is being controlled. Psychoanalysis was a great gift to me and my family. The purpose is to make the unconscious conscious so one has choices in life. I no longer would unconsciously repeat what had been done to me.

That I had been guilty of doing to my children what had been done to me was a tremendous blow, but at least I knew it, so I could spend the rest of my life developing new and healthy relationships with them. Union professor Dr. Ann Ulanov used to say: "Knowledge of the self is a blow to the ego." This certainly was true for me. The definition of love I learned at Union stayed with me as a guide: love is a presence, an affirmation, a union. Instead of trying to control or, worse, criticizing one's children, I learned to listen, affirm, and acknowledge who they were becoming. Don't send them away. Spend time together. Enjoy them. That's my new mantra.

Besides my daughter, Al was at my graduation, smiling, happy I had found some healing. He had not understood my emotional baggage I had brought into our new marriage, nor had I, but he was there with me. He always meant to be helpful, and he was. I could not have gone through the analysis without his love and support, and I had done it so our marriage, children, and grandchildren could thrive.

CHAPTER 21

My Father, Chicago, 1994

We must love one another or die.

—W. H. Auden

I had not been in Chicago for a while, since I was busy with my life in New York, but after graduating from social work school, where I had been taught to listen, notice, and understand my clients and to analyze what they needed, I decided it was time to go visit my family in Chicago. Margie had remarried and was busy with young children. Bobby had taken a prestigious position in the pathology department at Emory University and moved with his family to Atlanta, Georgia. Dad and his new wife, Laura, were busy with their lives. On my next trip to Chicago in 1993, I took time to listen to my older brother John who had had many hard struggles in life and had become deeply depressed. He told me that although he had contemplated suicide, he would not go through with it knowing how much Charlie's death had upset everyone. I consulted with my siblings Margie and Bobby. We decided that together we would do whatever it took to see that John was fine. We became our brother's keeper, and John in turn decided to spend his days praying for all of us.

John had heard Dad say he would like to go see Mapleton, Iowa, again, where he had been raised and where Mom had been laid to rest. Dad had ordered a stone bench for the cemetery, to be placed near his family's graves overlooking the cornfields, looking west toward the sunset. He wanted to go sit there. John, still trying to please his dad despite all his criticisms or perhaps because of them, set his mind and heart on accomplishing this daunting task. John became obsessed with arranging for his father to see Mapleton one last time, as Dad was ninety-five and feared he would not live for many more years. John called me over several months, pushing me to commit to a time to fly to Chicago and take part in the trip, and finally, we settled on a time.

We four grown children, minus spouses and our children, set off with Dad in an RV for Iowa. The RV was the only sensible choice because Dad was not strong enough to ride in a car and stop at motels. We divided the tasks by gender. Bob was the male nurse, caring for Dad. Margie and I were the cooks and housekeepers. John drove. We had become a Brady Bunch.

At the beginning of the trip, Dad complained bitterly and kept asking to go back home, but we persisted. Whenever he looked up at Bob, an accomplished physician from Atlanta, he would tell him to comb his hair. It was embarrassing, but Bobby seemed to flinch only slightly. Bobby had a distinguished career, and his father's criticism had not stopped him in life, although I am sure it was hard on him. It had hindered me, John, and even Margie.

We managed to get to Mapleton and see the cemetery and the bench, which had been installed before we arrived. The small midwestern American town was celebrating the Fourth of July. There were fifty flags flying on the roads through the cornfields leading to the cemetery. The Boy Scouts were on duty, and the local veterans were all in place. They made a huge fuss over Dad, a local boy made good who had returned for a hero's visit to his small town. Dad was in his wheelchair, all dressed up by Bobby and John in a snappy fedora, rich tan tweed blazer, white shirt, and tie. Bobby and Johnny had spent so much time and energy in getting Dad ready that they had had no time to shine themselves up and remained in their jeans.

When his two sons wheeled him up the hill at the cemetery, they presented a startling contrast: my father beautifully dressed and his two sons in old, casual clothes. The Boy Scouts gathered around his wheelchair for a photo, and the veterans acknowledged Dad. The local newspapers carried Judge Hunter's visit to the Mapleton Cemetery on the front page. The four of us were satisfied that we had taken Dad back to Mapleton one last time. We were surprised on the trip how critical and cranky he was with the four of us and how charming he was with his old friends from Mapleton when they came to say hello—the same pattern I had seen all my life—but we were thrilled that we four children did so well together. We were together in a new way, even if Dad was still the same old Dad.

A few years went by, and Dad was in and out of the hospital—at ninety-seven, that was not too surprising. Whenever I got a call saying Dad had another problem, I would drop everything and fly out to Chicago to see that he was well taken care of. Each time, I wondered if this was the end, and I wanted to be there with my father, whom, all my life, I had wanted to be with me.

He had always told me to go away, as he was too busy for me, saying, "Betsy, not now. I'm working," "Betsy, wait in the car while I go speak to these men about my cows," or "Betsy, go to bed." None of it sounds so terrible, but over time, it all added up to some lack in me. *It's not very good. You're not very good.* I would not do.

Yet I was going to him to take care of him. One Friday night in the winter of 1995, I got a call saying Dad was back in the hospital. I went directly from the plane to the hospital, but Dad was asleep. Having been reassured by the nurses that his condition was stable, his diabetes was under control, and his blood clots and infections were being managed, I arranged for extra care: a shave, which might make Dad feel a little better in the morning.

Saturday morning, at the start of the visiting hours, I walked into his hospital room, feeling a little harried from a poor night's sleep on the lumpy couch in his apartment on the Near North Side overlooking Lake Michigan. He was in a private room, and his bed was by a window. The winter light shone in on his winter-white hair, what little he had left. It was jarring to see him. He had been a big, strong man from western Iowa farm country. He'd worked in the fields starting at age eight and made his way in the world by fighting his way up. He had been the fullback on the football team and put himself through law school by being a professional wrestler and a pro football player. He'd fought his way through Republican politics to become the Republican candidate for mayor and ended up a chief judge. He'd raised prized bulls and sold them to Japan and Brazil. Now he was an old, shrunken man in bed.

He looked up with his clean-shaven face and beckoned to me with his finger. "Come here, Betsy. Come here. I have something to say to you."

My heart leaped. Was my ninety-seven-year-old father finally going to thank me for flying out to see him? Thank me for arranging for the shave? To say, "It's lovely to see you"?

I went to his bedside. "Yes, Dad, what is it?"

"Betsy, now that you are remarried, you will just have to do something about your hair," said Dad, looking up at me with his clear blue eyes.

Having been strengthened by therapy, self-knowledge, and an understanding of my family's dynamics and thinking about the saga with my brother John, I was fortified to answer Dad in a new way. I spoke up and told my father the truth. "Dad, you have devastated me. You have deeply hurt my feelings." No one had ever really stood up to him, but I did that day. It just poured out of me after all those years of hiding behind a smile, being the angel, and bottling up my feelings. "Dad, how could you tell me to fix my hair, when I've come all the way from New York to see you and to see to your care?" My whole being was ablaze.

He didn't give in. "Oh, Betsy, it's a father's job to tell his children when they need fixing," he answered, going back to his own childhood of belittlement. Here was another example of parents visiting their problems on their children. "My mother told me when I needed to comb my hair. She told me when I should put on a clean shirt. I'm just doing a father's job."

"But, Dad"—I started crying—"I am devastated."

"Oh, Betsy, don't be so sensitive." Dad paused for a few seconds and then proceeded to go into one of his well-practiced defenses: to change the subject and distract. "Here. Let me tell you about some of the plays I was in during my last football season as Iowa's fullback."

I interrupted the story I had heard often. "Dad, you have really hurt my feelings. I have been arranging for your care and taking care of your affairs, and I was hoping for at least an acknowledgment."

He stopped telling his story but didn't say anything. The physical therapist came into the hospital room. "Judge," she said, "it's time for you to get your exercise." She helped him up and strapped him to herself. The two of them walked down the white hall, with its tan and turquoise linoleum. Dad was wearing a hospital gown to his knees and a hospital bathrobe of soft patterned white cotton.

After fifteen minutes, Dad was brought back to the room, again strapped to a nurse for support. Even a big man grows old and weakens. It must be hard to grow infirm. The nurse helped him into bed, and I went over to speak to him. Then something happened I had never expected to see. Dad had tears in his eyes. I didn't remember ever seeing Dad with tears. He always had seemed like a wall to me. Now he had tears.

"Betsy, what a fool of an old man I am. You are my beloved daughter. When I got up this morning and looked in the mirror, I saw a white-haired, wrinkled, shriveled old man. When you came into the room, I threw it back on you. I'm sorry, Betsy. I never meant to hurt you. What a fool of an old man I am, and you are my beloved daughter."

I started crying as well. "Dad, I know you never meant to hurt me, and I forgive you. I love you and have always loved you." There was the connection I had yearned for all my life. There was the connection that could have freed my brother John to begin a life of his own. It could have freed me as well. Father and daughter, crying, finally acknowledging they loved each other, at ninety-seven and fifty-six. It had been a long time in coming.

Dad, at age ninety-seven, understood at that moment what he had been doing all my life. He couldn't tolerate the painful feelings inside himself, so he got rid of them by criticizing his children or, worse, being cruel to them. How I wished Mom and his children had spoken up to him long ago, but would he have listened?

Dad held on for two more years. There were no more conversations.

When he died, I called the Chicago newspapers and sent them his life story, a big write-up befitting a big man, which was published in the *Tribune*. The funeral was held at the large Fourth Presbyterian Church of Chicago, where he had been a trustee for many years. My sister and I talked with the minister, trying to tell him the truth about my father, but he only answered: "Your father was one of the finest men I have ever known. Did you know he used to have lunch with me from time to time and spent as much time trying to figure out his son John as you have spent trying to figure him out? He would often tell me about all of his children, but he told me again and again that he did not understand John."

Dad's funeral was beautifully laid out but sparsely attended. The truth was that he had been sick so long and was so old that all the people who had known him were themselves gone. I had a hard time accepting that truth. The minister's homily described how fine a person Judge Hunter had been. In my eulogy, I said it was not for cowards to be one of his children, but mostly, it was a service of praise for the life of my remarkable father, who had pulled himself up from the cornfields of Iowa to the big-city judicial chambers of Chicago.

Dad's personal bailiff from court attended the funeral. He had stayed close to Dad and Laura and sought me out at the reception in the church after the funeral. He was visibly upset. "Betsy, I have something I have to tell you. I had a dream last night where your father came and sat on my bed and addressed me."

The bailiff was shaking and told me the dream had seemed real. It was obvious it had upset him enormously. He continued. "He wanted me to tell you that he knew and appreciated all you had done to help the family."

I was amazed. In life, Dad could not speak, except that once, but in death, he spoke through his bailiff. I was deeply moved. I thought about the vision I had had as a tiny girl in my bedroom in Chicago of the Statue of Liberty outside my window, with the small figures of my father. In some inexplicable way, I, a self-effacing, invisible child, had grown up to become a strong woman who could help my family.

The next day, we followed the hearse out to Mapleton. Local people were gathered at the cemetery for the burial. Several people had come because they remembered reading the newspaper article two years before about the local boy who'd made good.

We gathered around the open grave, which was lined with a green indoor-outdoor carpet so we would not have to see the dirt. The pretty cherrywood casket my sister and I had picked out was suspended in a mechanical sling that would lower my father into the ground forever. We would not witness the actual burial. A small green tent had been placed beside and over the grave. Behind the grave, as far as the eye could see, stretched Iowa cornfields.

A local minister read the committal service. I was numb. Bobby brought me back to reality when I looked over and saw his tears, but it was my nephew John E. who brought truth to the burial for me. He stepped up and began to cry, clinging to the casket and speaking. The townspeople all seemed disturbed by the outburst, and some walked away, but I hung on every word. John E., John's son and one of Dad's grandsons, cried out hysterically, "Granddad, you sure made it hard on a fellow to love you!" John E. was the only one who spoke the truth. He had wanted to spend more time with his granddad but had known he would be greeted not with accepting love but with criticism and a lecture.

John E. had sent me a copy of a letter he had written to his granddad about five years before, when he was twenty-two. He had poured out his heart in the letter, saying that he was proud to call him his grandfather and that his granddad was his role model. He hoped he would be able to do as well in his life as his granddad had done in his.

I had also seen my dad's answer. He had written at the bottom of the letter, "Look how terrible your handwriting is." Dad had been unable to acknowledge the love and adulation of his own grandson. John E. had been desperately looking for a role model, for encouragement. My father hadn't known how to step up to the task and take in his love. His only response had been criticism.

My father always carried this great poem by Alfred, Lord Tennyson, with him:

Crossing the Bar

Sunset and evening star
And one clear call for me!
And may there be no moaning of the bar,
When I set out to sea
…
For though from out our bourn of Time and Place
The flood may bear me far
I hope to see my Pilot face to face
When I have crossed the bar

Dad had met his Maker, and we had to live on with the consequences. He left behind a great American example of a self-made man. He had done noble things, such as integrating the YMCAs of Chicago. He had been a tough father to all his children, with one memorable exception in the hospital, when I finally spoke up, and he finally said, "You are my beloved daughter, and I never meant to hurt you. What a fool of an old man I have been." He had expressed poignant and loving words, just once. His death made me sad because then I knew I would never have a relationship with him.

"Father, forgive us, for we know not what we do." Dad never knew what he did, as is the case for many of us. He had an enabling wife in Betty and silent and compliant children. He took care of other people's children through his good work at the Boy Scouts Council, the YMCA, and the divorce court's reconciliation service and as a trustee of the Presbyterian church. Being with his own children was something he did not know how to do. Other things were easier and always seemed more important.

After Dad's death, I continued to work toward mending our broken family.

CHAPTER 22

Patagonia, Chile, 2001

Al and I decided we had reached the stage in our lives when we should see the world and started taking big trips every year. As part of the plan, we visited Patagonia in Chile, where I decided to climb Osorno Volcano. It gave me the chance to reflect on our marriage and my life.

As I walked along the loose volcanic cinder rock of Osorno Volcano in Chile, I glimpsed Al, the tour guide, and the rest of the group on the hill below. It interested me that Al seemed to be carefully monitoring my progress up the volcanic mountain. I could see his head tilted upward as he watched me. I had decided to set out on my own up the mountain.

Another time when he had turned around to look at me flashed into my mind. It was the first time we met. He was in the jump seat in the back of a black limousine, facing forward. I was seated on the back bench, between a married couple, friends of both of ours. They had invited us independently to an exhibit of Hudson River paintings at the Newark Museum and to a dinner. Al's wife had died just two months before, and it was the first time he had accepted an invitation. He had not been told there would be a woman for him to meet. Had he been told, he would not have accepted. It was too soon. Since they had already gone several miles, it was too late for him to excuse himself and leave. Then he turned around and looked at me. Although we were total strangers, there was a spark of interest.

Something about being alone on the volcanic mountain, up above my husband and the rest of the group, made me reflect on our marriage.

It was highly unusual for me to be the one either above or ahead. My usual experience involved Al leading as I struggled to keep the pace. On other hiking trips, he had gone way ahead of me. He was a successful businessman who ran his own company; I struggled to make my own mark equal to his. I took on a physical challenge.

I looked up the volcano to the next rise. It was steep and high. I wondered if I had it in me, but a familiar feeling of grit pushed me forward. I would just keep putting one foot in front of the other. Earlier in the day, the tour guide had announced the several ways one could spend the hour appointed for the group to visit the volcano: stay in the shop and enjoy a hot chocolate and the view, ride the lift up the mountain, or walk up the mountain. I had planned to take the lift, until my husband announced, "I'm going to walk up."

It felt like a gauntlet thrown down. I knew it was his competitive nature bursting forth, and I didn't think he was putting me down. He probably thought he was just saying he wanted the exercise, or he wanted to prove himself to himself. Perhaps he wasn't thinking of me at all.

I looked down the valley again, and there was Al, staring up at me still. I learned later that after our unexpected meeting in the black limousine, he had cried when he returned to his home. It had been too soon after the funeral of his first wife. He had not wanted to meet a new woman; he had been devastated by her loss.

When the tour bus had reached the shop where one could buy tickets for the lift and also use the restrooms, my husband had said he was going to take advantage of the restrooms and would be back presently. I'd waited outside for a moment, seen the steep path to the right that led up the mountain, and decided to start walking. I'd asked a friend to tell Al I had started up.

The path had drawn me to it, beckoning to me. It was about the adventure, the challenge, and the path, steep and high. I looked up to the crest of the hill and set a goal to get there. I could make it, I told myself. I was alone. It felt exhilarating, and up I trudged, foot after foot.

After Al had seen me in the back of the limousine, two years had passed before he asked me if I would enjoy going with him to the antiques show. I had wanted to go. I had liked him from the start and looked forward to getting to know him. It had taken five years between that first backward glance in the limousine and the wedding. The wedding had entailed a prenuptial agreement, his daughter had cried because her father was remarrying, and the entire family of the late wife had come to witness the ceremony.

Al had come out from the bathroom and wondered where I was. I assumed it puzzled him that I had gone on off alone and had a considerable head start up the mountain. He was used to leading, so I thought it must have been a new feeling for him to watch me way out front.

We had been married for twenty years when we embarked on our journey to South America. At our wedding, I had felt a joy hard to describe. I wouldn't be alone anymore. He was my fantasy—an elegant, substantial, handsome, brilliant man with a vibrant spirit of creativity, a risk-taker, and a visionary. He fascinated me, and I was attracted to him, but despite all his magnetism, caring, and faithfulness over the last twenty years, he hadn't taken away my doubts about who I was as a person.

I finally made it to the crest of the hill, took a deep breath, looked up, and saw another steep slope above that I had not seen from below. Feeling confident and not too tired, I set off again with the same ambition: just to reach the top of the next rise. As I walked up the slope, I felt winded and stopped to take deep breaths. To my delight, I recovered. I went on. My hiking boots held firmly to the dirt path. The wind blew with increasing strength, but the boots worked, and I felt warm in my yellow slicker and waterproof pants. It occurred to me that the slicker made it easy for Al to spot me going up the mountain. I checked; he was looking up still.

Those twenty years of the marriage had been a long time, a great deal of life had happened, and we had helped each other. The four children from our first marriages had finished graduate degrees, married, had children, and bought homes. We had traveled the world; we worked at our respective careers. But my self-doubt, the fear that I did not measure up and would not measure up, persisted. It led to my equally painful question of whether Al really loved me. I could push it away from time to time, but then the doubts came back, nagging at me. I knew well the antecedents of this: my mother's and father's preoccupations and my father's belittling. But enough was enough. *Come on. Go on*, I would tell myself, but then there it was, nagging some more.

However, at that moment, there I was, by myself, climbing. I wouldn't have believed I could do it, but I was moving one foot in front of the other, up and up, step after step. I looked down, and the clouds seemed to part so that I could see the green valley below. Looking across, I could see more mist-covered hills in the distance. I had been admiring the dramatic snow-covered peaks of the Andes all week, but now I had a better view of the jagged peaks soaring up into the brilliant blue sky.

It seemed increasingly important to me that I keep climbing. I felt I was testing my will, strength, and ability. Could I succeed? Perhaps this climb had started with Al, but it ceased to be about him. My need went deeper. Could I make it on my own strength?

I was amazed to see I had walked above the green vegetation line and found myself in a valley of pebbly black ash from the volcano. It was hard going because my feet slipped on the loose black gravel, but across a flat part, the rangers had placed a walkway made of wooden slats. I carefully made my way across the boards toward a high hill of the ash with a wooden walkway going up, partially blown away by the strong winds. I had worked myself into a sweat, and to my surprise, my body felt like a well-oiled machine, raring to keep going. All thoughts faded away, except that I was going to make it to the top of that high hill of black.

It was steep, and my feet kept slipping. I had to stoop down when the wind gusted, so I would not be blown over. I looked down and saw that if I fell, it would be a long way down the volcanic heap, down the cliff. Again, I was glad I had on that yellow slicker to be easily spotted in case of an emergency.

Just then, I heard something behind me: "I think everyone needs a climbing partner, and I decided to be yours." It was Felicity, a member of the touring group, who was a few years younger than I. I was glad for the support.

Trudging up and up, finally, I got to the top of that high hill of black volcanic ash. Felicity stood a couple of yards below me. I think she wanted me to experience the top by myself. Seeing that I was safe, she headed back down the mountain.

I stood there taking deep breaths, trying to catch my breath. I was higher than if I had taken the lift. It felt great. I had done it. Flooding into my mind came all the other times in my life when I had made it. College had been extraordinarily hard, but I had made it. Losing my first husband in a car accident, raising my kids alone, and going through it all year after year had been extraordinarily hard, but I had made it; my children were great adults. My second marriage had been a challenge, but I had made it: we had forged a marriage bond. Yes, yes, yes.

Just then, I turned around, and to my surprise, there stood my husband on top of the same hill. He had come around from the other side, which was not as steep, and climbed up to meet me. I burst out laughing. He would not be outdone, and that was okay.

CHAPTER 23

Eminent Domain, Maine, 2005

So much had begun to heal in my life that I began to think there had to be a way to find peace in Tenants Harbor between me and the town government. If we could settle our disputes in this small town, perhaps there would be hope for peace in the world, I thought hopefully and grandiosely. The lavender blues and golds of the harbor beckoned. I heard the message from the tides: *It is possible. It is possible to connect and move forward. We are dependable; we are steady. There is a way for houses, people, marriages, and towns to live in happiness and peace. Keep searching, keep talking, and keep listening.* The beckoning continued: *There is a way.*

Front Street, the small gravel roadway between the sail loft and the ocean, was used by the public but was private and continued to be a source of friction with the management of the town. I wanted to get the matter straightened out. I did not want to live with unsettled problems and did not want to pass them on to my children. The tax map clearly showed it was a private easement, and state law said one had to close a private easement for one day every twenty years to keep the easement private. My mother had closed Front Street as required, and I planned to do the same, but the management of the town objected. I wondered what the best way would be to settle the dispute. I planned to call the town manager to work out a settlement.

In the meantime, Al and I planted another garden down by the water, to be designed by Harriet Pattison, the landscape gardener who had collaborated with the famous architect Louis Kahn. Harriet was the aunt of my talented friend Peggy who had also designed parts of our landscape. She had laid out a multi bush hedge of French lilacs, bush roses, hydrangeas, and others on the house side of Front Street to minimize the effect of our property's having been cut in two. She added an orchard of apple trees to shield us from the public landing and a row of trees to shield us from our neighbors.

The garden Harriet built on the far side of the road was a large circle overlooking the tides, a garden of peace. Harriet placed large boulders in a crescent so we could sit and look out at the harbor, with lavender, heather, and evergreens around the boulders. A small hedge on the far side completed the circle. The people of the town began to stop to admire the gardens. Many said, "We always take a walk down your lane in order to see the flowers."

Al and I strategized how to open up the Maine house to enhance our customary six weeks there every summer. We added windows to let in the light from the harbor so we could sit in our living room and bedroom and feel the warmth of the sun and see the beauty of the harbor. We watched the movement of the sun from early morning, when it peeked up over Southern Island, to dusk, when its setting light bathed the harbor in a golden glow. We watched the steady tides. We added flowering trees, shrubs, and perennial flowers. We started adding herbs, fruit trees, and berry shrubs that nourished and delighted us. The deep swings in myself and our marriage receded as we listened more.

Since sleeping in the yellow room with my brother and sister as a little girl, I had looked out toward the tiny speck of Two Bush Island on the horizon and watched the light on the lighthouse and the great expanse of the dark sea. Now, as a remarried woman and grandmother, I looked out my front door and across the little gravel way, Front Street, to my lawn and garden beyond. I walked down to the peaceful new circular garden, sat on one of the boulders, and took in the view. I walked back up the lawn, across gravel Front Street, and up the steps to the deck. I looked out to the harbor and sea beyond.

In the summer of 2005, I called the town manager and the assistant town manager, who was also the chief code enforcement officer and the highway superintendent, and said, "It's time we settled all outstanding issues. Let's meet and talk." They said they would come talk, but any agreements would have to be brought up with the board of selectmen.

I hired the best surveyor in the area and a local lawyer and initiated a series of talks with the town. We met together in our big downstairs room, the old storeroom. We spread out maps and agreements made by my ancestors and all the historical deeds to the property and tried to make sense of them. We went from one trouble spot to another, making compromises and agreements. The surveyor told me, "Betsy, it's hard to decipher property lines that measure boundaries from trees that no longer exist or the marine railway that was torn down a hundred years ago, but we'll try."

In our initial meetings with the officials of the town, I felt burdened with all my mother's unsettled fights of the past and how hurt she had been by the people of the town turning against her, but slowly, I began to realize how difficult it had been for the town to deal with me. Listening to them, I was able to hear the town and their point of view. Though the roadway was on our land, Front Street gave secondary access to the public landing and was particularly important in bad weather for the big lobster boats coming in or out of the water. The town needed Front Street, but how wide did it need to be?

Boundaries had never been established since the original deed dated back to the 1840s. When my ancestors had given the town perpetual ownership rights to the public landing in the 1950s and an easement for playing ball in the field behind our house a few years later, they never had discussed Front Street or exact boundaries.

As I read through all the old letters and records regarding Front Street and took in clearly the needs of the town, I had a change of heart. I realized the people who lived and worked in town year-round needed access to the launching ramp given to them years ago by my ancestors.

I decided to offer the town a perpetual easement on Front Street. I asked in return they leave the roadway one lane wide and unpaved with gravel so that the property would not be cut apart legally or visually. Forrester Smith checked with the man who hauled the boats across the road, who said he had no trouble hauling and launching boats up to forty-five feet. I was also thinking of the safety of the little children who had to cross that road to get to the water. We worked amicably over a period to make an agreement about all issues between my property and the town. We shook hands.

I asked my longtime Maine lawyer to write up what we'd decided, and he sent the town a letter formally summarizing all our agreements. Then we heard nothing. We wrote to the town a couple of times to inquire how the settlement was proceeding in discussions with the selectmen.

During the next summer, all was peaceful. I did not hear further from the town about any issue, and I told my circle of friends that peace had finally come to Tenants Harbor. I felt all the issues were settled. Al and I closed up the house and returned to New York and our busy lives, Al as a banker and I as a therapist. The back-and-forth from Maine to New York and back again, like the tides, was working. We even had winterized the sail loft and came up in February for a conference and to see our friends. Then a huge assault from the town hit us. It reminded me of a northeaster—everything seemingly was calm, and then a great storm appeared.

On the Monday morning before Thanksgiving 2006, I was sitting at my desk, getting ready for my first patient of the day. I opened an email from my lawyer in Maine, with whom I had been working for the past years. It said, "Betsy, I have not had time to read the enclosed, and I don't have time to work on it or attend the meetings, but there will be a meeting next Monday night in the town office to vote on the order of eminent domain. I won't be there, as I have to drive my son back to boarding school."

I read the attachment, four carefully typed pages. The town planned to seize two parcels of my property the next Monday night at six o'clock and have a special town meeting at seven o'clock to ratify the action. They would send me a check for the value of the property, as determined by a surveyor, which was surprisingly little.

I held my head in my hands and wondered what in the world I had to do. I called Al, who immediately told me I had to fight and said he would help me. My thoughts wandered to the beautiful new circle garden, the sweet place to sit on a summer's day. It felt endangered. They planned to make Front Street a public road. I ruminated on what this might mean to me: Would they widen and pave Front Street in the process of taking a thirteen-foot strip of land that contained the rose hedge and perhaps even the tip of the new garden? Would the town's plan take away the privacy of the garden? Would traffic speed down the road, endangering the crossing for my grandchildren? Would this new plan make my waterfront property a nonconforming lot, officially cutting it in two? I was in shock.

I learned later the municipal officers of the town had planned for ten months to take the land. Beginning in February 2006, they engaged a prestigious lawyer from Augusta. The lawyer scrutinized the law to guarantee to the selectmen that what they planned to do was legal. For example, since the law required the town to give notice, in the middle of winter, they tacked a notice on a telephone pole near the sail loft, knowing I would never see it. I was told later the lawyer had bragged, "I have arranged a slam dunk."

"We can do it, and we are going to do it," a municipal officer had reportedly said.

I picked up the phone. "Is the town manager there? This is Betsy. I am calling to complain bitterly about what you are doing to me. You are taking my land without notice. You made an agreement with me and then have not talked to me in ten months. Now, without notice, on Thanksgiving week, you announce you are seizing my land. Do you remember making an agreement with me?"

"Yes, Betsy, we made an agreement with you," the town manager responded, "but then the selectmen overruled me, and they are the ones in charge."

"Why didn't you ever tell me in the years you negotiated with me? I went to the considerable expense to have a survey made, hire a lawyer, and spend my time in good faith."

"Betsy, we have a letter here from your lawyer dated last February stating that you were no longer willing to make an agreement with us. We had no choice but to start legal proceedings against you. Once we started these proceedings, we were forbidden to talk with you, because we were in a legal action."

"What?"

"I have the letter here in the town office."

"What letter? I have no memory of any such letter. To the contrary, I have repeatedly asked for a meeting with you."

The letter to which he referred was a letter from my lawyer stating more conditions for the agreement. It had been a big step for me to go against what my mother had wanted and give the perpetual easement to the town. Nervous, I had wanted reassurance from the town that they would carry out the agreement into the future. Evidently, the town did not like the conditions and decided the easiest way to handle it was eminent domain. They thought as a summer person, I had been too demanding.

I called each of the five selectmen in turn and said, "Please talk with me. What are you doing?"

One after another said one or more of the following: "I cannot talk to you about town business except in an open town forum," "We have the letter saying you wouldn't negotiate further," "We have a file drawer of meetings with you," "We don't need to hear from you anymore," "We have spent so much money in legal fees that we are not spending any more money," "We have no time to meet with you," and "We need to get rid of this and do it."

I was in New York; the house in Maine was closed for the season. We had planned to spend Thanksgiving with our children in the Hudson Valley. I had no lawyer. I called Forrester Smith and asked what to do. "You must fight this legally, politically, and with the media," he advised. "Call reporters, write letters to the editor, call all your friends, and find a new lawyer." All in the three days before Thanksgiving. "By the way, you have to get your letter in by Thursday so it will be published with the Saturday edition."

I next called my nephew in Washington, DC, who was an aide to Senator Susan Collins of Maine. "Who's the best real estate lawyer in Maine?" I asked.

"Try John Cunningham with Eaton Peabody. He's the expert."

John Cunningham's office said he was on vacation that week. "But," the receptionist said, "we will send around your information to see if any lawyer is willing to take this on."

A man named P. Andrew Hamilton called me back. He first checked my references and then looked over the eminent domain seizure papers and agreed to take the case. But he was not optimistic. "Your legal chance of winning is in the basement. I just have to be honest with you," Andy Hamilton said. "Your only legal recourse is to sue them after they have passed the order and seized your land, to try to collect damages. The chance of finding a way both to stop the selectmen from voting the order to seize your property and to stop the townspeople from ratifying it by vote, all on the same night, is nil."

I called my longtime friends in Tenants Harbor. They said they were incensed and would get on the phone and start calling their friends and neighbors.

Al and I had Thanksgiving dinner with our grown children and our grandchildren in Rhinebeck, New York. At ten o'clock on Thanksgiving night, we started on our trek to Tenants Harbor, a seven-and-a-half-hour drive. *What am I doing?* I worried. *What am I doing to Al?* The wind pushed our heavy car around, and the rain made it hard to see at night. We even managed to miss our exit, which cost us an extra half hour. We arrived at the sail loft at five thirty in the morning, three days before the dreaded seizure of the property. The lobstermen were in their boats, heading out; the stragglers were in their pickups, heading toward their morning coffee.

"Al, where's the flashlight? I can't quite see to get the numbers for the combination lock to get into our house," I said.

"What's the number to disarm the alarm?" Al asked, exhausted. I told him the number, and we entered the house.

The housekeeper had been nice enough to open it up, and our carpenter, caretaker, and friend came over on no notice to turn the water back on. He said, "You know, Betsy, I have already drained all the pipes in your house for the winter, and it's a lot of work to go reopen that house. But I'll go down. Do you need the dishwasher and washing machine?"

We did not.

"By the way," said the caretaker, "they did the same thing to the Indians. They made them out to be bad people so they could steal their land."

Al and I were so keyed up that we couldn't sleep, so we set up our respective workstations, getting ready to man them for the coming onslaught. Al's station was in the master bedroom. We hooked up the fax, set up a desk, and laid out his papers. My station was in a corner of the old chandlery downstairs, including my desk, my computer and printer, paper, and notes. All looked ready.

After a few hours of sleep, I decided to get up and walk around to smell again the ocean and admire the house and garden. Yes, it was all worth fighting for. Since taking ownership in 1974, I had worked hard, steadily gentrifying the old run-down commercial building, and it had become a comfortable and pretty home. It had never been easy, to say the least. Through the years, I had replaced much of the wood in the old building because it had been rotten, as well as the siding and windows because they had leaked. I'd hired the landscapers and created a sanctuary by the seaside in my ancestral home built by my great-great-grandfather in 1848. I loved the old sail loft.

I hired an appraiser to determine the value of the land the town was seizing. He was sympathetic. "Why do they want your front garden? Do they want to plant trees so you can't see the view? This land is worth fighting for; it's worth at least fifteen times what they plan to pay you."

I worked late into the night to get my letter to the editor ready so it would meet the deadline for the Saturday paper.

My letter, plus three or four articles that appeared in the local press, raised the questions clearly: "Do you want a town government taking your property with one week's notice? Is any property owner safe? Call your selectmen, and let them know what you think of these proceedings."

I called more townspeople and asked them to help me fight.

"Betsy, I'm coming and bringing three friends," said one.

"I'm going to help you because I'm sick of this government," said a year-round resident.

"I'm coming and voting no because if they get away with it with you, I'm next," said a nearby neighbor.

I ran up the stairs to tell Al: "Even our neighbor is planning on voting with us. She doesn't like this any better than we do".

Al interrupted me. He said that Andy, the lawyer called to tell us the town manager was quoting a deed to the wharf that proved they had a right-of-way to the wharf and a claim to Front Street.

"That right-of-way was about a different road, Commercial Street", I said.

All too quickly, it was Monday night, the day of the selectmen's meeting and the public meeting about Front Street. The Eaton Peabody lawyers suggested a small gathering of my friends at my house before the meeting to prepare. Forrester was to ask that the whole order be postponed so there would be more time for discussion. Mac was to ask that I, a nonresident, be allowed to speak at the special town meeting. If all else failed, Jack was to ask that the compensation for taking my land be increased from the proposed $19,000 to the $297,000 the appraiser had suggested. We all then drove off into the night to the St. George Town Hall.

My caretaker stood next to me at the meeting. It was packed with supporters. His daughter, sitting in front of me, whispered, "You've never been a terrible person. My kids played ball down there."

My neighbor hobbled in on a cane with her husband, a political activist. I didn't know many of the people and kept trying to remember where I had seen some others before. They kept coming. The stream kept flowing on and on down the ramp into the basement room of town hall where the order of seizure was to be enacted. Usually, there were three or four members of the public. That night, they counted close to one hundred inside, squashed against the walls. There were no seats left, and people were outside the door, straining to get in. People sat on the steps. There was soft talking. I chose to stand in the back corner to see what was going on and to hide a little. My husband and our two lawyers sat in the front.

When we got there, the selectmen were already seated around two eight-foot Formica tables pushed together. The basement of the town hall had wood paneling and aluminum folding chairs. The chief selectman was in the middle, ready to preside. The sole female selectman looked snappy with her light green turtleneck. There was a retired lawyer, who looked a bit softer than the others; a minister; and another selectman sporting a freshly grown beard. Only one of the selectmen had been willing to talk with me. I had met his wife during the summer on an art tour. She was a charming and talented woman. The town manager, in a striped cotton shirt, sat next to the chief selectman. Their mouths were open, gaping at the size of the crowd.

Before the meeting started, Al made copies of the letters my lawyer and I had sent to the town stating the terms of our agreement, offering to discuss further, and asking for an update. These letters contradicted the story of the select board, including a short letter asking for a meeting. The letters reminded the selectmen that I had previously offered a perpetual easement.

The chief selectman officially opened the meeting, and another selectman immediately moved to go into executive session. The vote was unanimous. The five selectmen, the two town officials, and the town's lawyer rose, turned around, and walked out of the basement room. They left one hundred people standing around. Forty-five minutes later, they solemnly marched back into the room. I talked to people standing near me. They whispered to me that they were with me. Forrester walked over and said I was among friends.

When the forty-five minutes were over, the selectmen, the town manager, and the lawyer all marched back down the stairs, sat in their same chairs, and stared at the restless audience. One selectman announced, "We are not voting tonight on the order of condemnation, in order to give time for the negotiations to be reopened with the Scotts. We will have a public hearing, announced in advance, and the minutes will be made public. At the regular town meeting in March, the town will have the chance to vote." There would be no further action or discussion that night.

"What'd ya do it for?" asked a member of the audience.

"Since we have taken no action on the order, it is inappropriate to have public discussion at this time. There is no order on the table," replied the town manager.

"I move the town never again take eminent domain action against Front Street," a friend said.

"Since there is no order, there can be no motion," replied the town manager once more.

The meeting was adjourned, and the public meeting was opened with the nominating and voting of a moderator. Immediately, another motion was made to adjourn since there was no order on which to vote. The people streamed up the back stairs, out of the town hall, and into their cars to go home. I stood there stunned when my lawyer came over to me and said, "Betsy, you stared them down. Congratulations. The lawyers are impressed. You stared down city hall."

I asked John Cunningham, Maine's big-time real estate lawyer, "Have you seen other towns do similar things to their citizens?"

"Yes, they do it all the time. What is so unusual is that you won. You went to the newspaper, your friends, and the lawyers. We tell others to do the same, but they don't do it."

To the Editor
The Courier Gazette
Rockland, Maine

To my fellow Citizens of St. George:

Democracy has worked and how blessed we all are to live in a county where we the people have the right to be heard and when we speak, the government listens.

As you know, the Municipal Officers of St. George served an Order of Condemnation by Eminent Domain to seize two parcels of my property without any warning on November 20th, and the Order was to be enacted in one week's time. I asked in a previous Letter to the Editor if this was the way you wanted your government to treat you. Your response was a resounding no. You called, wrote, and appeared at the selectmen's meeting and the town meeting. It is estimated there were ninety people in attendance; a record turn-out. Your very presence made a powerful statement to the Municipal Officers.

Thank you very much to you all for your tremendous support. It means a great deal to me.

Because of your presence, the Condemnation Order was put aside in order to reopen the negotiations. Preliminary discussions have already occurred in an amicable and positive manner when the property was visited by town officers and selectmen on Tuesday and at the selectmen's meeting on Wednesday, when a proposal was made that was mutually acceptable. There will be an open meeting at 6 o'clock on Wednesday, January 24, in order to allow for public discussion, and a town meeting in March to ratify the agreement.

Although these unfortunate proceedings resulting from miscommunication and misunderstandings on the part of all parties have been difficult, I now see many positive things coming as a result in the form of a good agreement and increased public involvement in municipal affairs. Again, thank you one and all.

Al and I shortly thereafter went back to New York City and then trudged back to Maine in the middle of winter for the public meeting on January 24, 2007. Once again, it was packed.

I spoke at the meeting. "Hello. My name is Betsy Scott, and my grandmother Clara Watts Long was born in this town but was gone for thirty years as the wife of a Baptist missionary in India. The property in question came down to me through my mother's family. I wanted a quiet, safe summer home, particularly for my young children and now young grandchildren. I had wanted to close off Front Street, but now I realize the town needs the roadway for the launching of boats. Thus, I have offered the town a perpetual easement."

Al and I returned to New York again, only to return to Tenants Harbor a few days before the annual meeting, which would vote on the perpetual easement as long as the roadway remained gravel and one lane. We still had to settle on the exact width.

The next morning, we went to have a talk with the town manager, who said, "Well, Betsy, this whole thing is a matter of miscommunication. We are not planning to widen the road. We need to talk tomorrow night about roads. We need an area of shoulder to support the road and then another area where we can maneuver to keep a road in good repair. We can't go on your property and just trespass."

I thought to myself, *What a funny juxtaposition between all these rules and my experience of the town.* It reminded me of what my lawyer John Cunningham had told me about the town's taking land one foot at a time each year. To me, the recipient of this strategy, it felt like Chinese water torture.

The town manager continued. "The travel way can remain eleven and a half feet, and then we need a one-foot shoulder on each side to support the road. After that, we need another one foot on each side for maneuvering room. The whole thing comes to sixteen and a half feet."

Al looked over at me and raised an eyebrow. The town manager, in a seemingly nonchalant way, was making a compromise offer as though this were what he'd had in mind all the time.

The town manager continued. "Betsy, we've been making inquiries about moving the baseball field. It really is not a good place for a field. It isn't big enough, and there's no room for parking. What about making that your yard?" he asked in an innocent tone.

"But, sir, I love my front yard. I love my waterfront. There is no way I'm interested in giving up my waterfront."

Realizing I didn't like his idea, the town manager changed course once more.

"I will have to call the selectmen to see what they say," he said.

"You know, sir, with all due respect, you are the one who runs this town," said Al. We left, perplexed, to return in the morning.

When I awoke the next morning, I was mesmerized by the beauty of the morning sun on the cold harbor in front of me. It was a subtle powder blue with a light golden-tinged light. The quiet and beauty felt good to my soul. I had been hungry for contact with the sail loft. Maine was important to me.

Upon walking back into the town office the next morning promptly at ten o'clock sharp, we were shepherded into the town manager's office. He handed us the agreement we had talked about the night before, typed out clearly on his computer: sixteen and one half feet—really fourteen and one half with the two so-called easements on either side. The road would look exactly the same, minus my rocks, which I had moved voluntarily last November. After all this fuss, nothing would be changed.

Al began to argue over the grassy shoulders. The manager wrote down what Al asked for: "an eleven-and-one-half-foot right-of-way and grassy shoulders of one and one half feet on either side." I laughed to myself.

"What about saying *vegetated* instead of *grassy*?" the manager asked. The two men agreed, and this condition was added to the agreement. I realized the town manager was writing down an acceptable agreement.

The assistant town manager came in and said, "You have no idea how much we want this agreement and to get this whole thing behind us."

"Okay, Betsy," the manager said, "we will take the wording right from your lawyer's letter and add it to our agreement."

Finally, Al and I were satisfied. We had actually gotten what we'd agreed to long before. I wondered if anything in the wording would come back to haunt me someday, but in reality, we had agreed to a true compromise, with each side getting what we needed but not all we had wanted. One of the selectmen put it this way: "Now I know what a compromise is. It is where neither side gets what they want."

"Well, Betsy, with this agreement ends fifty years of acrimony in this town," the town manager said unexpectedly.

I nearly fell off my chair. What was he saying to me? Did he think this whole thing was about the fight between my mother and her first cousin? "Sir, have you ever looked at the full-length version of those wills? You know that codicil was written when my great aunt had been senile for years."

"I always figured I had been in the middle of a family dispute. You know, it broke my heart when everything in your grandmother's ancestral house was sold off after your cousin's wife's death. The ones who inherited that house were just interested in the money," said the town manager.

"I know," I answered. "It was very painful to come up that August and find everything had been sold without my ever knowing about it. A friend showed me a picture she had bought of a pretty lady. When she showed it to me, I exclaimed, 'That is my mother!'—a picture I had never seen. How strange it feels to have one's family heritage sold off to the highest bidder."

"Well, this is the fiftieth anniversary of that fight, and it's about time we brought this whole thing to a close. You know, your cousins did not speak well of your mother," said the town manager.

"My mother did not speak well of them," I answered.

"The cousins always told everyone that the baseball field was their idea."

"That's funny, because my mother always told me it was her idea." I was stunned. The town manager knew every detail about everything in my family. "By the way, where should I leave the Long and Bean shipbuilding papers?" I asked.

"You should leave them in Bath. We really don't have room here."

I knew that was a good idea because the Bath Marine Museum had proper storage to preserve the records.

My mind was trying to take this all in. The town manager had been following this family fight all these years, every last detail. But why had he done what he had if he knew everything? What was he after? Did he just have to test my mettle? Did he have to find out once and for all if I was a worthy opponent, if I really loved this place? That I was strong enough to be there and that I cared enough? The only thing I could think of was a theory of psychologist D. W. Winnicott, who said that at some point, children have to give their mother their worst, and if she is still there, then they will know they are truly loved. On the other hand, there were people in town who feared I would close the road permanently, but I had, on my own initiative, offered a perpetual easement. On the other hand, I realized I had been difficult.

At the town's annual meeting, the vote was ninety-nine for me and four against, an overwhelming victory. Forrester stood up at the meeting and said, "I think it is time we thank Betsy and her family for all they have given to the town instead of criticizing them. After all, they have been the most generous benefactors this town has ever had, giving us the pubic landing, the boat-launching ramp, and the right to use the ball field."

The whole audience broke into applause. Tears rolled down my cheeks. I only wished my mother, Betty, could have been there. It would have been a true healing of the heart, a welcome home. "May all our disputes be settled with such grace," emailed a local resident. I thought back to Clara and Betty, who had always felt Tenants Harbor was home, despite their being in India, clearly not home. They'd clung to Tenants Harbor, but the people of Tenants Harbor barely had known them; they had been gone too long. It is understandable the town manager wanted Tenants Harbor to be for the people who lived there year-round, but for my family, it was their heart's home.

I thought back to the time when a serviceman wouldn't even park in front of the house. He didn't want the people of the town to know he had agreed to work for me. How far we had come. I'd witnessed the fulfillment of my dream: to settle the dispute I had inherited from my ancestors and bring peace between myself and the village of Tenants Harbor. I had hoped it was possible. I had inherited a basic faith, perhaps from Clara and Hebron, that if one keeps seeking, one will find. To have come to that place in my life was deeply gratifying. I thought again of the people of the town clapping in appreciation for our family's generosity.

Later, when my granddaughter Darin came to visit me in Maine, we took a walk down into the circle garden and sat on one of the great rocks, looking out to the harbor, and she said, "Grandma, don't ever sell this house, because I want it." I realized then that my actions had ramifications for future generations. My granddaughters would not have to face the animosity I had inherited. I would pass the torch in peace.

Not many years after the settlement with the town, the tide again went out: Forrester was dying. He suffered a series of illnesses, and it became clear he was not going to last long. I made a special trip from New York to visit him in a nursing facility. He looked to be asleep when I entered his room. I went quietly over to his bed. He opened his eyes, and I whispered to him, "Forrester, I am so happy to see you. I want to thank you for being such a great friend to me."

Forrester raised his head and looked at me. He became animated. "Thank you for being a friend to me. We brought the harbor together." It made him happy to think the harbor was more united as a result of all we had done. I was deeply moved.

He then lowered his head. "Betsy, I'm tired now and need to rest. You need to leave."

I reluctantly obeyed. "Goodbye, Forrester. Goodbye," I said as I left his room. I knew I would never see him again.

CHAPTER 24

My Daughter and Blueberries, 2010

It was the end of August, the end of summer 2010. The nights were cooler, and the blueberries were bursting on the bushes I had planted more than a year ago. I hoped my granddaughters would come pick them with the same delight that I had experienced as a child with my mother and that my daughter had experienced with me.

It was getting on toward ten o'clock on a late August evening, and I was getting worried, sitting with Al at the old pine table with the wide boards in the cream-and-apple-green kitchen. Where were my daughter, Betsy; her husband, Ken; and Ellie, my two-year-old granddaughter? I'd thought they would be there by now. I thought to myself how blessed I was to have a daughter and a son, both of whom were successful in work and in love. I was looking forward to having my daughter and her family come visit in Maine. My son was too busy making his way in business to come up for a visit with his wife and my two other granddaughters, Darin and Kristen.

I rejoiced, particularly since blueberry picking with my daughter when she was a child had not been typical of our relationship through many years. There had been strains, many of which I had failed to understand, made worse by the terrible car accident twenty-six years earlier, when she'd lost her father at age fourteen. It might have felt to her as though she had lost her mother as well. I don't know for sure; I just know she became distant, sometimes refusing to see me. One time, when she was in her late twenties and working as the marketing manager of the Whitney Museum, I called. "Hi, Betsy. What day might you have free this fall when we could have lunch?"

She replied, "Mom, I don't know that I want to see you at all."

I was devastated, but I decided I wasn't going to stop trying to connect with my daughter.

Through the years, I reached out to her in every way I knew. I was heartened when she started talking to me. She told me, "I have decided to tell you every time you make me mad."

"I'm so glad," I replied, "because then maybe I will understand."

But that night, finally, she was coming to visit. It was the first time in the eighteen years I had been married to Al that she was going to visit us together in Maine. "Mom, I would like to introduce Ellie to Maine, to the blueberry picking, to the big tidal beach, to the apple orchard, to the sail loft," she'd said.

"Wonderful" was all I'd said, to try to make it seem perfectly natural, but I was restraining myself from jumping for joy.

Since Ellie had arrived, our relationship had improved dramatically. "Ellie is so lucky to have a grandmother who adores her," Betsy had declared one day. Besides, I had a special talent: I was able to rock Ellie to sleep when she refused to cooperate for either of her parents.

I heard a car door open at eleven o'clock at night in our driveway, and before I knew it, Ken walked through the kitchen door. "Hi, and shhh. Ellie is asleep, and I want to get her bed set up and not wake her up."

I had prepared the guest suite for them, but they preferred one large bedroom so Ellie would not be scared. I tore downstairs, and there Betsy was, sitting in the darkened backseat of the car with Ellie asleep in her car seat. "I have special blueberry pie," I whispered.

The next day, I announced I wanted to have a dinner party for Betsy and Ken and invite some young people, about fifteen all together. I was fearful she would object. To my surprise, Betsy replied, "It sounds like fun."

I began scurrying around, pulling out the table, shopping, cooking, and fixing flowers. I wondered what Betsy would wear to the party and wanted to tell her what to wear, when I stopped myself. What was I thinking of doing to my forty-year-old executive daughter? Would I really be so thoughtless as to ruin the whole visit? What if I had not stopped myself? I could imagine her conversation with Ken: "My mother is just awful. She has just insulted me, treating me as though I'm ten years old. Let's leave."

In that moment, it dawned on me that I had been giving her conditional love for a long time without even knowing it, just as my father and mother had done to me. My wonderful, beloved daughter. I had not been thinking. I had just been copying the generations before me.

Perhaps it all had started in Tenants Harbor with Clarissa, whose parents had thought they were better than anyone else and would not let their daughter marry the man she loved. I thought of Clara and Hebron, whose faith and works had been so important to them in India that they had been willing to stay in India and send their children away for months and even years at a time to get a good education rather than going with them. I thought of Betty in Chicago, who always had thought she knew what was right for her children without ever asking them or listening to them. I thought of my dad, who'd felt his work was so important that he never had time for his children. I thought of my own children and how often I felt I had the answer for them without ever even consulting them or how often I was concerned about making a good impression on others rather than concern for my own children's feelings and needs.

I looked out at the blue waters of the harbor outside the window of the old sail loft. In the afternoon light of August, the sun was just beginning to cast its golden glow. What grace suddenly entered my soul at that moment and saved me from criticizing her. I remembered with vivid clarity all the times I had made my children change clothes for some person whose approval I thought important. I had repeated this in a thousand ways I hadn't realized at the time.

"Has Ellie picked the blueberries yet?" I asked Betsy.

"We're waiting for you," my daughter replied. I stopped fiddling with my dinner party, realizing that it would be fine and that I needed to get my priorities straight and spend time with Ellie, the person I had been dreaming about ever since I planted those bushes for her and my other granddaughters a year before in the spring.

I grabbed my camera, and Ken grabbed his. We all met at the blueberry bushes. I sat on the grass, wearing my big green sun hat, and Ellie stood wearing her small green sun hat. "Ellie," I said, "you may pick the blueberries. You take your thumb and finger, and pull." I held her tiny, delicate hand in my large, aging, arthritic hand and let her feel the movement.

Betsy encouraged her. "Grandma planted these for you, Ellie," she said as Ken snapped pictures. Ellie got the idea and was soon popping blueberries into her mouth and a few into the basket.

"Let's get a picture of the three generations," said Betsy.

CHAPTER 25

India Revisited, 2011

In February 2011, Kusum and Rupi, two beloved Indian friends in New York, both Hindus, invited Al and me to come to India to see their India, the India of the educated and upper caste. Perhaps I finally could come to terms with my Indian heritage. Even though I had visited South India before and the sites of my mother's life there, Kusum sensed my continued anguish about my grandparents' thirty years in India as Canadian Baptist Foreign Mission Board missionaries and my mother's birthplace and home until she was fifteen. Kusum was right. I sensed there was still much I had to learn about what had happened in South India that had influenced my mother and how she had raised me.

Kusum arranged for us to meet and be taken care of by their Indian friends in South India, to see the great sites of Rajasthan in northern India, and to attend a Hindu wedding of their friend's son in New Delhi. They wanted us to experience the elegant life of the maharajas and the warmth and friendship among their friends, the successful businesspeople of India. In contrast, my grandparents had lived and worked mostly among the Dalits, the poor and lowest class in India.

Al and I embarked for India and Kusum's friends, but first, I wanted to take Al to Vizianagaram, the village in Andhra Pradesh in South India, my mother's birthplace. I wrote ahead to ask the minister of Syms Memorial Baptist Church of Vizianagaram if I could stop by to ask some questions about the Reverend H. Y. Corey, my grandfather, who had died in 1927, long before I was born, and I wrote to Mr. Sharma, the holy Brahman man, whom I had visited before.

We first went to visit the saintly Mr. Sharma. He lived in a comfortable one-story brick house on several acres of land. When I had visited more than a decade before, I had left a check for $1,000 to build a redbrick church in my grandfather's memory in a village where they'd assured me the people needed a place to meet. Subsequently, I had received a letter from Mr. Sharma with a picture of a half-built church, saying they needed another $1,000 to complete the church. I'd sent the money and had heard nothing since. Thus, when we arrived, I asked to see the church I had had built. Mr. Sharma answered, "The roads to the tiny village are so bad that I cannot not take you there."

Disappointed, I began to wonder if the church in memory of the Reverend Hebron Young Corey had ever been built. I realized I would never know, because I never expected to make another trip to India.

The children of the orphanage performed a charming dance for us. Mr. Sharma had mentioned during my initial visit how hard it was to find the necessary support for the work after the government threw out all foreign missionaries. On my second visit, he told us he felt blessed since he had found a church in the southern part of the United States to send both money and people. I wondered how long they would be a steady source of support for their work. I thought about how different our cultures were. Had Mr. Sharma been so desperate for support that he had made up a story about building a church to get enough money to feed the orphans? If so, I was glad my donation had helped. My grandfather had sacrificed everything to help these people of southern India, but they needed more. I wondered what would have to happen for all these people to have what they needed for the long run. Depending on missionaries and their descendants had not been sustainable. I admired what my grandparents had done to help the poor of India but did not admire the unintended consequences to their own family. Enormous resources would have to be committed through the government and private philanthropy.

Next, we decided to visit Pastor John, thinking we would be led into his study and have a brief talk about my grandfather. I had arranged to come the day before, but it had gotten late, so I'd called and said we would come the next day. Pastor John had asked the driver, "Can't you come today?" but the driver had said it was impossible.

When the car arrived in front of the church, I started fumbling in my purse for my comb, but Al said, "You have to get out. They're waiting for you."

Children waiting in line to greet us at Syms Memorial Baptist Church, Vizianagaram, Andhra Pradesh, India 2010.

I turned around, and there were two long rows of schoolchildren, barefoot and not in uniform, unlike most Indian schoolchildren. They were waiting for us in front of the church, lined up by size, with the smallest in front, looking adorable and expectant. They held welcoming leis to place over our heads, like the garlands of flowers the cherubim carry. I finally understood why Pastor John had continually called our driver to see what time we were arriving. The children must have been all lined up waiting for us yesterday.

The children proudly put the leis over our heads with beautiful smiles, and Pastor John led us to the front of the church, where two red velvet throne chairs were set up. Their English was minimal, and our Telugu was nonexistent, but mostly by sign language, they invited us to sit. I thought of my grandmother Clara, who had arrived in India speaking only English. Pastor John's son, Noble John, who was seventeen years old and knew a smattering of English, and one other member of the congregation became our translators, although I had a hard time understanding their English.

The pulpit above the red velvet throne chairs was decorated with orange Shasta daisies, and the altar was covered with purple cloth. Red, orange, and pink tinsel garlands lined the front of the church. Above the chairs hung a large banner painted in orange, pink, and yellow, with a turquoise stripe across the bottom: "Hearty welcome to Mr. Alfred Scott and Mrs. Betsy Scott, USA grandchildren of late Rev. and Mrs. Chory, former pastor of Syms Memorial Baptist Church." Although my grandfather's name was misspelled and I wondered if he had ever been the pastor of this particular church, it did not dampen the effect the gesture had on me.

We looked in the church, and to our amazement, a large congregation were waiting patiently for us in the cavernous church. The men wore bush shirts and trousers, and the women wore brilliantly colored saris. As we'd had no idea we were to be the honored guests at a big celebration, I was dressed simply in white slacks and a pink overblouse, with my camera case and purse slung over my shoulders. Noble John, with a radiant smile, handsome and tall, came up to our red velvet throne chairs. "Auntie, give me your camera. I will take pictures for you," he said, and I gladly complied.

Pastor John came to the front with the translator and told the congregation in Telugu that we were grandchildren of missionaries. An elder came up to greet us and, with his hands folded in front of him, bowed and said, "Namaste." We bowed back. He placed on both Al and me large tan pashmina shawls—ceremonial robing and a mark of honor, Kusum told me later.

One by one, men and women of the congregation came forward and placed over our heads brilliant and generous fresh floral garlands of pink, orange, green, and white. Each had a picture taken with us. Al and I ended up with ten garlands apiece. They piled up nearly to our noses. We were moved with the outflowing spirit.

Betsy and Al sitting at the front of Syms Memorial Baptist Church
with all the congregation giving greetings and presents, 2010.

Next came a procession of gifts: a wooden cutout of the church with
100 printed on it, evidently the one hundredth anniversary of the church
the year before; a book about the one hundred years of the church's history;
a triangle of pink and white roses; bouquets of brightly colored zinnias and
marigolds; and platters of sweets. No Old Testament celebration for King
David could have been so grand, I thought.

Betsy's eyes tearing up as she thinks of Hebron, Clara and all the
Canadian Baptist missionaries to the Telugu of South India.

My eyes welled up, my mouth opened, and I took a deep breath. I pictured my entire extended family sitting on the thrones and being celebrated. I pictured all the families of all the missionaries who had given so much of themselves and their lives for these people similarly placed. "But, Betsy, was the sacrifice worth it?" my sister would always ask.

Noble John handed me a microphone and asked me to give a speech.

"I have come a long way to visit you, and never had I thought you would celebrate," I said. "You have melted my heart and made me deeply proud of all that was accomplished by the Canadian missionaries." I felt as though I heard the seraphim singing.

When it was Al's turn to speak, he said, "I am deeply honored."

The wife of the pastor, clad in a brilliant red-and-gold sari, came forward with an angelic smile and offered a prayer in Telugu. Next, the head of the school came forward and placed an envelope in my hands. Inside was this letter:

> Dear Mrs. Betsy Scott,
>
> We are so grateful for all that your grandfather did to establish our church and school, and now we need a new school. Won't you carry on the work of your grandfather and build us a new school? We need $60,000.

I was surprised. Maybe I shouldn't have been. This was not just for money, my spirit cried out; these people were telling us the truth. The people of the church were still poor, the old school building had been damaged when the road was widened, and the school was currently being held in temporary sheds. There was no money for uniforms, shoes, or a school building. They needed a new school, but I had not come to India expecting or prepared to make a major donation. It had been the Indian government's decision to eject all the missionaries in 1970, thus leaving many small churches and church schools without means of support. The Canadians had tried to make the Indian churches and schools self-sustaining but this school was struggling.

I looked at Al, asking him with my eyes what he thought was an appropriate amount to give. We both felt on the spot. I felt guilty and wondered what we should do. We did not speak Telugu and could not communicate. All the misunderstanding made me sad. In the end, we were glad to leave them a token check to help them with their new school. I wished I had had a way to communicate with the congregation for I would have enjoyed the dialogue of what we had each experienced over the years, possibly finding a way to help them move forward with their goals at the same time having them understand the unintended consequences for my family of my grandparents having spent those nearly thirty years on India. It is a far-fetched dream of mine that this book might serve as a bridge.

A reporter from the local newspaper interviewed us and said he would send us a copy of the story (which we never received). They led us on a tour of the church's courtyard, where there was a plaque listing all of the church's pastors over the years. The Reverend Hebron Young Corey was not among them. I wondered if Hebron had just preached at this particular Baptist church but never been their pastor. Or had he never been there at all?

We were shown the bookstore, which looked meager, and then asked to sit on two white plastic chairs out in the school's courtyard. As many as fifty women gathered around in a semicircle to have their pictures taken with us. They reached out to touch our shoulders. It seemed important to them to touch us. At the end, an older woman, all wrinkled and with a broken tooth, came up to us and shyly touched my shoulder. She smiled all over, a radiant smile. We connected through our smiles. Although we couldn't speak to each other, I wondered if her grandmother had been one of those baby girls Hebron picked up off the village street and brought to an orphanage. The missionaries had done a lot, and the old lady made me understand why my grandfather had chosen to remain in India for so long, even to the detriment of his own children. His son Cedric had been dropped on his head by a Hindu ayah and never learned to talk; his son Harold had died as an infant from cholera; and his son Charlie, left alone in Canada while his father saved the orphans of India, had committed suicide at age twenty-seven. No wonder my mother, Betty, always had been afraid of what would happen and never had gone back to India.

It was time to leave, as we had arranged to have lunch at the home of the former maharaja and maharani of Vizianagaram, friends of friends of Kusum. But first Noble John came over to speak to us and told me proudly he was going to become a Baptist minister like his father "in order to bring light to the darkness of India." I winced. He assumed I was an evangelical Baptist like my grandparents, but I was not. I had come to believe there were many paths to the one Spirit. I had long ago left behind any thought of the literal interpretation of the Bible. I did not think India was "dark India." To the contrary, I thought I had much to learn from the ancient Hindu scriptures and had been studying them. I had no idea how I could explain my theology to Noble John and all the others. Going back to visit the Indian Christians left over from my grandfather's mission had become sad. The gulf between us was as wide as the oceans that separated America from India.

I needed to leave, and it was time for our luncheon. The maharaja and his wife spoke perfect English. The maharani, a well-spoken, beautifully educated, handsome Indian matron, said she had been educated in missionary schools in Madras and reiterated that the missionary schools had been the best schools. Our Indian friends explained the maharajas were still considered the nobility of India, even though their power had been taken away from them at the time of Indian independence in 1947, and their government payments (privy purse) had been taken away in 1971. Consequently, many lived in much reduced circumstances.

As we lunched on Indian delicacies in their airy gray stone house set in a private garden behind a big white wall, the maharani said, "The missionaries used to live in this house, and on the column in the veranda were the scribbled names of children who grew up here, but we covered them over a few years ago."

I said I was sorry not to know the names of the people who had lived there, and I was curious about the place of Christianity in India today. The maharaja, a distinguished gentleman who had held a number of posts in the government of Andhra Pradesh, told us that traditionally, they had welcomed the work of the missionaries for their excellent social work and fine schools. "However," the maharaja said, "Christianity became politicized in our area, and the Indian Christians were buying people houses if they would become Christian and vote with the Christian party."

"What a dispiriting story of Indian Christians forty years after the missionaries left," I replied. "The spirit was absent."

As Al and I left, I felt heavyhearted. On the road, we passed the Canadian Baptist Foreign Mission Leper Asylum. It was in ruins, with weeds growing everywhere, abandoned.

After leaving Vizianagaram, we took a plane to Coimbatore in Tamil Nadu State, where Kusum's friends Lakshmi and his wife, Swarna, lived. They had invited us to stay with them in their gracious, elegant marble family compound and offered to drive us up into the Nilgiri Hills to let me visit again the Hebron School, where Mom had gone to boarding school.

Early the next day, Swarna took me shopping to a local shop that sold women's clothing, and I picked out several Indian outfits. Now I wish I had bought many more, since I have found them comfortable to wear, charming and dirt cheap. How my attitude had changed from my first trip to India, when I had felt awkward in wearing Indian clothes.

Swarna and Lakshmi generously and amazingly took off several days from their own busy lives to take us in their private car with chauffeur on a lovely trip up into the Nilgiri Mountains so I could once again visit the school Mom had attended and also see their beautiful county home. Kusum had written that she felt it important I see the school once again since she had the sense I still needed to understand more about what had happened to Mom so many years before.

Although I had written ahead, it seemed the school had not received the letter, and they were not expecting me, so I had to persist to get through the security and be allowed to enter the school. The students—boys and girls, Indian and Western—wore uniforms of navy blue and white and looked very young to me, some eight years old or younger. The school was nearly all boarders. A secretary called for someone to help me. The wife of the headmaster, named Lynn Noonan, appeared and offered to talk with me and take me around.

Lynn, a middle-aged woman from South Africa who was a bit roly-poly and had short blonde hair, greeted me in Western clothes: a white blouse and a dark skirt. She would have fit in perfectly in England, but we were on top of a hill in South India. We talked in their waiting room. I told her I had come seeking to understand what it had been like for my mother to be a student at the Hebron School when she was eight years old and five hundred miles from the village where her parents were stationed in 1916.

We looked quietly at each other, and she began telling me the stories of the past, which appeared to be very much on her mind at the present. "They used the cane liberally back in those days—and continued the caning up to a couple of decades ago—and the children were disoriented. They didn't know where home was."

I was surprised she began immediately with the harshness of the school decades ago.

She continued. "Today we never ask the children where their home is. We only ask where their parents are, since these children's parents keep moving to different posts or assignments as diplomats, businessmen, or missionaries."

I looked at her and held my head, wide-eyed. What was I hearing?

She noticed my response. "I am sorry, and we are now trying to make it right," she said as her own eyes welled up.

I couldn't stop my eyes from watering. I couldn't stop myself from crying. The school was apologizing to me for what had happened to the little girl Betty so many decades ago. She undoubtedly had been beaten with a cane for going off to care for a mangy donkey, talking when the lights went out, or not folding up her clothes neatly enough. I could picture her in her small navy-and-white uniform, fearful and frightened, eight years old, always trying to obey so she wouldn't be caned and, at the same time, feeling terribly homesick for her parents. She would not have been sure where her home was, since the missionaries moved around so much, and likely had cried at night and been caned for making noise.

"We are sorry, and we are now trying to get it right," the headmaster's wife said again. She told me what they were doing to make it better for children. "Many graduates have come back to heal. We had our centenary with a psychologist from England working with people to heal their wounds from our school. There are now big conferences on the MKs and the TCKs," she said, using their shorthand for *missionary kids* and *third-culture kids*. "It is an area of study today."

TCK Betty Corey wearing her Indian sari as a graduate student at Northwestern University in Evanston, Illinois, circa 1930.

I have since learned that TCKs were children who were born in one culture, raised in second culture different from their parents' primary culture, and then developed a third culture, a combination of the first two. I thought of my growing-up years on the South Side of Chicago as the result of my mother's being a TCK: Mom had wanted me to wear a navy-blue pleated skirt and white blouse, had wanted me to stay away from the ruffians down the street, and had been so controlling, so afraid of what could go wrong. She had had good reason to be afraid. I had misunderstood her fear, thinking she thought I was the one who was wrong.

The headmaster's wife said, "Let me run upstairs to get some names and addresses for you of people you can call to ask their experiences. Just wait right here. Or better yet, why don't you come up to my office? I can show you some of the books, such as *The Wounded Healer* by Henri Nouwen." I had read Henri Nouwen's book in seminary.

In the hallway on the second floor, I saw a teacher standing in his dorm apartment. When he was told I was there to understand what had happened to my mother in the second decade of the twentieth century, he said he was a former student. "Yes, they used to use a cane on me." He proceeded to tell me he had spent many years working with a therapist to heal. Now he was trying to give the children under his care a different experience, keeping his door open so the children could come talk and receive comfort when feeling homesick.

I met a fortyish mother with her curly-haired ten-year-old daughter standing by her side, pulling at her shirt. The mother told me she was dropping off her daughter as a boarder to join her two older sisters. I asked, "Why would you put your three daughters in boarding school?"

"We are working with the prostitutes in Calcutta," she answered, "teaching them skills so they can get a job. There was no safe, good school for my children, so I have sent the three of them here to Hebron School."

I thought to myself, *Here we go again. Missionaries taking care of some of the "least of these" and sending their own children away.* I shuddered, hoping her children would fare better than Clara and Hebron's had.

"You really like it here, don't you?" asked the mother to the child. The child shrugged and continued to cling. "You like being here with your two older sisters better than being home," the mother said hopefully, trying to convince the child. The child clung some more, looking up at me, seemingly overwhelmed. I felt sad upon seeing the same pattern all over again.

I went to see the children's dormitory room. There were four little beds to a room, and each room was filled with stuffed animals, colorful quilts, clothes, and shoes. I saw that the children were surrounded by things that might make a child feel okay. They each had brought a stash of comfort foods from home, crackers or mints. They had a binge night once a week when the children could go into their stash and indulge.

A twenty-five-year-old with a lovely smile was introduced to me next as one of the dorm parents. "I love working with these kids," she said. I had the sense she was wonderful with them and did a good job in helping them navigate their daily lives: lights out, lights on, baths, teeth brushing, school dress, meals, playtime, homework time, dinner, reading, and bedtime. I could see her working around the clock like a camp counselor to keep the kids on track and happy. The enthusiastic young dorm parent's description contrasted greatly with what life had been like for little Betty.

On my earlier trip to India, I had seen the original Hebron School for girls in Coonoor, a few miles down the mountain from the current Hebron School. It was now an orphanage. The boys' and girls' campuses initially had been separate but had been combined decades after Betty left. The dormitory rooms had been stark and barren compared to those at the current Hebron School. There had been little iron bunk beds, twenty to a room, with nothing colorful around anywhere. I thought to myself that had been Betty's experience. I could imagine the matron from England telling the children there would be no talking when the lights were put out. They'd had to line up for meals, class, and baths with no talking. When the children had disobeyed, they had been caned. No one had listened to them. No one had been interested in what they thought or felt. It seemed to me the woman from England had been interested in order, quiet, and control. I could see where Betty had learned her controlling ways and her belief that children should be told, not asked. Mom used to say, "If it were not true, I would not say so. Children couldn't possibly know and should be told what to do. How would children know? They don't have the experience."

This was what I had traveled halfway around the world to find: what had happened in India that had influenced my mother's whole life and mine as well. Occasionally in life, there is a link without which one's life does not make sense and does not hold together. All my struggle, all the deep inner turmoil over a lifetime, now made more sense. I couldn't stop crying.

I had learned so much with this visit, but I forced myself to say good-bye to the Headmaster's wife as Swarna and Lakshmi were waiting in the car outside and I didn't want to delay them longer. They has made wonderful additional plans for us. Kusum had told Swarna and Lakshmi that Al would be having his eightieth birthday while visiting them. An eightieth birthday is a major event in India, and they decided to plan a celebration. The evening we arrived back, a festive dinner party was held in Al's honor at their daughter's house, which was part of the compound where the family lived. The third house of the compound belonged to Lakshmi's parents, and there was a central cook house. This Indian family had four generations all living in the same compound, not separated and scattered like my own. They all took good care of one another.

The dinner party, where an array of servants brought foods just for the Western palate, ended with a beautiful cake decorated in a glaze with many local fruits. Swarna presented Al with a Ganesha statue for his eightieth birthday present. Ganesha consists of an elephant's head and a human body with a rotund belly. One can rub the tummy when one needs to get over an obstacle.

Swarna and Lakshmi also arranged a ceremony for Al in their private family temple the next morning before we left. It was their custom, they explained, that on the eightieth birthday, a person retakes his or her marriage vows. Surprised and somewhat fearful, we went to their family temple, a small, rectangular limestone building with a portico enclosed behind a big iron fence. Inside, it was dark, lit only by candles. Several priests wearing loincloths and beads were there, as well as baskets of fruits, flowers, and coins.

Looking down the center of the Hindu temple toward the inner sanctum, a part of the temple where only the priests were allowed, I saw the statue of a Hindu deity, a black statue with piercing black eyes, looking at us. Two bare-chested priests with the image of the deity painted on their foreheads chanted blessings and prayers in Hindi, holding the baskets of fruits and flowers in their arms. They beckoned to us to place our hands on the baskets. Then they carried the offerings up to the inner sanctum to chant and sprinkle the flowers onto the statue of the deity. We were then brought leis made of fresh small white jasmine flowers and red cockscomb flowers—the prettiest I had ever seen or smelled. I started to put one on myself and was told not to. I was to place mine around Al's neck, and he was to place his around my neck. That was the sign of our taking each other again or, perhaps better said, giving ourselves to each other again. The sweetness and freshness of those flowers imprinted on my soul: I felt like a new bride, fresh, young together, and holy.

Swarna and Lakshmi with Al and Betsy in front of a private family
Hindu temple in Coimbatore, Tamil Nadu, India 2010.

After the ceremony, Swarna suggested I leave the flowers, thinking we couldn't take them on the plane, so I gave them to her. I started to place one over her head, and she shuddered. "Oh no!" It was like giving another your wedding ring. I gave those sweetest of garlands to her. I felt bereft. I wished I had insisted on taking them with me on the planes I would take that day. Swarna said she would place them on a Ganesha in her home.

A Christian missionary's granddaughter participated in the renewal of her wedding vows in a Hindu temple. Even though the symbols, images, prayers, and rituals were foreign to me, the spirit refreshed me. I said to Al that he was far from home on his birthday, and he said, "I can't think of anything I would rather do than to be with you on my birthday."

Some Christians keep wanting converts, wanting to "bring light to the darkness of India," but this Christian wants to learn from the ancient Hindu traditions. They have much to teach me. When we finally left India two weeks later, I knew I had seen the Hindu India and culture my grandparents had not seen.

CHAPTER 26

One Spirit Seminary, New York, 2013-2014

After the trip to India, where I had had the opportunity to understand my mother better and experience the deep spirituality of the Hindu ceremony and the amazing hospitality of its people, I decided to enroll in the One Spirit Seminary in New York City to study the world's major religions. I wanted to know more about all religions, realizing there were many paths to the Holy Spirit; I hoped to be ordained an interfaith minister; and I felt keenly the need for still another spiritual renewal. I had learned that the journey of life continued for all of one's life. It was as if one could see just one mountain at a time, but as that mountain was climbed, another appeared. Finding ways to climb these mountains are steps on the journey of healing.

I hardly knew anyone when I arrived with a busload of people from around the world at the church retreat center of the One Spirit Interfaith Seminary in Stony Brook, New York, an hour outside New York City. I had been a distance learner, doing the work by the computer and not in person, for the past year at the seminary, located at 247 West Thirty-Sixth Street in New York City. To become an interfaith minister involved a two-year part-time program and an intensive three-day weekend of seminars, presentations, and ceremonies mandatory to complete the first year. We had spent that first year studying scriptures and rituals of the world's major religions. The weekend was to be devoted to the bringing together of our work from the past year. It had become clear to me that all religions were a path to the one Spirit deep within the soul.

The retreat center had buildings made of cinder blocks and restrooms down the hall, but it was a heavenly late-May day, and lush green lawns provided a parklike setting for the gray cement buildings. My fellow students, more than a hundred, represented various religions, races, ages, and backgrounds: elegant Jewish matrons, African Americans from California who wore multiple beads, gay professors from local colleges, musicians, Muslim women in head scarves, and one elderly Hindu woman in a sari.

I was curious about the agenda for the intensive, which had not been announced in advance. We were soon told the major event of the retreat was the acceptance as a candidate to be an interfaith minister. I wondered if I was ready. In addition, I didn't think I could stay, because my step-granddaughter was graduating from high school on Saturday, and my husband planned to pick me up Friday afternoon. It seemed like a family command appearance, and there was no transportation from the retreat center to our farm over the weekend.

"I have to leave early to attend a family event," I said to my dean, Joan, a slight woman with lots of curly blonde hair, who all year had written insightful and clarifying comments on my monthly papers on one of the world's religions.

"Are you planning on missing your own initiation? It's like missing out on your own life," she said with deep intensity.

How would I explain missing a family event? I wasn't sure what I wanted to do, but fate seemed to take over. I felt a scratch in my throat, probably a result of spending the last weekend with my own granddaughters, who had had sniffles and fevers. I knew from long experience that germs would not be welcome at the farm, so I could dare to stay and attend my own initiation. Also, it dawned on me that I could rent a car and be free. I found Joan and told her I was staying.

"You've made my day," she answered.

It amazed me that even after all those years, it remained a struggle to claim my own life. It showed again that the roles we take on as children—in my case, the pleaser—become so firmly fixed in us that a lifetime of trying to change does not take those roles completely away. We can become aware of what we are doing and have some choice, but the emotional pulls from our early years don't completely go away.

When they handed out the agenda for the weekend, the first event was a purification ceremony, for which they required us to wear all white. I had not brought any white clothing so was happy to find a little shop nearby. I found an attractive white top with a V-neck, pulled in just above the waist, and a pair of flowing white pants. A pure-white silk scarf made in China with a handmade fringe was so soft that I couldn't resist buying it to complete the outfit.

The purification was a letting go of the past. We wrote letters to all the people we still needed to say things to. Then all the white-clad figures went outside, stood in a big circle around small fire pits, crumpled up our letters, and burned them. I thought of all the people who had gone before me and their stories: my grandmother Clara, who'd had five children in India; my grandfather Hebron, who'd put his missionary work before the needs of his own children; Harry, who'd died at three months; Cedric, who had been injured at birth and abandoned by his family; Charlie, who'd committed suicide and broken my mother's heart; and my mother, who'd tried to make it all better by burying all the tragedy that had occurred in her family but instead had acted it out. I thought of my father and how much he had had to fight to make a place for himself in the world. That helped me now. I had forgiven him long ago; he never had known what his criticism and absence did to his children—none of us do. I kept going through the people of my life, releasing them to their own lives so I might be free to go on to my next chapter.

We walked back into the retreat center in silence. I went to my room, changed into something comfortable, and went back out. First, one of my peers played a classical piano piece. Then a circle of drummers played out their feelings and danced them off into the night. I picked up a tambourine and thought of the Old Testament Miriam playing and dancing.

The next night was the initiation. We were told to wear celebratory garb, so I wore a batik Indian tunic in white, deep pink, and purple over my new flowing white pants, with the white Chinese silk scarf. I was ready.

Walking in a long line two by two, we went into a candlelit sanctuary. A radiant Diane, the head of the seminary, greeted us, clad in golden embroidery, with her hands out in a sign of blessing. I gasped at how lovely the moment was.

After a song of commitment in which we sang, "You have called me; I have answered," each of us went up one at a time to the front to be with Diane.

My turn came. Diane placed a white scarf decorated with a symbol of each of the world's religions around my neck, saying, "Here is your mantle. Welcome home."

Tears rolled down my cheeks, and my eyes burned. I could barely speak. I had finally taken the step to become a minister like my grandfather but one who wanted to be an instrument of bringing all peoples together.

The next morning, during a time of sharing, I offered my story.

"I am the granddaughter of Canadian Baptist missionaries to India, and although I never knew them, I love them dearly. They had great faith, which led them to sacrifice nearly thirty years of their lives to help the Telugu of South India. Their children suffered greatly, as did many of the Telugu families. They were part of the British Empire. They sincerely believed they had the truth and felt it was their duty to teach it to the heathen. They had the best of intentions. They helped a lot of people in poverty to get an education, medical care, and renewed hope for their lives, but there were many tragic unintended consequences. They had colonial superiority and did not know it. For all the hurt they unknowingly caused and for all those in my family, including me, I am sincerely sorry.

"And there is another side of this story I have finally understood. My mother, born and brought up in India, always told me I was special and that I shouldn't play with the other kids down the block. I have finally understood that being told one is special translates to a lonely, isolated, empty life separated from others and from one's self. *(I suddenly thought of the tragedy of Clarissa back in Tenants Harbor in 1862 who died because her parents thought she was too special to marry the man she loved.)*

"Yes, it has been a long journey. I stand here today feeling connected to all of you and even to all my family.

"I think my missionary grandfather might be turning in his grave right now."

"No, I don't think so," said one of my fellow students. "I think he is happy with you." The affirmation made me happy, but I wondered.

In the second year, we continued our studies of all the major religions, and a number of times, my spirit was enlivened and blessed by a tradition other than my own, even though I have remained an Episcopalian.

An American Indian spiritual teacher preached about filling ourselves up with the energy of the earth and then giving it all away in love. I followed his directions perfunctorily. He told us to stand up on the wooden floor and imagine deep roots going down into the earth. I stood up and thought about roots growing down into the earth, when all of a sudden, I heard a swishing noise. *Swish!* I wondered what it could be. I looked around to see if anything had happened, but no one else seemed to have had anything special happen. However, as I looked at the other people in the classroom, I was startled to realize that my perception had been changed. Every single person seemed different. I saw them all with a new sense of compassion and empathy.

I thought about the people in my life whom I had found difficult, such as Al's sister, and it dawned on me that of course she had not been happy to see me come into their family. I saw in a new way how hard it had been for all of Al's family to have a new person enter with her own history, children, and home. It was okay with me suddenly. It didn't bother me anymore. I understood. I could see more clearly. This sudden clarity was a mystery that I had no way to explain.

I went to the head of the seminary and asked her about my experience with the swish of the sound of the wind changing my perception. "That is called grace. Buddha was also enlightened under a tree," she replied.

That was particularly startling to me since I am a descendant of the Pilgrims on the *Mayflower*, who came to America's shores seeking to develop a theocracy in the new world. The Native American Indians had helped them survive the harsh winter. Wouldn't those Pilgrims have been surprised to learn that four centuries later, a descendant of one of those American Indians had used his religion to help a descendant of the *Mayflower* Pilgrims?

Looking back at my life, I realize I have been helped along my path from isolation to connection and from emptiness to fullness by many people, including the very people my mother, Betty, was taught to shun as a child and in turn taught me to shun. They took mercy on me, understood my anguish, and held out their hands to lift me up.

At the end of the second year, I took the oath of ordination as an interfaith minister in the hope I could become a force toward peace in this broken world, passing on to others all that had been given to me.

Ordination ceremony of One Spirit Seminary at
Riverside Church in New York City, 2014.

Betsy in a choir robe and stole with two
granddaughters after her ordination, 2014.

Al and I established a wedding barn in the Hudson Valley near Hudson, New York, called the Hill, where couples from all religions and backgrounds come to be married. Our site has broad lawns, mature trees, horse pastures, and views of the Catskill Mountains, as well as an antique Palladian barn. Hindus, Muslims, Jews, Protestants, Catholics, agnostics, and those who say they have no religion have come seeking blessings for their marriages. They all are welcome, and I have had the privilege of officiating at a few of their weddings.

CHAPTER 27

Twenty-Fifth Wedding Anniversary, Maine, 2016

In the summer of 2016, our children and grands gathered to celebrate our twenty-fifth wedding anniversary at the newly shined up sail loft in Tenants Harbor, Maine. It was thrilling to have everyone there for parts of the summer, as Al's family had also come to love the sail loft. There were eighteen of us in the blended family. Our four married children all had children of their own. Between us, we had eight grandchildren, who all celebrated holidays together.

Al and I had turned the sail loft building into a comfortable summer home, and everyone wanted to come. It had a garden down by the sea filled with dahlias, an apple orchard, and a circle garden, and the refurbished house itself had new windows, new paint, and a new deck. Inside, there were lots of new paintings, many by my daughter and myself. The house looked greatly loved, nothing like the abandoned-looking building I had inherited more than forty years before.

My son planned a cookout on the shore. He had carefully brought down wood and started the fire so the coals would be hot. He tended it the same way he tended everything: carefully. "I like being up here, Mom. It's what we have, and it is not that bad," he said. I think he was talking about his heritage. His children were there on the shore with him, gathering sticks to be used later in the evening to roast marshmallows.

I walked with Bob's daughter Darin down to look at the dahlias, and I reminded her of what she had told me some years before: "Grandma, don't you ever sell this place, because I want it."

"That's right," said Darin.

"Well, I won't sell it, dear. I will arrange to give it to your father and your aunt so you can always come here."

"Thank you, Grandma. I love you so much."

My daughter and her daughters were in the kitchen, cooking. I decided to walk up and join them. They were cooking together at the warn cherry table where I had started out my journey. They were making an anniversary cake. Flour had spilled onto the floor, and they had bits of batter on their faces. Together they were having a marvelous time.

I stopped and watched the scene in wonder. Those children were not told to go away, as I had been told as a child, and they were not being criticized. Instead, they were cooking together with their mother and enjoying being with one another. My dream had come true—what I had always wanted to happen for my children and their children. I hoped for generations to come the unhealthy cycle had been broken.

Al and Betsy's twenty-fifth wedding anniversary celebration on the deck of the Sail Loft in Tenants Harbor, Maine with some of their children and grandchildren.

My daughter told me, "Mom, I suddenly realized you had become a presence of accepting love in our lives, and we want you around." She started calling and suggesting outings we could all take together.

My son told me, "You are now fun to be around."

His wife, Kristen, told me, "Our door is always open to you."

My sister declared, "We are now a family."

The tide that had gone out with the demise of the wooden shipbuilding industry, with the attendant loss of income and way of life for my ancestors and most of the village, had had deleterious effects down through the generations. When people lose their whole way of life, there are not only economic repercussions but also social and family ones. Those ancestors had to find a way to survive. Deep shame developed in generations of children as a result of their turning against themselves as the children's way for protecting themselves against full knowledge of their parents unexplainable lives. Clara fled to India but could not escape her depression, which manifested in her being sickly and helpless. Her husband spent a lot of time away. Her children suffered by being depressed themselves, and the depression resulted in Charlie's terrible suicide. Clara's last child, Betty, my mom, hurt by her loneliness, abuse in India, and deep feelings of abandonment from Charlie's suicide, hid her pain in layers of control. She married a man who himself had been deeply hurt and who buried his hurt by criticizing others and withdrawing. I unconsciously made the decision to turn against myself as a child to protect myself from the criticism, control, and withdrawal of love. In the process, I gave up my soul and became a pleaser. I knew something was wrong, but I did not know what it was.

To heal, I studied my family history, learned to speak up and finally had to face the excruciating truth that I unknowingly had repeated the cycle of criticism and control with my own children. To change, I had to feel the enormous hurt feelings within me through the painful process of psychoanalysis. I discovered peace and joy within for I had come home to myself, the safe harbor. The love of my husband, children, and friends pulled me through. In the midst of my quest, the unfathomable mystery, the Holy Spirit, through grace, entered my life and restored my soul. I am filled with deep gratitude. For now, after the long struggle and great gifts, the tide has once more come into the blue, lavender and golden harbor. Myself, the family and the community that were worlds apart have been connected.

Love is a presence, an affirmation, and a union.

ACKNOWLEDGMENTS

I wish to thank the writing teachers at the West Side YMCA Writing Center in New York City, Patty Dann and Mindy Lewis, for their many years of working with me to write this family history and autobiography. They worked tirelessly and I thank them for all they taught me. The limitations of this work are solely my own.

I want to thank readers Lisa Foxmartin, Lee Kravitz, Reverend Eileen Epperson, Nina Frost, and Kusum Gaind and my sister, Margie Palmer, for their perceptive and encouraging comments. I want to thank Kusum Gaind and Rupi Puri for their tremendous assistance in helping me to understand India, for arranging our great trip to India, and for their dear friends Swarna and Lakshmi, who did so much for us in southern India and took us personally up to the Hebron School in Ooty and to Coonoor, even riding the blue-engine cog railroad with us.

I want to thank both my children, who read this manuscript early on. My son told me he was grateful I had written it, for it brought us closer together, and his children will like to read it one day. My daughter told me she found it exciting to read and loved it.

I wish to thank my sister, Margie Palmer, for reading the book a second time and telling me she not only loved the book but felt as if I had written her a love letter, as it articulated so many things for her.

I want to thank my Vassar '62 classmates who listened to my presentation on this book in progress at our fifty-fifth reunion and encouraged me to have it published. I want to thank the many friends, including but not limited to Susie and Jody, who have helped in many ways over many years.

No list of thank-yous would be complete without my thanking my beloved husband, Al, for his many years of patience and encouragement while I worked on this manuscript.

SOURCE MATERIAL

Corey, Albert B., editor *Conference on Canadian American Affairs Held at Queen's University, Kingston, Ontario, June 1922, 1937.*

Corey, Charles Henry. *A History of the Richmond Theological Seminary: With Reminiscences of Thirty Years' Work among the Colored People of the South.* Richmond, Virginia: J.W. Randolph Co. 1895.

Craig, John, and J. R. Stillwell. *Telugu Trophies: The Jubilee Story of Some of the Principal Telugu Converts in the Canadian Baptist Mission in India, 1874–1924.* Toronto, Canada: The Canadian Baptist Foreign Mission Board, 1924.

Orchard, M. L., and K. S. McLaurin. *The Enterprise: The Jubilee Story of the Canadian Baptist Mission in India, 1874–1924*, Sagwan Press, 1924.

Scott, Elizabeth Jacks. *Widowhood: A Doorway to Calling and Conversion*, New York: Xlibris Corporation, 2009.

ABOUT THE AUTHOR

Elizabeth Jacks Scott, author, coach, and minister. Practiced psychotherapy and family therapy in New York City for two decades, former grief group leader at St. Bartholomew's Church, cofounder of Hudson Valley Weddings at the Hill. Ordained interfaith minister and clinical social worker. Vassar College BA, the University of Chicago MA, Hunter College School of Social Work MSW and Union Theological Seminary M.Div. Certificates in family therapy from the Hunter College postgraduate program and in psychoanalysis from the Object Relations Institute of New York City. Graduate of the One Spirit Seminary in New York City. Author of *Widowhood: Doorway to Calling and Conversion.* Member of nonprofit boards including Society for the Relief of Women and Children, and the Emma Adams Fund. She and her husband reside in New York City, the Hudson Valley, the coast of Maine and combined have four children and eight grandchildren.

LIST OF PHOTOGRAPHS FOR JOURNEY TO SAFE HARBOR

1. The former Hebron School for girls in Coonoor, which currently is an orphanage but still has the monkeys Mom used to talk about.
2. Brown bunk beds at an orphanage in Coonoor, India.
3. Betty and Bob's wedding photo, Evanston, Illinois, 1936.
4. Ships' graveyard—five-masted schooners left to rot as the sailing ships of the coastal trade were made obsolete by the introduction of the steam engine.
5. Oxcart in a river in India.
6. Cedric as a baby, 1898.
7. Campaign card for Dad running for mayor of Chicago in 1951.
8. Corey family back from India in Wolfville, Nova Scotia, 1924.
9. Clara with her son Charlie, Nova Scotia, circa 1926.
10. Betsy and her two children as a recent widow, 1984.
11. Children waiting in line to greet us at Syms Memorial Baptist Church, Vizianagaram, Andhra Pradesh, India, 2010.
12. Betsy and Al sitting at the front of Syms Memorial Baptist Church with all the congregation giving greetings and presents, 2010.
13. Tears welling up in Betsy's eyes as she thinks of Hebron, Clara, and all the Canadian Baptist missionaries to the Telugu of South India.
14. TCK Betty Corey wearing her Indian sari as a graduate student at Northwestern University in Evanston, Illinois, circa 1930.

15. Swarna and Lakshmi with Al and Betsy in front of a private family Hindu temple in Coimbatore, Tamil Nadu, India, 2010.
16. Ordination ceremony of One Spirit Seminary at Riverside Church, 2014.
17. Betsy in a choir robe and stole with two granddaughters after her ordination.
18. Al and Betsy's twenty-fifth wedding celebration on the deck of the sail loft in Tenants Harbor, Maine, with some of their children and grandchildren.

Comments on
JOURNEY TO
SAFE HARBOR

Elizabeth Scott seeks the answers to two questions as she embarks on her epic journey of self and family healing: "Why did my parents show me so little love growing up? And how can I break my family's centuries-old cycle of dysfunctional parenting?" Probing the psyches and behavior of three generations of women in her family, including herself, she gives the reader a front-row seat at the unfolding of three historical dramas: the rise and fall of Christian missionary work in India during the British raj; the fight for civil rights in 1940s Chicago; and the technological and economic changes disrupting a small shipbuilding town in Maine. The answers she discovers along the way will give you a fresh perspective on how to parent (and grandparent) more effectively, in tune with your deepest aspirations and values.

—Lee Kravitz, author of *Unfinished Business* and *Pilgrim: Risking the Life I Have to Find the Faith I Seek*

Love can conquer all, but the adage seems trite compared to what this memoir shows: that the hardest of the struggles in life is love based on acceptance of oneself in order to fully love others. The real story centers on the psychological verities of this family saga and the personal and emotional sacrifices that were made in the name of mission, commitment, and duty. The emotional culture is tragically the same through three generations, until the narrator, through the hardest work imaginable, changed it. What comes through in the penultimate section is the triumph of the narrator's determination to break the chain and reach the top of the volcano alone but knowing there is support from others below. The metaphor of Tenants Harbor represents the binding thread of the saga, leading to the seaside garden yielding sweet blueberries for the fourth and fifth generations to pick. Now the granddaughters eat many, and a few go into the basket to be made into jam for future use.

—Lisa Fox Martin, former instructor of
classics at Brooklyn College

Rev. Scott's family journey illustrates the extraordinary commitment of one person to find her life which was lost and make a profound difference to the people she loves. The author demonstrates seemingly endless resilience and courage in her determination to make sense of her ancestors, her parents, her childhood, and then her husband's sudden death, which left her to raise two young children. All along the way, Rev. Scott struggles to answer the question "Where is God?" In the process, the child with no voice becomes the Amazon we see at the close of the book. Clearly, the author thinks it is important for the reader to know that it takes perseverance and determination to work through one's demons. And that cannot be done alone. This is a book worth reading slowly while pondering.

—Reverend Eileen L. Epperson, Presbyterian minister